The Strategic Role of Marketing

The Strategic Role of Marketing

UNDERSTANDING WHY
MARKETING SHOULD BE CENTRAL
TO YOUR BUSINESS STRATEGY

Adrian Davies

McGRAW-HILL BOOK COMPANY

London · New York · St Louis · San Francisco · Auckland
Bogotá · Caracas · Lisbon · Madrid · Mexico
Milan · Montreal · New Delhi · Panama · Paris · San Juan
São Paulo · Singapore · Sydney · Tokyo · Toronto

Published by
McGRAW-HILL Book Company Europe
Shoppenhangers Road, Maidenhead, Berkshire SL6 2QL, England
Telephone 01628 23432
Fax 01628 770224

British Library Cataloguing in Publication Data
Davies, Adrian
Strategic Role of Marketing:
Understanding Why Marketing Should be
Central to Your Business Strategy
I. Title
658.8

ISBN 0-07-707854-3

Library of Congress Cataloging-in-Publication Data
Davies, Adrian.
The Strategic role of marketing: understanding why marketing should be central to your business strategy/Adrian Davies.
p. cm.
Includes index.
ISBN 0-07-707854-3
1. Marketing. 2. Strategic planning. I. Title.
HF5415.13.D357 1995
658.8′02–dc20 95-7927
CIP

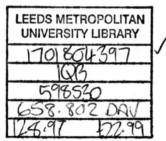

12345 BL 98765

Typeset by BookEns Limited, Royston, Herts.
and printed and bound in Great Britain
by Biddles Limited, Guildford and Kings Lynn.

Printed on permanent paper in compliance with ISO Standard 9706.

Contents

PREFACE vii

CHAPTER 1 The marketing environment 1

CHAPTER 2 The strategic context 13

CHAPTER 3 Strategy formulation 33

CHAPTER 4 Strategic planning 43

CHAPTER 5 The marketing concept and the marketing process 59

CHAPTER 6 Organizing for strategic marketing 71

CHAPTER 7 Marketing planning 89

CHAPTER 8 Marketing implementation, practice and controls: 1 105

CHAPTER 9 Marketing implementation, practice and controls: 2 121

CHAPTER 10 Marketing audit and corporate self-renewal 139

CHAPTER 11 Strategic marketing beyond the second millennium 147

APPENDIX 1 **Mission statements** 159

APPENDIX 2 **Strategic planning techniques and their practical application** 163

GLOSSARY 193

INDEX 198

Preface

In his book *Commonsense Direct Marketing* Drayton Bird records his surprise at finding that few marketing professionals admitted to having formal business plans. Many of those who did plan did so to meet the requirements of their organization–'few evinced any great enthusiasm for planning'. This experience is not unique and it is because strategic marketing is greatly discussed and little practised that I have been moved to write this book.

My target audience is primarily comprised of company directors, who need to understand fully how marketing can be used to shape and deliver key business strategies for which they are accountable. This book is also intended to be helpful to marketers who wish to fulfil the strategic role which their profession is primarily called upon to encompass. As it is aimed at a top management audience I have not structured the book as a manual, but as an intelligent person's exploration of the complex issues surrounding strategic marketing.

When I went to the Harvard Business School in 1966 on the first British-American Marketing Course the concept of marketing was virtually unknown in the UK and was in its pioneering phase in the USA. Since that time marketing has moved to the centre of the stage and its relevance has been recognized in many ways, not least in the award of a Royal Charter to the Institute of Marketing. Vast sums of money are invested in marketing departments, media advertising, market research and the whole panoply of sales promotion and yet few businesses have been able to secure a sustainable competitive advantage.

Close examination of what happens in many companies shows that the activity of marketing is often not fully linked to the strategic objectives of the business, in the same way that so many of the other functions have operated independently. Whenever I hear the words 'IT strategy' I am concerned to know whether it is driven by professional IT interests or, exceptionally, is fully articulated to the strategic need of the business to win and retain customers.

The recent upsurge of interest in 'business process re-engineering' is a sign that the need to reintegrate businesses behind a clear customer-focused strategy has been recognized as urgent for future prosperity, if not for survival. Reintegrating the marketing function is probably the biggest challenge in re-engineering business processes. The unique focus of this book is on the linkage between corporate strategy and marketing strategy which enables customer-focused strategies to be delivered effectively and sustained over time.

Much marketing activity is at a tactical level. This is not a problem where there is a clearly stated and understood strategy which drives this activity. Often, however, the emphasis on techniques and excitement which characterizes many marketing departments masks a lack of rigorous analysis at a strategic level to develop winning strategies. Even worse, few companies have managed to make an all-pervading marketing ethic part of their culture; Marks & Spencer does not have a large marketing department (its core skills are in buying and merchandising) but it has a culture which creates and sustains great loyalty in its customers.

Since the Second World War the growth of television and other media, with a market that initially favoured sellers, has created a heavy bias in the 'marketing mix' towards advertising. With increasing emphasis on market segmentation and the growing individualism of consumers the effectiveness of advertising has become harder to substantiate. Advertising is aimed at selected crowds; marketing now has to be able to target individuals.

It is harder and perhaps more expensive to target individuals, so great skill is needed in identifying those at whom to 'pitch' and greater skill must be deployed to develop and sustain an ongoing relationship with these particular individuals. Even in marketing to companies it is essential to target individual people–a principle highlighted by Aubrey Wilson nearly 30 years ago and still imperfectly practised.

In 'pitching' to individuals how many marketers, even today, try to see the transaction they seek from the standpoint of the customer? Julius Rosenwald, the founder of Sears Roebuck, once expressed a wish to be able to stand on both sides of the counter at the same time. Marketing is a two-sided process and the winning insights mostly come from the customer's side of the counter. To create a customer-orientated market why not change the 'New Products Department' into the 'New Solutions Department'?!

The growing emphasis in recent years on competitive strategy is healthy and realistic. Michael Porter's exploration and codification of competitive strategy has helped marketers to grapple with issues of competitive advantage with greater clarity and purpose. There is, however, a danger that competitive strategy becomes an end in itself and not a means to a more fundamental end. The objective of marketing is to win and retain customers not to concentrate on demolishing competitors. Market share may be won by competitive strategy, it can only be sustained by building customer loyalty.

Much has been written in recent years about excellence, total quality and customer care. Historical attitudes are, however, all product-orientated and have led to the self-serving attitudes, cartels and restrictive trading practices which characterize 'fair trade'. Only when organizations place the customer unequivocally at the centre of their culture and take the risks of living by the values of quality and customer service will they create the climate in which strategic marketing can build for them a long-term prosperous future.

This book–what it is and is not

This book is not primarily a treatise on marketing strategy. That subject has been well covered by a number of authors, most recently by Paul Fifield. The main objective of this book is to reintegrate marketing with the long-term strategic direction of the business and to ensure that it can fulfil its strategic role of helping to shape corporate strategy and of acting as the main agent implementing that strategy.

The book is constructed in such a way that the reader will hopefully be able to:

1. Appreciate where marketing has come from and where it is capable of taking us in the future.
2. Understand in broad outline the 'mysteries' of strategic planning, with emphasis on the 'logical incremental' model, and the crucial role of marketing in providing external intelligence and understanding to the strategic planning process.
3. Understand how strategies are formulated or can be adapted to respond to emergent opportunities or threats.
4. Recognize that the implementation of corporate strategy has often been inadequate, partly due to the failure of management to link corporate strategy and marketing.
5. Demonstrate the effectiveness of integrating marketing and the total strategic management process, using a number of case studies.

The case studies follow the earlier parts of the book which explore the different stages of strategic management and of strategic marketing. Some readers may find that this does not fit their favourite pattern of learning; for them the case studies are signposted earlier in the text and can be read at that stage if desired.

The marketing environment

CHAPTER 1

Origins of marketing and development to date

Trading is one of the oldest social activities in the world and occurs whenever people share an activity, as in marketing, or where there is an economic surplus to be exchanged for goods or services in short supply. Even the so-called oldest profession in the world is based on trading!

Evidence for the scale of trading in pre-Christian times is regularly uncovered by archaeologists. Copper goods from the Mediterranean are found at late Iron Age sites in Britain; the trade within the Hellenic and Roman worlds was on a scale which was not repeated until the sixteenth century. Between these times societies had become more secluded and self-sufficient; the manorial system of feudal times was virtually an enclosed economy until the Black Death in the fourteenth century and the growth of the craft system broke it down.

The three fundamental issues that an economy must resolve are seen by Paul Samuelson (1992) to be:

1. What commodities shall be produced and in what quantities? That is, how much and which of alternative goods and services should be produced?
2. How shall goods be produced? That is, by whom and with what resources and in what technological manner are they to be produced?
3. For whom are goods to be produced? That is, who is to enjoy and get the benefits of the goods and services provided? To put it another way, how is the total of the national product to be distributed among different individuals and families?

All economies, from the most primitive to the most sophisticated, have faced and had to resolve these issues. In earlier times priorities were mostly set through the power system–royalty, the nobility and the priesthood had first claim on resources and their wishes steered both production and innovation. It was also the wishes of those in power that drove the trading system and for centuries, when most people were preoccupied with survival, cultivated the taste for the novel, the unusual and the personal which fuelled the growth of civilization.

Most of the trade in earlier times would have been local and involving utilitarian items–food, clothing, tools, etc. All would have been traded as commodities with values established by custom but conditioned by major fluctuations of supply and demand. Trade in less utilitarian goods would have mainly been over longer distances, a picture of which is evoked by John Masefield's poem 'Cargoes':

> 'Quinquireme of Nineveh from distant Ophir,
> Rowing home to haven in sunny Palestine,
> With a cargo of ivory,
> And apes and peacocks,
> Sandalwood, cedarwood and sweet white wine.'

Few such luxury goods were differentiated other than by origin and it was only over time that clients began to prefer a statue by Phidias or a building by Ictinus. Such preferences must have existed in the choice of weapons and even of some tools, but the names of such super-armourers and outstanding blacksmiths are lost in time. Superior performance was beginning to have a growing importance as the world became more competitive and the rewards of success more enticing to kings such as Croesus and conquerors like Alexander the Great.

With the progressive collapse of the Roman Empire and the onset of the Dark Ages this extensive and mostly free trading pattern was broken and societies largely turned in upon themselves. Trading was still important to the courts and still a source of wealth in certain commodities (e.g. wool). The Crusades were partly mercantile in character and kept open supply routes from Asia. The depredations of the Vikings were accompanied by a significant expansion of trade within a limited area. Nevertheless, the extent and volume of trade retracted in the Dark Ages and did not begin to expand again significantly until the Age of Discovery, which blossomed from the end of the fifteenth century.

The earliest voyages of discovery were mainly made by the Spanish and Portuguese. They were financed by or for their courts and aimed at finding and monopolizing the treasures of the East. The treasure found was mainly in the West but was subjected to strict exclusivity and brought back for hoarding and for financing further conquest. The British, Dutch and other traders were excluded from the Iberian trading system, and operated either on the fringe of the system or plundered it as pirates. Sir Walter Raleigh, Sir Francis Drake and others developed the ability to live by their wits but were in reality as mercantilist as the Spaniards. The slave trade which developed in the seventeenth century was as closed a system as the gold and silver trade of Spain and Portugal.

The ideal of free trade, lost since the demise of the city-states of Greece, did not re-emerge until the Iberian system was in decline and Britain was established as the strongest maritime power in the world and the cradle of the Industrial Revolution. Adam Smith's *The Wealth of Nations* was published in 1776, and articulated for the first time the arguments for free trade. The doctrine of the 'invisible hand' shows the working of free market forces, while recognizing areas where the state must take the lead (e.g. providing bridges and lighthouses). Individuals pursuing their own best interests will collectively maximize the wealth of all nations. These ideas reflected the limited intervention of government in industry and markets in eighteenth-century Britain, which enabled that country to outstrip France and other Continental countries in the race to industrialize. With the Napoleonic Wars, the development of the Continental System and increasing government intervention, the nineteenth century saw the return of mercantilism in most major economies and the corruption of Smith's ideas into the doctrine of *laissez-faire* in Britain and the USA.

The Great Depression in the 1920s and 1930s was seen as the ultimate consequence of unbridled *laissez-faire*. Statist doctrines based on Marx, Rocco and others gained greater credence and the corporate state became the preferred economic model in Russia, Italy, Germany, Spain, Argentina and elsewhere. As Samuel Brittan states (1977):

> 'The 'corporate state' rests on the fallacy that the national interest is the sum of the interests of trade unionists, farmers, employers, shopkeepers and so on. Even if it were true that everyone is a producer, and there were no such people as housewives and pensioners, it would still be a fallacy. For it ignores the interest that everyone has as a consumer, which is diffused among thousands of products and activities aside from his particular industry. A producer-orientated society is likely to make its own members worse off because of their apparent interest in shoring up each other's special interests and restrictive practices. The result on an international scale leads to tariffs, quotas, trade wars, competitive devaluation and similar aggressive phenomena which cause political as well as economic harm.'

The failure of statism has recently been confirmed by the collapse of the key role model, the economy of the USSR. Mercantilism survives in pockets despite the very real contribution of GATT since the ending of the Second World War. The difficulty of penetrating the Japanese market and the consequent rise of US protectionism, allied to fears about the openness of the European Community to outsiders, have created a situation where the march of freer trade has halted. Much hangs on developments following the successful outcome of the Uruguay Round but the progressive move to global markets in the last forty years should be unstoppable and the free working of the 'invisible hand' should make all nations richer as the twenty-first century comes into sight. Given the wider working of markets and competition, it could be said that the Age of Marketing has dawned. In such an age 'success goes to those who combine the highest degree of aggression with the fullest application of intelligence', in the words of Robert Heller (1987).

What is marketing?

As Robert Louis Stevenson said in *Across the Plains*: 'Everyone lives by selling something'. Even where no money passes we all spend much of our time selling ourselves to others; how quickly even a baby understands the value of its smile! Selling is, however, only the culmination of the marketing process. In the words of Professor Peter Doyle: 'Selling is making people want what you've got, while marketing is selling people what they want.'

Peter Drucker (1954) sees the only valid purpose of business as the creation of a customer. In his view there are only two basic functions of business–marketing and innovation. 'Marketing is the distinguishing, the unique function of the business'. If this is true then for centuries people have been marketing unknowingly, just as Molière's Monsieur Jourdain was surprised to find he had been speaking prose all his life! Business-people have obviously prospered increasingly since the dawn of civilization; some, like Henry Ford, despite their insistence on anti-marketing stances such as selling only black cars. Yet the word 'marketing' would have had little meaning until after the Second World War. Drucker quotes it as being in a GE Annual Report for 1952, but the date of first use remains obscure.

We have seen earlier the pattern of economic history and of the growth of world trade. Only in periods of peace and prosperity have free market policies been in evidence. Since the Second World War we have had the longest uninterrupted period of world peace and expansion of trade for which meaningful records are available. It may be no coincidence that this same period has seen the recognition of marketing as a generating force for prosperity and as a key instrument of competitive advantage in a world of increasingly deregulated markets. In his book *Management Controls in Marketing* (1973) R. M. S. Wilson states: 'The distinction between marketing and sales is highlighted by the distinction between strategy and tactics–marketing is basically a study of strategy, whereas selling is essentially a tactical operation.'

In the same post-war period business has expanded and grown by merger and acquisition in order to achieve ever more competitive economies of scale. The resources deployed now have to be planned with greater care and investments have to be made over longer periods.

Businesses can no longer plan over shorter periods; budgeting is now supplemented by corporate planning. Business can only be managed strategically in modern conditions, despite the difficulties of planning in turbulent times, and marketing has become a key element in the process of establishing and delivering corporate strategy. Selling is now directed strategically through marketing; the marketing process should ensure that the focus of strategy is constantly on the customer.

The term 'marketing' is born out of the age-old process of trading in markets. The New Market in Istanbul is said to be a thousand years old and the 'marketing concept' can easily be traced back to Adam Smith and his belief that consumption is the sole end and purpose of production. What distinguishes marketing from selling, as we saw above, is the emphasis on the customer–as Ted Levitt said (in terms little different from those of Peter Drucker): 'The purpose of a business is to create and keep a customer.'

Marketing is defined by the Chartered Institute of Marketing to be 'the management function responsible for identifying, anticipating and satisfying customer requirements profitably'. Baker quotes a less portentous definition–'marketing is selling goods that don't come back to people that do'! I prefer this definition to the many alternatives that are both more detailed and more confusing. It does, however, beg the question about differentiating marketing from selling. Levitt (1975) sees this as follows:

> 'Selling focuses on the needs of the seller, marketing on the needs of the buyer. Selling is preoccupied with the seller's need to convert his product into cash, marketing with the idea of satisfying the needs of the customer by means of the product and the whole cluster of things associated with creating, delivering and finally consuming it.'

Marketing and selling may also be seen on a continuum, in which marketing analyses customer needs and market conditions and prepares the salesforce to achieve the sales. This is also the continuum between planning and implementation. Frequently there is also a trade-off between the effort invested in marketing and the ease of the sale. Yet what about the next sale, and the one that follows? This is where marketing becomes strategic.

Strategic marketing is the building of competitive and sustainable long-term customer relationships which give continuing value to both parties. The key factor in strategic marketing is relationship; as in a marriage, that relationship has to be nurtured continuously and to be of sustained value to both parties by comparison with any alternatives. All relationships are subject to competition and all depend for long-term success on a shared set of values and compatible objectives. Obtaining value from a relationship is not only a commercial consideration, although this must be of fundamental importance, but is also an issue of working to create ongoing compatibility.

Limits to consumption–new strategies for opulence

Marketing emerged as a coherent force at a time when the ending of wartime shortages began to restore some market power to buyers. Many of the earlier techniques were based on manipulation and were later challenged by populists like Vance Packard and Ralph Nader. Some of these techniques, such as the cruder uses of direct mailing, still reek of manipulation, as anyone who has tried to escape from the attentions of some well-known practitioners can testify. It has been claimed that some products (for example, insurance) are not bought and can only be sold. This phenomenon is seen more recently in the high-pressure selling of timeshares in popular holiday resorts, involving practices more redolent of customer abuse than customer care. The growth of such excesses, seen also in pyramid franchises, 'network marketing', high-pressure telephone selling and other predatory practices, shows that concern for the customer is little more prevalent than in earlier days of foot-in-the-door salesmanship and the purveying of snake oil and other magic remedies.

Marketing has also thrived on the growth of competition. The breakdown of many of the cartels and restrictive practices which enhanced producer power, and the remarkable expansion of world trade in the last forty years, have opened markets to an extent unknown for over 200 years. Before the Second World War an average car cost some £150 and an average house approximately £600. This represented 100 per cent and some 400 per cent of the average yearly wage. Today these figures are some £7000 and £50 000, respectively, representing 46 per cent and 333 per cent of average annual earnings, despite the higher taxation levied, particularly on cars. The smaller decrease for houses reflects the distorting effect of tax subsidies. Even more remarkable, when the growth of competition combines with advancing technology, is the example of computer power. A modern personal computer has the processing power of the largest early mainframe installation. Its cost is a fraction of 1 per cent of the cost of that installation. The remarkable proliferation of new routes and multiple fares following the deregulation of internal airfares in the USA during the 1980s contrasts with the stultified growth of many international routes which remain hampered by bilateral government treaties and high entry barriers to prospective new carriers.

Despite the best efforts of producers, distributors and most governments, the pressure to liberalize markets has been growing in most parts of the world. The European Commission took the lead in obtaining legislation to create a free internal market for the Community from 1993 onwards. It is unlikely that this process will be achieved on time or without challenge, but a momentum has been created which is being copied in North and South America and will probably have echoes in the Pacific Basin (Australia and New Zealand have already moved to free mutual trade). Success with the Uruguay Round should make these movements converge in a rapid surge in world trade; had the GATT negotiations failed it could have left the world with a 'triad' of trading blocs pivoting on the USA, Japan and the European Community. As a result of GATT and other treaties trade will be liberalized within a wider space and competition will increase markedly in most markets.

These developments will lead to an expansion of certain under-developed markets (e.g. Asia, Eastern Europe) and John Naisbitt (1984) sees no limit to the economic growth he expects in the 1990s. Growth requires both the means of its achievement and the desire to go on increasing consumption. The emergence of a vocal and growing concern about the environment, and the beginnings of a recognition of the dangers of further rapid growth in population, give pause for thought about the implications of unlimited consumption. Many of the scares of the past–Thomas Malthus, the Club of Rome and, most recently, *Report on the Year 2000*–have proved to be exaggerated if not totally misconceived. Evidence for global warming is still incomplete and some of the excitement about tropical rainforests has been 'unscientific', yet environmental issues, combining with an increase in religious belief in some countries, linked to a wider recognition that happiness is more than greater consumption, may be driving a change of perception. It is said that new recruits at Cadbury's chocolate factory were encouraged to indulge themselves in the company's products, leading 'the appetite to sicken and thus die'. Perhaps we now seek or recognize the need for options other than the acquisition and consumption of goods and services.

Human beings who are less unsure of themselves than their forebears, and hopefully better educated than them, will have the luxury of a wider choice in how to run their lives. Instead of living to work they will have the option of working in order to live. For them, living may mean more than subsistence, more than conspicuous and peer-driven consumption, hopefully a greater degree of self-fulfilment. Even the process of self-development generates a demand for libraries, art galleries, musical instruments, antiques and other relevant goods and services. For all the self-fulfilment that painting can give, it requires a modest outlay on materials in order to produce finished work of however great an added value. Consumption will move into new and more elusive channels which will challenge the imagination and ingenuity of marketers as never before.

Some of the self-fulfilment may be solitary, like lone sailing in yachts and the isolation sought by latter-day hermits. Most self-fulfilment, however, depends on peer involvement–it is hard to climb major mountain peaks without assistance, birdwatchers like to compare notes and even stamp collectors form mutual-interest groups to advance the frontiers of their hobby. At present, most of these peer groups are voluntary and loosely organized. As their scope and number grow greater, investment and organization will be necessary; the modern golf club bears little resemblance to its predecessor of the 1920s. As work becomes a means not an end for a growing majority, the professionalism developed to succeed at work will switch into maximizing the process of self-fulfilment, which will become a new battlefield for the competitive spirit. This process is already well advanced in the field of sport and is evident in many of the arts. As it moves into wider areas of self-fulfilment new markets will emerge which are as yet dimly foreseen. The tourist industry was built by Thomas Cook and his imitators out of religious excursions and dilettante walks in the Swiss Alps; many new industries will be born out of the growing search for personal self-fulfilment in the 1990s.

Markets in the 1990s–the immediate challenge

In the 1980s marketing became the key function both to restore and then to fuel the growth of prosperity. Greater emphasis on service industries strengthened marketing relative to most other functions, and marketing was seen in many quarters as the cutting edge to increase the growth of profits needed to facilitate mergers and acquisitions and, later in the decade, to fund the growing burden of debt needed for management buy-outs and buy-ins.

The influence of marketing can be seen behind John Naisbitt's 'Megatrends' for the 1980s:

1. Industrial society moving to information society
2. Forced technology moving to high technology/high touch
3. National economy moving to world economy
4. Short term moving to long term
5. Centralization moving to decentralization
6. Institutional help moving to self-help
7. Representative democracy moving to participative democracy
8. Hierarchies moving to networking
9. North moving South (the demographic move in the USA to seek a better quality of living)
10. Either/or moving to multiple option

Not all these trends were accomplished in the 1980s; short-termism is still a powerful force, reinforced latterly by recession. The battle to liberate the National Health Service from bureaucracy still rages, for example, though the growth of consumer awareness is now forcing more choice and greater responsiveness from producers and even some institutions. The consumer movement, started in the 1960s and personified by activists like Ralph Nader, gathered strength through the 1970s and 1980s. A major consumer expert Jim Turner sees consumerism as 'the economic expression of the American Revolution'. The growth of consumer power in the US by the early 1980s was such that Jim Turner stated 'consumers are to economies what voters are to politics'. A study by Lou Harris in 1977, *Consumerism at the Crossroads*, warned that producers had no more than ten years to begin to bring consumers into the corporate decision-making process or there would be a return to the militant consumerism of the 1960s and early 1970s. Unfortunately, too many producers see consumers as a threat and consumerism as a menace to their profitability. Consumerism is seen by some writers (e.g. Vance Packard) as the shame of marketing. Michael Baker sees consumerism as a cry for help, drawing attention to the need to re-establish balance in the marketplace between producers (and distributors) and their customers. The pressure of producers in the major economies to seek to wreck the Uruguay Round negotiations demonstrated starkly that the balance in the marketplace remains far from restored.

At the threshold of the 1990s John Naisbitt and Patricia Aburdene wrote *Megatrends 2000*. The Megatrends of the 1980s, identified above, are seen to 'continue pretty much on schedule'. They are, however, now seen to be supplemented by a new set of forces, namely:

1. The booming global economy of the 1990s (derived from Megatrend 3 above)
2. A renaissance of the arts (derived from Megatrend 1 above)
3. The emergence of free-market socialism (derived from Megatrends 5 and 6 above)
4. Global lifestyles and cultural nationalism (derived from Megatrend 3 above)
5. The privatization of the welfare state (derived from Megatrend 6 above)
6. The rise of the Pacific Rim (derived from Megatrend 3 above)
7. The decade of women in leadership (derived from Megatrend 8 above)
8. The age of biology (derived from Megatrend 1 above)

9. The religious revival of the new millennium (derived from Megatrend 6 above)
10. The triumph of the individual (derived from Megatrends 6–10 above)

From these Megatrends emerges a picture of a society of global scope, enriched by the reduction of defence expenditure and following success in the Uruguay Round, hopefully, by further freeing of world trade and the greater use of information, breaking down hierarchies and barriers to achievement by minorities, encouraging individuals to greater self-fulfilment in a caring society. Individuals will be liberated; no longer will they have to work against their own interests as consumers in the guise of an 'organization man', to employ William Hyde Whyte's chilling expression. They will have more scope for living, greater choice of goods and services, less government and more involvement in the decisions which affect their lives. The assumption must be that people will become more responsible, more educated, less greedy for material satisfaction and more concerned for spiritual, artistic, environmental and cultural issues. Allowing that this picture omits the workings of original sin, the threat of crime, drugs and desperate migrations to fight for a better life and other menaces to the Megatrends, what are the implications for marketing in the 1990s?

The most obvious implication of the Megatrends is that individuals will become more self-aware and progressively more confident about their values. These values will increasingly come from education and self-improvement and less from peer groups or external pressure. Much of today's advertising appears to be aimed at a mental age of eight years and urges conformity; it is interesting that Guinness has seized on the opportunity to promote non-conformity in its 'Man in Black' advertisements, and this may become a new trend.

Marketers will need to deal with customers more as individuals. At present, customers are analysed by demographic socio-economic and other groupings. The ABC socio-economic classifications were devised over fifty years ago at a time when society was both simpler and more static. Not only are some marketing tools out of date but they are increasingly inadequate without validation by closer customer contact. Even consumer panels are too mechanistic to make the fine qualitative judgements on which effective marketing will increasingly rely in the future. When Peters and Waterman (1982) cited 'close to the customer' as a source of excellence they were not talking about market research techniques but about close personal relationships. Research by Doyle, Saunders and Wong in 1985, quoted by Baker and Hart (1989), shows that successful customer contact needed visits by company executives and not just sales staff. Tetra-Pak's territorial managers are expected to spend at least half their time talking to customers. Most important in the future, as Peters and Waterman emphasize, will be not customer education nor mere customer contact but obsessive listening to customers. In the words of Malcolm McDonald (1984): 'The customer rarely simply buys a product; he buys a relationship with his supplier.'

With the triumph of the individual will come both a greater requirement to match product offer with customer needs and a commitment to offer choice. In *Marketing Myopia* (1975) Ted Levitt stated:

> 'People buy solutions to problems, not products, and successful marketers are problem solvers. They differentiate their products/services from the competition with tangible features and intangible promises and metaphors that present customers with the answers to their problems.'

Many customer needs are not perceived, let alone articulated, and may only emerge when a solution presents itself–as in the case of 3M's Post-it Notes. Such latent needs are likely to increase as life becomes richer and more complex. The need to offer choice is already recognized by some companies. Volvo offers a range which has more than 20 000 permutations. Choice can be confusing to customers who are unsure of themselves; tomorrow's better educated and more demanding customers will use choice only to achieve an optimized solution to their needs.

References

Baker, Michael and Hart, Susan, *Marketing and Competitive Success*, Philip Allan, Deddington, 1989.

Brittan, Samuel, *The Economic Consequences of Democracy*, Temple Smith, 1977.

Drucker, Peter, *The Practice of Management*, Harper and Row, New York, 1954.

Heller, Robert, *The Supermarketers*, Sidgwick and Jackson, London, 1987.

Levitt, T., 'Marketing myopia', *Harvard Business Review*, September/October 1975.

McDonald, Malcolm, *Marketing Plans*, Heinemann, London, 1984.

Naisbitt, J., *Megatrends*, Futura, London. 1984.

Naisbitt, J. and Aburdene, P., *Megatrends 2000*, Futura, London, 1990.

Peters, T.J. and Waterman, R.H., *In Search of Excellence*, Harper & Row, New York, 1982.

Samuelson, Paul, *Economics–an Introductory Analysis*, McGraw-Hill, New York, 1992.

Smith, Adam, *The Wealth of Nations*, 1776.

Wilson, R. M. S., *Management Controls in Marketing*, Heinemann, London, 1973.

The strategic context

CHAPTER 2

Few words create more confusion than 'strategy'. Igor Ansoff (1979) quotes an unknown source–'strategy is when you are out of ammunition and keep right on firing so the enemy won't know'! A glossary covering this and other terms may be found at the end of this book. The *Concise Oxford English Dictionary* defines strategy as 'generalship, the art of war (literally and figuratively); management of an army or armies in a campaign, art of so moving or disposing troops or ships as to impose upon the enemy the place and time and conditions for fighting preferred by oneself'. Kenichi Ohmae (1982) draws powerful analogies between military and business strategy in his book *The Mind of the Strategist*–'grasping the state of the market, objectively assessing the strengths and weaknesses of one's business, changing direction with flexibility when required, and calculating the amount of profit or loss likely to result from each management action'. If this is linked to the idea of imposing on competitors the place, time and conditions of battle the analogy is almost complete. Ohmae warns 'both the business strategist and the military planner are prone to be trapped by perfectionism'–no strategy is likely to be perfect and none should be inflexible. In the land of the blind one eye is enough to make you king.

Strategy can only be realistically developed in a situation where there is a clear objective and there are one or more antagonists who seek to prevent you from achieving it. Strategy without direction and competition is only a policy which explains the rationale and difficulty of bringing market forces to bear on government departments. The process of establishing objectives and the strategies needed to achieve them is known as the 'strategic process'.

The strategic process begins with a clear definition of the purpose of the enterprise. For businesses this has traditionally been to maximize shareholder profits and company law has been built on that foundation. Many businesses now seek a wider purpose; some wish to satisfy a range of stakeholders (shareholders, employees, customers, suppliers, local interests, etc.), others have broader horizons (The Body Shop seeks to protect the environment). Komatsu stated that its purpose was 'to encircle Caterpillar' and has moved far towards achieving it. Other Japanese companies declare similar competitive purposes which are powerful long-term motivators to their employees and other stakeholders. Honda countered a strategic threat from Yamaha to its dominance of the motorcycle market with the mission: 'We will crush, squash, slaughter Yamaha' and proceeded to do so.

In a powerful article in *Long Range Planning*, George Binney (1991) argues that there is an inhibition in British companies against open statements of any purpose other than maximizing shareholder profits. Charles Handy (1985) propounds the 'existential organization' dedicated to maximizing its potential and 'striving for immortality'. Given the gap between the power of a clear purpose adopted by all stakeholders and the inadequate performance of many British companies, there is a need for most of them to make a radical restatement of purpose. The customers of The Body Shop are not offered the cheapest prices but are, in a large measure, loyal to a purpose which is wider than pure profit. As more and more countries move up Maslow's (1954) 'hierarchy of needs' from material satisfaction towards self-realization such a phenomenon should become more common.

Given a clear purpose, the business needs to articulate a strategic vision. This is a picture of the business at an indeterminate time in the future when it has materially achieved its purpose. This will identify the size, scope and activities of the business and provide a model towards which stakeholders can strive. Campbell, Devine and Young (1990) in their book *A Sense of Mission* criticize strategic vision as a motivator, since, in their view, a tangible vision is soon achieved and loses validity and a remote vision fails to motivate. This is true at the extremes, but a well-articulated vision which is not too remote remains a powerful focus for leadership and a beacon to maintain strategic direction in the midst of storms. Such a vision, to be 'the world's favourite airline', has galvanized and sustained British Airways through the recent crisis in the airline industry. *The Economist* (1991) reports that a sample of 20 visionary companies selected by American top managers was shown to have outperformed Wall Street by a factor of 50 (based on investing $1 in each share in the mid-1920s). Strategic vision is therefore the distant objective, strategic direction is provided by the company's sense of mission.

Mission is defined by Campbell, Devine and Young as 'the combination of purpose, strategy, values and behaviour standards' (see Figure 2.1). The Strategic Planning Society defines mission as 'the core tasks which an organization intends to carry out to achieve the corporate purpose within the constraints of corporate vision'. Mission is often expressed in 'mission statements', which typically set out the corporate purpose, define the businesses in which the company will engage and the competitive posture to be taken, and detail the values and behaviour standards which characterize the culture of the company and the relationship sought with all stakeholders. Current thinking favours the definition of key or core

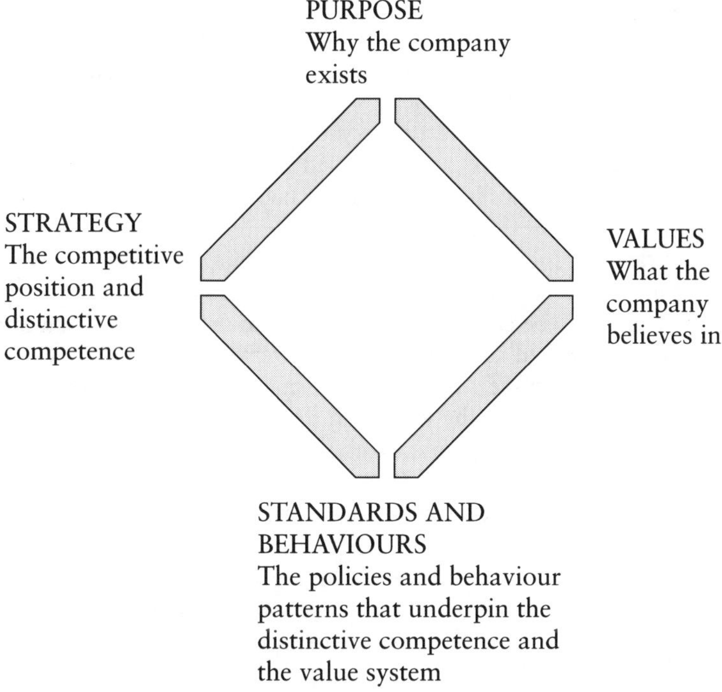

Figure 2.1 The Ashridge mission model (Campbell *et al.*, 1990)

competences in mission statements as well as, or rather than, defining specific businesses. This avoids trapping the future of the business in the cage of today's thinking. Some examples of mission statements are shown in Appendix 1. To be effective a mission statement must be a well-publicized document inside and outside the company. It will not, therefore, detail the specific strategic objectives of the company nor the precise strategies for achieving them; these are crucial elements of the corporate plan.

Strategic objectives are set for the longer term, usually beyond the period of the current corporate plan but often short of achieving the competitive or market postures targeted in the mission statement. They will usually be larger in number and more specific than the ambitions shown in the mission statement. Some companies like to have quantified strategic objectives (e.g. a return on nett assets of 20 per cent per annum). Such precision is laudable in principle but gives a hostage to fortune. To take our example, a return of 20 per cent might be inadequate if sustained by heavy borrowings at a high rate of interest at some future time, or if shareholders came to expect a better performance by comparison with other potential investments. It is usually more meaningful to set an objective such as 'the highest rate of return on nett assets in our industry', which is flexible but remains a stretching challenge in all circumstances.

The strategic objectives are approached over time through shorter-term goals. These are usually detailed in the corporate plan and should be specific and quantified. The delivery of the targeted goals is driven by detailed strategies. These are discussed later in this chapter, and the formulation of strategies is addressed in Chapter 3 and corporate planning in Chapter 4.

The strategic process, having started with purpose, must logically end with achievement. The implementation of the strategies developed by the company needs to be closely monitored, and in the same way that budgets are closely monitored to ensure that they remain on track, it is essential that corporate plans are subject to performance review and that strategic control is exercised over the long-term direction of the business.

Strategic control complements the financial controls that are well established in most businesses. Financial control is essential to provide the resources to achieve objectives; strategic control ensures that the company's long-term direction is maintained, its strategies remain effective, its values and culture are not corrupted and that its vision remains valid in conditions of turbulence and change. Strategic control processes in the experience of Michael Goold (1990) offer the following advantages:

1. Greater clarity and realism in planning
2. Encourage higher standards of performance
3. Provide more motivation for business unit managers
4. Permit more timely intervention by corporate management
5. Avoid 'back-door' financial control
6. Make decentralization work better by defining responsibilities more clearly.

The form of strategic control will depend on the nature of the business, but the process adopted should be consistent with the culture of the company (e.g. no covert recentralization of a decentralized business) and be responsive to emergent change. From his research Michael Goold identified both formal and informal strategic control processes. Formal processes normally require the setting of 'milestones' at intervals on the path to achieving specific objectives. Only 15 per cent of his respondents had explicit milestones for their key strategies; most other companies concentrate on the key financial aggregates of their business and allow strategic deviations to emerge through regular management contacts. With sensitivity and good communications an informal system can work well, but informality can often hide a lack of purpose and be exploited by the devious.

Conglomerates do not seek to establish any strategic controls. Goold and A. Campbell in earlier research (1987) identified three strategic control styles among companies. Companies such as GEC, BTR and Hanson had a 'financial control' style which was based on financial targets or ratios, leaving strategic management to the individual subsidiary, if it wished. At the other extreme lay companies such as Shell, NatWest and Digital Equipment, which had a 'strategic planning' style in which strategy was agreed jointly between subsidiaries and the centre. In the middle were companies such as ICI and Courtaulds, which largely delegated strategy to business units and exercised control through agreed strategic and financial performance targets—the 'strategic management' style.

Despite some notable exceptions, the use of strategic controls by British companies is underdeveloped and less than fully effective. In highly diversified businesses strategic control from the centre is difficult and a portfolio approach to managing the group may be the only practical solution. This does require, however, extreme care in the acquisition of businesses and a ruthless approach to performance and, if necessary, disposal. Many British conglomerates have a good track record in this respect. For businesses which attempt to build a core competence with sustainable competitive advantage the need for strategic controls is more pressing. Frank Harrison (1991) shows that weakness in strategic controls is also evident in US business. He quotes examples of successful use of strategic controls in the mergers of Chevron with Gulf Oil and of Wells Fargo Bank with Crocker Bank as well as the restructuring and recovery of Bank of America. A survey carried out by Harrison showed, however, that chief executives scored higher in the creative and planning end of the strategic management process than in strategic control. Improving performance in strategic control will no doubt be a key issue for Anglo-Saxon management as worldwide competition with countries with a more strategic culture, such as Japan and Germany, accelerates and intensifies.

Strategies

We have examined the strategic process and followed its logical steps through from establishing purpose to exercising strategic control over the achievement of progress in the chosen long-term direction. It is important to set carefully conceived and evaluated objectives, but the motive force of the whole process comes from strategies. Only sustainably successful strategies can move the business from its present stance to the achievement of its vision.

We saw earlier that the concept of strategy is based on the interplay of two or more antagonists. As in war, strategy will be the sum of a number of substrategies whose interplay is aimed at achieving competitive advantage. These substrategies will, in turn, break down into lower-level strategies and the specific tactics needed at an operational level to move those strategies forward. Such tactics are in business usually defined as tasks and built into programmes aimed at delivering the overall strategy (see Chapter 4 for more detail). For the purpose of clarity top-level strategy is usually referred to as corporate strategy, supported by business strategies which are in turn supported by functional strategies. A key functional strategy is that of marketing, which is discussed in Chapter 7.

Each of the company's objectives will need one or more strategies to ensure its achievement. Some of these strategies will be developed through conscious planning, others will be 'emergent' strategies which evolve out of changes in circumstances affecting the company. Strategies are the means to an end, achieving the strategic objective, which, if well chosen, should not readily be changed. Strategies should be selected with care and be as robust as possible to changes in assumptions, but should be pursued only as far as they may realistically be expected to achieve the strategic objective over time. Strategies consume resources and must prove themselves to be effective within the expected timescale or must be subject to stringent reassessment and, if necessary, abandonment.

What form do strategies take? An early practitioner of business strategies, L. C. Sorrell, had strategies like 'strike while the iron is hot', 'time is a great healer', 'pass the buck' and 'conserve your gunpowder'! The controls of such strategies may be surmised and may well have been successful. Michael Porter (1980) is preoccupied with competitive strategy, and in his book *Competitive Strategy* identified three 'generic' strategies:

1. Overall cost leadership } industry-wide
2. Differentiation }
3. Focus (1 or 2 above directed at a market niche)

This approach appears oversimplistic; Porter does not exclude tailored strategies but maintains that they will almost certainly have at least one foot in one or more of his generics. His book explores a number of industry-specific derivative strategies; for declining industries he examines the options of (1) seeking market leadership, (2) creating and defending a selected niche, (3) 'harvesting' by controlled disinvestment and (4) divesting quickly. The case studies in Chapters 8 and 9 explore other specific and successful strategies.

Peter Drucker in *Innovation and Entrepreneurship* (1985) identifies four specific and distinct entrepreneurial strategies (using folksy language reminiscent of Sorrell):

1. Being 'firstest with the mostest' (leadership with a new product)
2. 'Hitting them where they ain't' (improving someone else's pioneering product)
3. Finding and occupying a specialized ecological niche
4. Changing the economic characteristics of a product, a market or an industry

There are three distinct ecological niche strategies identified:

1. The tollgate strategy
2. The speciality skill strategy
3. The speciality market strategy

Drucker characterizes the tollgate strategy as producing the component without which a key product cannot function (e.g. Alcon produces an enzyme essential for cateract operations and without which they are likely to fail). Given the size of the market, there is no room for a competitor and entry barriers would be high. The speciality skill market may be characterized by the Michelin guides which have built an infrastructure and reputation which for prospective competitors present a high barrier to entry. An example of a speciality market strategy is the development of the worldwide market for biscuit machinery by Baker Perkins, a medium-sized subsidiary of APV.

Changing values and characteristics involves creating a customer by (1) creating utility and (2) delivering what represents true value to the customer.

Peter Drucker quotes Rowland Hill's Penny Post as a reform which created utility by making the post more efficient and accessible to a larger number of potential users. By doing so, it also stimulated interest in learning to read and write and multiplied its market many times over. The Xerox business was built on the policy of pricing by the number of copies rather than selling the machine. Not only did this avoid capital appropriations but it met the real need of the user. Here also availability helped to multiply the market size. Cyrus McCormick could not sell his harvesters until he offered farmers instalment payments over three years to be paid out of the savings made by his machines. He had to adapt to the economic reality of his market. Delivering true value to the customer is characterized by Drucker in the case of a medium-sized supplier of heavy lubricant which offers contractors a maintenance programme and a guarantee of minimal downtime due to lubrication problems. He sells oil, they buy trouble-free operations.

Earlier we differentiated between consciously planned and emergent strategies. Henry Mintzberg (1991) distinguishes between visionary, planning and learning models of strategy formulation. The visionary model depends on deep experience of the business sector and insights about the future owned by an outstanding leader. Mintzberg's vision serves as an umbrella under which detailed strategies can emerge but must remain informal and personal to allow it to stay rich and flexible. The planning model provides closed-end analysis, programmed strategies and orderly implementation. The learning model is not driven solely by conscious thought and involves anyone in the organization capable of contributing to strategy formulation which is an informal, often spontaneous and usually collective process. Formulation and implementation tend to be intertwined. This approach is favoured also by Ralph Stacey, author of *Managing Chaos* (1992). He sees businesses as dynamic feedback systems, subject to chaos and responding through self-organization. Learning is the driver of strategic management rather than intent.

Although Mintzberg's preference seems to lie with a less formal approach to strategy (he also contrasts favourably a 'grassroots' model with a 'hothouse' model of strategy formulation), he recognizes that businesses are likely to generate 'intended' strategies which will merge with 'emergent' strategies, dictated by random opportunity or threat, to produce a stream of realized strategies over time. Mintzberg is concerned with adaptability and sustainability; he quotes the Duke of Wellington:

> 'They [the French] planned their campaigns just as you might make a splendid piece of harness. It looks very well and answers very well; until it gets broken; and then you are done for. Now I made my campaigns of ropes. If anything went wrong, I tied a knot; and went on.'

There is no doubt that many businesses have prospered, in both the past and the present, without any conscious attempt to shape winning strategies. Much can be achieved by native wit and by personal relationships, particularly when there is a seller's market. Consumers are now more aware and buyers have the initiative. Ample supply and increasingly open markets are increasing competition to levels never previously known.

Producers can only survive, let alone prosper, by distinguishing themselves from other producers in an increasingly crowded market. To distinguish yourself on a sustainable basis requires more than native wit: it entails an understanding of your competition and the peculiarities of your market and new insights into the real or latent needs of potential customers. It requires also the ability to distil and exploit the 'critical factors for success' in meeting customers' needs. The process of building this understanding and ability, as we shall see in Chapter 3, is the process of crafting strategies.

The sources of competitive advantage

Michael Porter (1985) identifies two basic types of competitive advantage–cost leadership and differentiation. These, of course, relate to his generic strategies referred to earlier in this book. Competitive advantage is judged by the customer or buyer, not the seller, and relates to the buyer's values. Porter uses this perception to define a 'value system' in which the market operates where the value placed by the end customer can be built up through the 'value chain' of his suppliers, their suppliers and so on. Competitive advantage depends on the most advantageous relationship to the value chain of the next purchaser.

The value chain of a specific firm displays total value and comprises 'value activities' and margin. Value activities are the building blocks of the final product or service and margin represents the premium over total cost which the product can command from the buyer. An example of a generic value chain is shown in Figure 2.2. This shows that value activities can be divided into two main categories: 'primary activities' and 'support activities'.

Primary activities are identified as inbound logistics, operations, outbound logistics, marketing and sales, and service. The relative importance of each of these categories will vary from company to company; logistics will be crucial for a distribution company, operations for a restaurant and service for a supplier of cash dispensers. Each user of the value chain technique needs to make its own analysis of primary activities, probably breaking down operations in more detail, so that the real stages of adding value emerge. Support activities will comprise all tasks which the firm undertakes that are not encompassed in primary activities; Porter defines four generic categories–procurement, technology development, human resource management and firm infrastructure. The last comprises the general management, finance and other functions which complete the organization structure and the sum of costs and added value in the firm. The value chain for a copying machine manufacturer is shown in Figure 2.3.

The search for competitive advantage starts with mapping and analysing the value chains of key competitors. This process is more revealing and creative than any amount of study of your own value chain. The process of striving to understand the dynamics of a competitor's business brings new

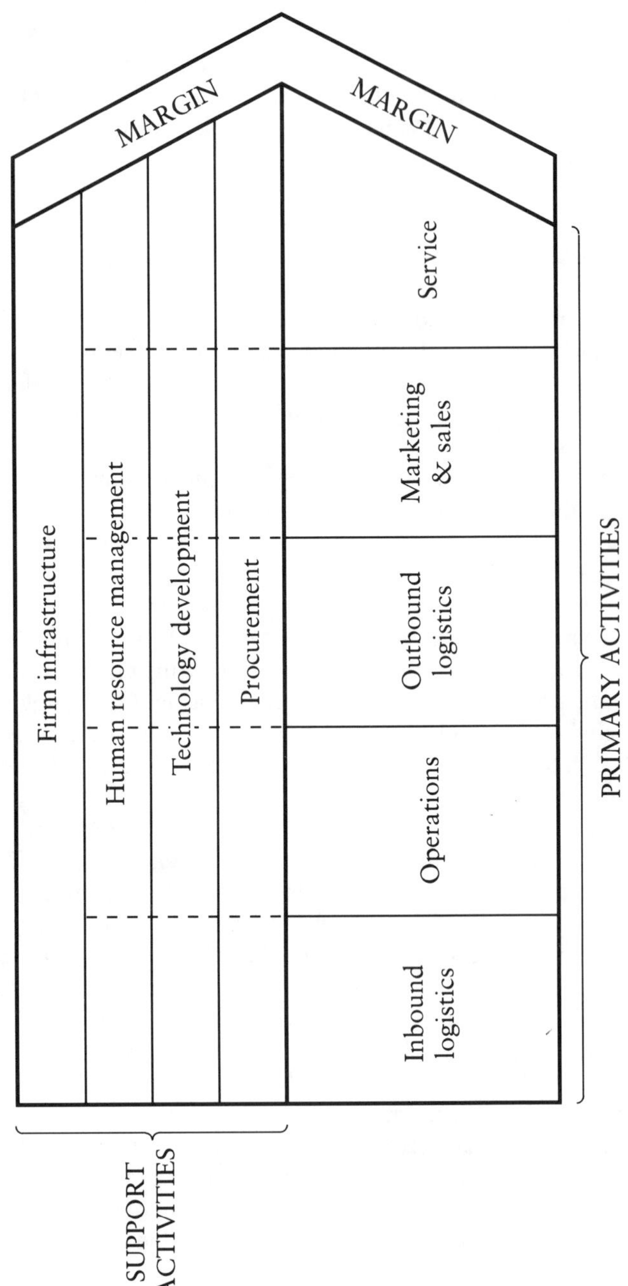

Figure 2.2 The generic value chain (Porter, 1985)

	INBOUND LOGISTICS	OPERATIONS	OUTBOUND LOGISTICS	MARKETING & SALES	SERVICE
	Firm infrastructure				
HUMAN RESOURCE MANAGEMENT		Recruiting Training		Recruiting Training	Recruiting Training
	Design of automated system	Component design Design of assembly line Machine design Testing procedures Energy management	Information system development	Market research Sales aids and technical literature	Service manuals and procedures
PROCUREMENT		Materials Energy Electrical/Electronic parts Other parts Supplies	Computer services Transportation services	Media agency services Supplies Travel and subsistence	Spare parts Travel and subsistence
	Inbound material handling Inbound inspection Parts packing and delivery	Component fabrication Assembly Fine tuning and testing Facilities operation	Order processing Shipping	Advertising Promotion Sales force	Service reps Spare parts systems

MARGIN

MARGIN

Figure 2.3 Value chain for a copier manufacturer (Porter, 1985)

insights into the key factors in the marketplace and provides sharper terms of reference for criticizing your own business. Comparison of competitor value chains with your own adds an extra dimension to your analysis and throws up gaps and wastage which might not otherwise be evident. For example, a successful competitor may be found to devote more resources to new products than your own firm, or may use direct marketing where you have relied on the use of media.

Comparison of competitors' and your own firm's value chains should not be a static exercise. Insights will be sought and found but most markets are increasingly dynamic and no analysis is complete without an attempt to evaluate the value chains from the standpoint of both your competitors and your targeted customers. It should not be assumed that competitors will be unaware of their weaknesses and will not be debating whether to address them or to build on their strengths. Nor should it be forgotten that customers are becoming increasingly demanding and will seek to enhance the value obtained from their suppliers. Analysis needs therefore to identify the direction in which the market is moving and likely reactions from competitors and customers.

The main sources of competitive advantage fall into two categories: cost leadership and differentiation. Porter identifies ten 'cost drivers', any of which, individually or by interaction, may affect each of a firm's value activities. These are economies of scale, learning, the pattern of capacity utilization, linkages, interrelationships, integration timing, discretionary policies, location and institutional factors. Examples of the effect of these drivers are shown in Table 2.1.

After mapping the costs attaching to each of the firm's value activities it is necessary to identify the cost drivers which do or may affect each of those value activities and determine the interworking of those cost drivers within each value activity. The effect of changing output rates, investment, training and other key factors can be estimated and the impact of such changes on other value activities explored. It may be found that a higher purchasing price for a partly finished part may save making costs and reduce scrap later in the process. Once this process is complete and comparisons have been made with competitors' value chains, it should be possible to establish whether cost leadership is achievable and develop a strategy to work towards it. If cost leadership is not achievable and sustainable a strategy to exploit the insights achieved and to minimize costs is still necessary if only to minimize the competitive advantage of the cost leader. The main thrust of competitive advantage will, however, need to be sought in differentiation.

Differentiation is usually a qualitative factor whereas cost leadership must largely be quantified. Differentiation is basically a search for uniqueness in a feature that is valued by customers. Differentiation is not based on price; if it creates a real value it should lead to a price

Table 2.1 Drivers of the unit cost of purchased inputs

Cost driver	*Cost driver applied to procurement*	*Description*
Economies of scale	Purchasing scale	The volume of purchasing with a given supplier affects bargaining power
Linkages	Linkages with suppliers	Coordinating with suppliers on specifications, delivery, and other activities can lower total costs
Interrelationships	Shared purchasing with other business units	Combining purchases with sister business units can improve bargaining power with suppliers
Integration	Make versus buy	Integration may raise or lower the cost of an input
Timing	History of supplier relationships	Historical loyalty to or problems with suppliers may affect input costs, access to inputs during tight periods, and services provided by suppliers
Policies	Purchasing practices	Purchasing practices can significantly improve bargaining power with suppliers and the willingness of suppliers to perform extra services, for example: ■ Selection of the number and mix of suppliers ■ Hedging procedures ■ Investment of information on supplier costs and availability ■ Annual contracts versus individual purchases ■ Utilization of by-products
Location	Supplier location	Location of suppliers can affect the cost of inputs through the cost of transportation and the ease of communication
Institutional factors	Government and union restrictions	Government policy can restrict access to inputs or affect their cost through tariffs, taxes, and other means. Unions may affect the ability to out-source or whether nonunion suppliers can be used.

From Porter (1985)

premium. Differentiation may be achievable over a wide sector of the market, as Marks & Spencer achieves with its quality and 'value for money' image, but most differentiation strategies will rely on market segmentation to achieve their full effect. A striking example of differentiation is Burmah Castrol, a medium-sized oil company which has prospered in recent years by developing a global niche in lubrication. This has differentiated Burmah Castrol from the oil majors, who are seen as energy businesses.

The sources of differentiation may be found anywhere in the value system. They may be based on the qualities of inputs into the value chain (e.g. jewellers can command a premium for using Welsh gold). They may be based on ease of handling for distribution companies at the output end of the value chain. Most of the sources of differentiation are likely to lie in the firm's value chain, in its detailed profile compared with that of competitors and in the detailed interface with the value chain of buyers. An overall view of the potential for differentiation is shown in Figure 2.4.

Porter (1985) sees differentiation as derived from 'uniqueness drivers'. These are classified as policy choices and linkages. Policy choices will, according to Porter, typically include:

- Product features and performance offered
- Services provided (e.g. credit, delivery, repair, etc.)
- Intensity of an activity (e.g. rate of advertising spend)
- Content of an activity (e.g. information provided in order processing)
- Technology employed (e.g. precision of machine tools, computerized order processing)
- Quality of inputs to an activity
- Procedures (e.g. service procedures, nature of sales calls, frequency of inspection sampling)
- Skill, experience and training of personnel in each activity
- Control information (e.g. number of variables controlled in a chemical process)

To this list one might add:

- Responsiveness to public policy (e.g. health, environment)
- Adapting the product or service for use in foreign markets
- Creating scarcity (Morgan Cars limit production)
- Scale of investment (few can match Boeing in the civil aircraft market), etc.

	INBOUND LOGISTICS	OPERATIONS	OUTBOUND LOGISTICS	MARKETING & SALES	SERVICE
FIRM INFRASTRUCTURE	Top management support in selling; Facilities that enhance the firm's image; Superior management information system				
HUMAN RESOURCE MANAGEMENT	Superior training of personnel	Stable workforce policies Quality of work life programmes Programmes to attract the best scientists and engineers		Sales incentives to retain best salespersons Recruiting better qualified sales and service personnel	Extensive training of service technicians
TECHNOLOGY DEVELOPMENT	Superior material handling & sorting technology Proprietary quality assurance equipment	Unique product features Rapid model introductions Unique production process of machines Automated inspection procedures	Unique vehicle scheduling Software Special purpose vehicles or containers	Applications engineering support Superior media research Most rapid quotations for tailored models	Advanced servicing techniques
PROCUREMENT	Most reliable transportation for inbound deliveries	Highest quality raw materials Highest quality components	Best located warehouses Transportation supplies that minimize damage	Most desirable media placements Product positioning and image	High quality replacement parts
	Handling of inputs that minimize damage or degradation Timeliness of supply for the manufacturing process	Tight conformance to specifications Attractive product appearance Reponsiveness to specification changes Low defect rates Short time to manufacture	Rapid and timely delivery Accurate and responsive order processing Handling that minimizes damage	High advertising level and quality High sales force coverage and quality Personal relationships with channels or buyers Superior technical literature & other sales aids Most extensive promotion Most extensive credit to buyers or channels	Rapid installation High service quality Complete field stocking of replacement parts Wide service coverage Extensive buyer training

MARGIN

MARGIN

Figure 2.4 Representative sources of differentiation in the value chain (Porter, 1985)

Linkages may be inside or outside the value chain. For instance, a total quality approach will reduce defects at each stage of manufacture and ensure a lower level of final rejects. Such an approach may be enhanced by moving total-quality disciplines back into the businesses of suppliers. Internal linkages are crucial also for expediting the rapid supply of urgently needed goods or for bringing urgent product modifications through to market. Supplier linkages are important at all stages from design, through tooling, to supply. Distributor linkages are important for all products not sold directly to the end user. These may involve financing, joint selling, promotional support and staff training. Distributor quality is crucial for companies like Caterpillar, and in some markets the distributor may become more powerful than the manufacturer (e.g. the food industry). Timex Products has a powerful grip of the luxury watch industry through a system of exclusive agreements.

Uniqueness may also, according to Porter, come from factors such as:

- Timing (first mover or late mover) (see Table 2.2)
- Location (critical in the retail trade)
- Interrelationships (Lloyds Bank selling insurance)
- Proprietary learning (Amersham International has unique nuclear competence)
- Integration (American Express business travel implants in key customer premises)
- Scale (the Post Office has 22 000 retail outlets and had unique coverage for selected products)
- Institutional factors (Ordnance Survey has unique authority in the map business)

Uniqueness may also come from:

- Changing the market rules (Firstdirect/Midland Bank) (see case study in Chapter 8)
- Powerful branding (Coca-Cola)
- Adding value to the product (Rolls-Royce is not just a car)
- Patronage (Simmonds of Kensington is the building firm with the Queen's Warrant)
- Historical authority (Lloyd's of London)
- Specialized market knowledge (British Antarctic Survey) etc.

Table 2.2 Technological leadership and competitive advantage

	Technological leadership	*Technological followership*
Cost advantage	Pioneer the lowest-cost product design Be the first firm down the learning curve Create low-cost ways of performing value activities	Lower the cost of the product or value activities by learning from the leader's experience Avoid R&D costs through imitation
Differentiation	Pioneer a unique product that increases buyer value Innovate in other activities to increase buyer value	Adapt the product or delivery system more closely to buyer needs by learning from the leader's experience

There has recently been significant criticism of the Porter and other models of competitor analysis. Gary Hamel and C. K. Pralahad (1989) have observed:

> 'Few Western companies have an enviable track record anticipating the moves of new global competitors. Why? The explanation begins with the way most companies have approached competitor analysis. Typically, competitor analysis focuses on the existing resources (human, technical and financial) of present competitors. The only companies seen as a threat are those with the resources to erode margins and market share in the next planning period. Resourcefulness, the pace at which new competitive advantages are being built, rarely enters in'.

Xerox failed to appreciate the seriousness of Canon's challenge to its copier business, or the power of its strategic intent to produce low-cost copiers and to market them through a different distribution channel.

Sustainable competitive advantage depends on the 'strategic intent' to which Hamel and Pralahad refer. This is identified with 'an obsession with winning at all levels of the organization' and with maintaining that obsession 'over the 10 to 20 year quest for global leadership'. In order to drive this strategic intent there is a need to identify the key objectives which will enhance performance in the areas where it is essential to seize and maintain competitive advantage. This process involves what Gregory Watson (1993) calls 'strategic benchmarking' in his book of that name. It involves setting goals based on challenging external standards–'companies selected for benchmarking because of their key business process knowledge and performance indexes can serve as a basis for establishing challenging, yet realistic and achievable goals'. He quotes the case of Hewlett-Packard, where John Young challenged the organization to think differently and to change its processes in order to drive for a tenfold improvement in hardware reliability. Change is a key element in strategic benchmarking and many companies can only achieve it through total re-engineering of their business, process by process. Strategic benchmarking is a key element of modern strategic planning and its place in the process is shown in Figure 2.5.

Strategic benchmarking depends on identifying the 'best in class' in respect of the key long-term objectives of the company. Many such paragons will be in different industries and it is important to search as widely as possible for the most challenging benchmarks. GE is a well-established strategic benchmarker and has created a network of partners with whom it shares strategic direction and methodology. It plans to build its network to include no more than sixteen customers, suppliers, strategic allies and pacesetters outside the electrical engineering industry. The

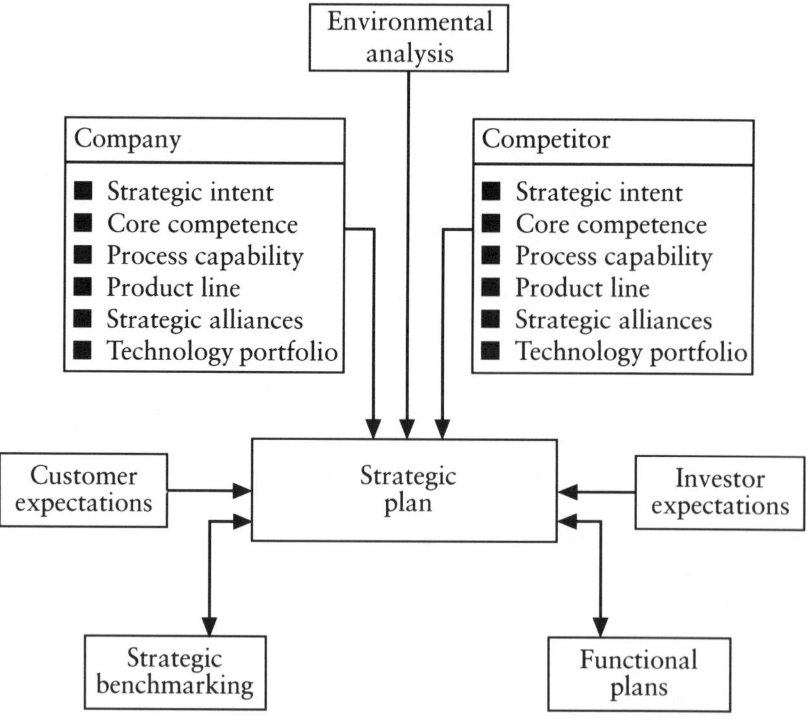

Figure 2.5 The application of strategic benchmarking (Watson, 1993)

basic principles of benchmarking, according to Watson, are reciprocity (sharing information and learning), analogy (that the methods used must be transferable), measurement (baseline and improvements over time) and validity (ensuring that the process produces real benefits).

The essence of strategic benchmarking is aggression. Too many companies settle for a 'good performance'; effective strategic benchmarking should force companies to move to levels of performance which they may initially have believed to be impossible. Some company, somewhere, is achieving spectacular increases in key performance measures–strategic benchmarking should hunt them down and learn how to beat them. Progress is rarely a gentle continuum; more typically it derives from leapfrogging those who are currently out in front and running like hell to avoid being leapfrogged in turn!

References

Ansoff, Igor, *Corporate Strategy*, Penguin, Harmondsworth, 1979.

Binney, George, 'Shareholder dominance–time to ask if the emperor has any clothes', *Long Range Planning*, December, 1991.

Campbell, A., Devine, M. and Young, D., *A Sense of Mission*, Hutchinson, London, 1990.

Drucker, Peter, *Innovation and Entrepreneurship*, Heinemann, London, 1985.

The Economist, 'Sample of visionary companies', 9 November 1991.

Goold, Michael, *Strategic Control*, Hutchinson, London, 1990.

Goold, Michael and Campbell, A., *Strategies and Styles*, Blackwell, Oxford, 1987.

Hamel, G. and Pralahad, C.K., 'Strategic intent', *Harvard Business Review*, May/June 1989.

Handy, Charles, *Understanding Organisations*, Penguin, Harmondsworth, 1985.

Harrison, Frank, 'Strategic control at the CEO level', *Long Range Planning*, December 1991.

Maslow, A., *Motivation and Personality*, Harper, New York, 1954.

Mintzberg, Henry, Conference with Strategic Planning Society, November 1991.

Ohmae, Kenichi, *The Mind of the Strategist*, McGraw-Hill, New York, 1982.

Porter, Michael, *Competitive Strategy*, Free Press, New York, 1980.

Porter Michael, *Competitive Advantage*, Free Press, New York, 1985.

Stacey, Ralph, *Managing Chaos*, Kogan Page, London, 1992.

Watson, Gregory, *Strategic Benchmarking*, John Wiley, New York, 1993.

Strategy formulation

CHAPTER 3

Strategies may be shaped in numerous ways, varying from the most painstaking to the most informal. Many strategies are developed by experimentation until a formula that achieves a competitive advantage emerges; this was the experience of a small damp-proof treatment company in London which found that a twenty-year guarantee gave it an edge over its rivals. Some strategies are opportunistic, such as the discounting of goods following the Resale Price Maintenance Act. Others are subservient to the strategies of others, as in the case of key suppliers following car manufacturers' new factories all round the world. Many of these strategies are 'emergent', in the term used by Henry Mintzberg, and are crafted as they develop to maximize their effect. Few emergent strategies give a lasting competitive advantage, however, as they are often available to competitors. As I wrote in *Strategic Leadership* (1991), 'It should be recognized, however, that reliance solely on emergent strategies militates against innovation, and the bold but calculated initiatives that are the real stuff of competitive strategy'.

Effective strategies are based on a deep understanding of customers and of the marketplace in which they may be approached. Some of this understanding may come from accumulated experience, it may be helped by a whole range of techniques, but it will mainly be based on systematic hard work. Much of this effort will be devoted to the process of strategic analysis, including the value chain analysis discussed in Chapter 2.

Strategic analysis–external

The object of strategic analysis is to obtain and process sufficient relevant information about the market environment to enable the company to distil a wide range of strategic options. From these options the most effective strategies can then be synthesized and evaluated. The scope of strategic analysis can, in theory, be virtually limitless, but consideration of cost and time usually limits the process to the factors most likely to be significant in the company's chosen business. The range of considerations which is likely to be relevant is shown in the 'environmental wheel' of Narchal, Kittappa and Bhattacharya (1987) shown in Figure 3.1. From this diagram it can be seen that the core of the analysis is the 'business system' relevant to the company. This has to be set in the context of its wider environment, since it is this wider environment, over which the company will exercise virtually no influence or control, that will condition the working of the business system.

Few strategic planners give the attention to the wider environment which its potential impact on their business clearly justifies. It is an area which is in parts poorly documented, in others swamped by data, where great vision and judgement are needed to shape meaningful pictures and capture relevant trends. Some companies, particularly Shell, have invested considerable resources in an understanding of the wider environment, not least because of the size of the investments they have to make and the long gestation time before profit streams emerge. In the 1960s Shell developed a technique of building scenarios based on differing political, economic and

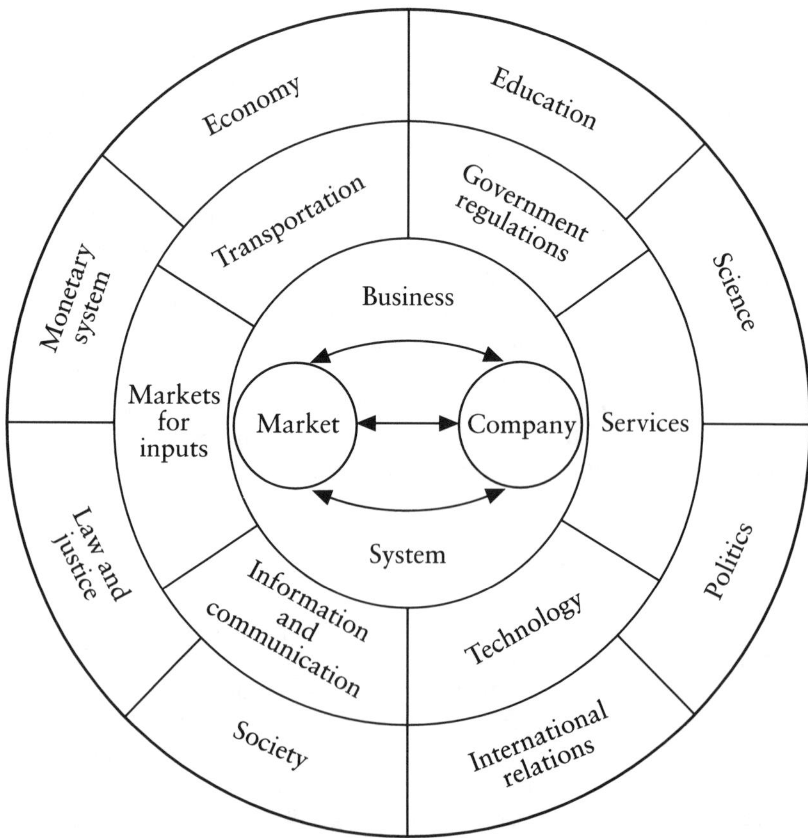

Figure 3.1 The environmental wheel (Narchal *et al.*, 1987)

market assumptions which has been very powerful. Use of scenario planning enabled Shell to anticipate the 1970s OPEC crises and their consequences in the marketplace. More details of scenario planning are given in Appendix 2. Many other large companies devote significant resources to understanding the dynamics of their environment but most do not give this dimension of their planning the attention or resources required. How many companies were able to foresee and pre-position themselves for the break-up of the Soviet bloc?

The importance of modelling and understanding the external environment is such that companies are increasingly seeking to monitor changes in their environment dynamically. Monitoring systems are discussed in Chapter 4, but for the purposes of developing strategy the kind of factors to be considered include:

1. *Political/societal factors*
   (a) Government impact on the company (policy, taxes, laws, etc.)
   (b) European Community impact
   (c) International policy effects (GATT, UN, etc.)
   (d) Demography (employment, age patterns, etc.)
   (e) Sociological changes (expectations, lifestyle, social values, families, mobility, etc.)
   (f) Environmental protection issues
2. *Economic, industry, technology factors*
   (a) Macroeconomic (balance of payments, GNP, inflation, exchange and interest rates)
   (b) Microeconomic (investment, wages, productivity)
   (c) Present and future industry structure (dynamics of change)
   (d) Factors effecting entry or exit to/from the industry
   (e) Technologies likely to influence the industry directly
   (f) Technologies which may impact the industry indirectly.
3. *Competition, markets, suppliers*
   (a) Known competitors
   (b) Potential competitors (also in potential markets)
   (c) Present markets
   (d) Potential markets
   (e) Established suppliers
   (f) Potential suppliers

Many of these factors will interact, e.g. if the company is considering entry into the Japanese market (under 3(d)) it will need to build a background picture of that market in respect of all other factors in the list (and probably more). Demographic changes will interact with sociological and microeconomic factors and environmental issues will interact widely over the range of factors. After the hard work of researching these factors and recording relevant data comes the patient search for insights into their trends and interaction which gives your strategies an edge over those of competitors.

The amount of data collected will depend on the relevance of each factor to your business. It will certainly increase as you work down the list from the political framework to competitor and market data. It will need to be supplemented as it is examined closely and interactions emerge. There will be many gaps in the data; where these cannot be filled without difficulty, judgements will have to be made, either from experience or from cross-interpretation of other data series. In recording data it is important to note the data's credibility (possibly as a percentage); judgements should be clearly labelled as such and also given a credibility rating. These ratings will be important when strategic options are developed and evaluated later.

Data collection should be built ideally on information available from commercial sources. These include Dun & Bradstreet, The Economist Intelligence Unit and many sector specialists. Onto this basic framework can be built the specific information which has to be sought by the researcher and which will provide deeper insights which can yield competitive advantage. Some of this additional information can be found in shared databases (e.g. Internet) but much of it will need to be gleaned by personal contact or by targeted questionnaires, focus groups and commissioned research.

The data collected should be set out in a format that is easy to use and to update, and codified for simplicity of access and cross-referencing. Care should be taken to protect the data not only because of their competitive value but also to avoid any temptation to 'improve' them by unauthorized employees.

Strategic analysis–internal

While great care has been taken to detail and analyse the external environment of the company, equal attention has to be given to record and evaluate information about its internal capabilities. The external analysis will have highlighted a number of opportunities and threats; the internal analysis is required to assess the ability of the company to respond to them.

A company comprises a number of resources. These include financial resources, physical assets, intangible assets and people with a variety of skills. In the same way that detailed information on external factors needs to be gathered and collated, an inventory of internal resources must be prepared so that it can serve the process of strategic analysis. We saw earlier how the value chain can be used both to identify resources and to highlight their relevance and effectiveness. The value chain also emphasizes the linkages between resources (e.g. the impact of training on the utilization of physical assets).

A mere inventory of resources is of limited value. It is necessary to evaluate the capability of the company in using those assets and relate that capability to that of its competitors. It is not sufficient to give a value for stock, for example; it is necessary to calculate how many times that stock turns over each year and relate that figure to competitive stockturn. It is the same for employees; it was only when US car firms confronted the reality that their annual production of cars per employee was less than one third that of Japanese competitors that they began to tackle their productivity problems with vigour.

Resources are scarce and their use has to be optimized relative to alternative employment. Financial markets are very sensitive to effective use of invested funds, employees are increasingly sensitive to better outlets for their talents. TSB received an endowment of over £1 billion when it was floated on the Stock Exchange in 1987; by 1992 this had largely been dissipated in acquisitions which made losses. It will be a long time before TSB will have easy access to fresh equity capital. Many key employees left Salomon Brothers to pursue their careers with untarnished employers following sanctions by the US authorities against the firm for manipulating auctions of US government securities in 1991.

Optimizing the use of resources can most meaningfully be achieved by benchmarking to best external practice. Earnings per share is seen as a key indicator of shareholder value and will, as well as return on nett assets, be subject to close scrutiny in financial markets. Such measures do not, however, focus on the real use of assets since they leave open the option of gearing through borrowing (in different forms, from debentures through junk bonds to unsecured overdrafts) and fiscal manipulation. Lord Hanson is famed for requiring his managers to 'make their assets sweat'. This means that gross assets are benchmarked and stock, debtors and other current assets are expected to turn over competitively and fixed assets such as buildings and equipment have to make a competitively acceptable return on their replacement cost rather than historical cost.

Resources which are not on the balance sheet may be critical in the value chain. Employees are a critical resource, particularly in service industries. Brands have increasingly been recognized as a key asset and some companies (e.g. Reckitt & Colman) now value them in their balance sheet. The current value of Reckitt & Colman's acquired brands now approaches £700 million. Goodwill is usually associated with the premium over nett asset value paid for acquisitions and shown in the balance sheet as an asset until written off against future profits. Left on the balance sheet, goodwill reduces the productivity of tangible assets and of other intangible assets such as patents. No company can tolerate 'sleeping assets' in these turbulent and competitive times.

A framework for evaluating company resources might be developed from Table 3.1. This will require considerable analysis of company operations, allocating costs and identifying where value is added, in order to build a model of the business which is generally accepted. It will also, to the extent that external benchmarks can be determined or reasonably well estimated, enable the areas of competitive strength and weakness to be identified. It is also necessary to estimate the productivity of marginal increases in each resource to help guide investment decisions. This work needs to be painstaking and harshly realistic. Much of its value is in gaining self-knowledge and in questioning the 'sacred cows' which are happy to graze in any business. The tighter the result of this analysis, the easier will be the task of making sound judgements in respect of the external world, which dominates the company but over which it can exercise little influence.

Table 3.1 Evaluating resources

(a)	*Overall performance*	*Measure*	*Immediate benchmark*	*Wider benchmark*
	Number of ordinary shares	Earnings per share	Best earnings per share in own industry	Best EPS on stock market
	Nett assets	Return before tax on nett assets (%)	Best RONA in own industry	Best RONA on stock market
	Total assets	Return before tax on total (gross) assets (%)	Best ROTA in own industry	Best ROTA on stock market
(b)	*Individual resources*	*Measure*	*Immediate benchmark*	*Wider benchmark*
	Investments (long term)	Return on investment (%)	Best ROI in industry	Best ROI in marketplace
	Land	Notional rent per ft^2/yr	Best rent ratio in industry	Best rent ratio in marketplace
	Buildings, installations	Notional rent less costs per ft^2/yr	Best rent less costs ratio in industry	Best rent less costs ratio in marketplace
	Plant, machinery	Nett value added p.a.	Best nett value added in industry	Best nett value added anywhere

Other equipment	Nett value added p.a.	–	–
Vehicles	Nett value added p.a.	–	–
Other fixed assets	Nett value added p.a.	–	–
Stocks Bought in	Nett value added × stockturn/yr up to next stage	Nett value added × stockturn in industry up to next stage	Best nett value added × stockturn anywhere up to next stage
Work in progress	As above for each stage	As above for each stage	As above for each stage
Finished goods	As above excluding earlier stages	As above excluding earlier stages	As above excluding earlier stages
Debtors	Debtors–Sales (%)	Best ratio in industry	Best overall ratio
Short-term investments	Return on investment (%)	Best ROI in industry	Best overall ROI
Cash and equivalent	Interest p.a. (%)	Best ratio in industry	Best overall ratio
Intangible assets Goodwill	Goodwill: total assets (%)	Lowest ratio in industry	Zero ratio
Patents, copyright, etc.	Royalties: p.a: balance sheet value (%)	Best ratio in industry	Best overall ratio
Brands	Premium over industry average margin: balance sheet value (%)	Highest premium over average in industry: balance sheet value (%)	Best ratio anywhere
Personnel Productivity	Pretax profit per employee	Best ratio in industry	Best overall ratio
Skills	Gross profit per employee	Best ratio in industry	Best overall ratio
Loyalty	Staff turnover p.a. (%)	Best ratio in industry	Best overall ratio

Critical success factors (CSFs)

Strategic analysis is a long and demanding process, requiring great rigour and considerable ingenuity to explore all areas which may be of relevance to the future development of the business. It is as if Sherlock Holmes were investigating in depth the causes of past success and failure and the weather bureau was seeking to forecast the future patterns emerging from that investigation! The danger of being swamped by data is very real and the ability to detect meaningful patterns in the mass of information accumulated is essential for formulating successful strategies. A key process in evaluating the data is to establish the critical factors for success in the chosen marketplace.

Critical success factors are meaningful only if evaluated from the standpoint of the prospective customer. Having a wide choice of products might seem to be a critical success factor but may lead to excessive costs which undermine price competitiveness. Features on a product which are not preferred by customers may also undermine competitiveness. Identifying and evaluating critical success factors is therefore a task which requires rigorous adoption of the customer's viewpoint, not just in isolation but through market research, focus groups and other customer involvement. One of the features of aluminium is its ability to be re-used almost without waste. This feature has led aluminium manufacturers to place heavy emphasis on recycling and environmental protection, particularly in Germany, where there are strong recycling regulations. This strategy is aimed at creating a perception of aluminium as an environmentally friendly material, thus increasing demand for it at the expense of steel, plastics and other materials, which are less easily recyclable.

Many critical success factors will seem to be obvious–customer service, price, product quality, and so on. To be effective, analysis has not only to identify such factors and focus on how the customer will perceive them but it must also recognize probable trade-offs (price: quality, etc.) and establish a likely ranking of critical success factors. This may well vary between market segments and must be both recognized and regularly tested.

The number of critical success factors is unlikely to be more than six for any given market. Beyond this number the criticality of the factor declines rapidly and the ability to weigh the relative value of each factor declines. In some markets one factor may be clearly predominant (e.g. price in the discount grocery market). Many users of CSF analysis find it meaningful to attach weightings to factors as well as to rank them, so that the ranking of critical success factors for the discount grocery market might emerge as:

Price	(45%)
Convenience of location	(23%)
Freshness of products	(18%)

Quick-to-find products	(8%)
Speed of checkout	(6%)

Such an analysis would relegate issues such as choice, pleasant surroundings, amenities, product advertising, etc. to a non-critical level, whereas these issues may well be critical for grocers such as Sainsbury.

The value of such analysis depends on frequent market testing and on awareness of possible changes in customer priorities. The attempt to add relative weights to each of the factors should be treated with caution and be subject to constant testing. It does, however, help in marketing planning and in gauging the value of proposed changes (e.g. investment in location versus investment in store layout).

No examination of the process of strategic analysis is complete without a health warning. Analysis is seductive, and there will always be the temptation to pursue further analysis and thereby delay decision and action. 'Paralysis by analysis' is the cardinal sin of strategic planners and cool judgement is needed to know when the time for analysis is over and when decisions leading to action have to be made.

References

Davies, Adrian, *Strategic Leadership*, Woodhead Faulkner, Cambridge, 1991.

Narchal, R.M., Kittappa, K. and Bhattacharya, P., 'An environmental scanning system for business planning', *Long Range Planning*, December 1987.

CHAPTER 4

Strategic planning

In his book *The Rise and Fall of Strategic Planning* (1994) Henry Mintzberg draws a distinction between strategic planning, which he sees as an analytical process, and strategic thinking. He hypothesizes that strategic planning is really strategic programming, articulating existing visions and strategies rather than opening up the business to new thinking and learning. Strategic planning fell into disrepute at an earlier date, when failure to foresee the probability of the oil crises in the 1970s damaged most Western economies. On both occasions the process of strategic planning had become mechanistic and driven by numbers. Too little attention had been given to capturing and interpreting signals from the external world and to thinking through their potential implications for the specific business.

The development of chaos theory, or the science of non-linear dynamics, has shown that many systems apparently subject to physical laws (e.g. the weather) could in fact be highly unstable and unpredictable. This has demonstrated the impossibility of forecasting many major developments (e.g. population) and has been used by some as an argument against strategic planning. It has now emerged that many systems which are apparently subject to chaos can in fact be kept in relative control by anticipatory intervention. This offers the prospect not only of better control but also of achieving more useful results. The implications for strategic planning would seem to be positive rather than negative, allowing deeper insights into exogenous systems even though control remains elusive. More details are given in an article in *The Economist* (1994).

Despite a history of poor performance, the need for strategic planning has not disappeared. The bureaucracy of earlier planning systems, driven by large planning departments and linked to a formal and mechanistic cycle, has increasingly been dismantled. Corporate planners are now lone agents or in small teams and the process of planning is driven by line managers who have to deliver the plans they produce. The planners are responsible for the planning process, the various planning techniques which line managers might wish to use to assist them in preparing plans, and act as facilitators of the process. A survey by *Business International* in 1991 of eighteen leading global companies indicated that the ten main functions of corporate planners were now:

1. Compiling information for top management
2. Competition research
3. Forecasting
4. Consulting services
5. Creating a common language
6. Communicating a corporate culture
7. Establishing and communicating corporate objectives
8. Group facilitation and team leadership
9. Guardianship of the planning system
10. Developing planning methods

Strategies are formulated, emerge or are sometimes imposed by circumstances (e.g. Honda's reaction to the sale of Rover to BMW). Strategic planning is the process for ensuring that actions are taken to implement strategies effectively. It is in order to ensure commitment that strategic plans should be prepared by those who have to deliver results, and any effective strategic planning process will need to penetrate to all parts of the organization which it is intended to drive.

Strategic plans

Strategic plans normally include a number of key elements of which the first three and the seventh were discussed in Chapter 2; others will be discussed further below:

1. Vision for the organization
2. Mission of the organization
3. Long-term objectives
4. Objectives for the plan period
5. Key issues affecting the plan
6. Plan assumptions
7. Strategies to deliver the plan and projects affecting the plan
8. Resources needed for the plan
9. Sensitivity analysis/risk analysis

10. Key action programme for the plan period
11. Contingency plans
12. Supporting plans (marketing, manufacturing, R&D, etc.)

Objectives for the plan period

These relate to the long-term objectives and represent measurable steps towards their achievement, often known as 'milestones'. Where the long-term objectives usually relate to strategic market positioning and competitive profitability, plan objectives will be related to the progress needed in key parameters in order to maintain the strategic direction of the business. Examples of long-term and related plan objectives for a typical business are shown in Table 4.1.

Key issues affecting the plan

These are the specific challenges, opportunities and threats faced by the company which the plan needs to address. The board will usually refer to these in preparing its plan framework but others should emerge from the planning process and also be addressed in the plan.

Table 4.1 Objectives over time

Long-term objectives	*Plan objectives*
1. To be market leader in all countries where we trade	1. To achieve No.3 market position in the UK by 1997
2. To have the highest return on capital employed of any company in our sector	2. To achieve a return on capital employed of 17.5% by 1997
3. To maximize earnings per share	3. To achieve earnings per share of 13.5p by 1997
4. To optimize the use of debt	4. To achieve a debt/equity ratio of no more than 0.7/1 by 1997
5. To maximize the efficiency of product renewal	5. To achieve a ratio of new products (less than two years old) to all products of 0.1/1 by 1997
6. To maximize employee productivity	6. To achieve pre-tax profit per employee of £30 200 by 1997

Plan assumptions

Plans need to address issues which are internal and external. Whereas a company may have some degree of control over internal issues, it will have limited or no control over most external factors. These need to be identified and, where they affect the possible outcome of the plan, an agreed assumption for each will need to be made for planning purposes. A set of assumptions is usually provided in the planning framework but will be subject to modification and/or expansion as the plans develop. Examples of assumptions are shown in Chapter 7.

Strategies and projects

For each objective in the plan there will be a need to develop strategies capable of achieving them. Strategies were discussed generally in Chapter 2, but those used by specific businesses will be conditioned by the objectives set, the resources available and the competitive situation faced. Case studies relating to specific strategies are developed in Chapters 8 and 9.

Projects are, in effect, longer-term strategies which may have started before the plan period and/or may finish after it. In many businesses projects may last long periods and involve large sums of money. Each plan will need to identify, appraise and quantify the effects of all projects on its planned outcome.

Resources

Plans will need to identify the financial and human resources needed for their achievement. Where there are limits on the resources available, plan objectives and strategies will need to be scaled down or priorities will need to be set between them.

Sensitivity analysis/risk analysis

Plans need to be tested against a significant movement in key assumptions. For an oil company the assumed average price per tonne of crude oil will be critical and movements either side of the assumed price will affect profitability significantly. Where a factor is critical it may be necessary to establish a contingency plan (see below).

All strategies involve risk–'nothing ventured, nothing gained'. Plans need to assess the different risks to which the company will or may be exposed in implementing planned strategies. Such risks may include political risk (such as being expropriated overseas), trading risk (not being paid for exports), currency risk (where trading in foreign currencies), contractual risk (being sued for non-performance), etc. For international companies the personal risks faced by their employees in certain markets (kidnapping, assassination, robbery, etc.) are an increasing area for concern.

Key action programmes

When plan strategies have been determined it is essential to establish a control mechanism to guide them. A well-proven means of doing this is to break down each strategy into a series of actions needed to complete it, to place these along a critical path and to set dates for completing each action and name the individual who is to be accountable for meeting that deadline. In preparing key action programmes it is essential to identify the interactions between different departments. Where actions are controlled along process lines, involving multifunctional teams, interactions are easier to identify and control.

Contingency plans

It will be necessary, where certain factors may have a very damaging effect on the business, to prepare contingency plans. A typical example would be a plan to cope with a major fire at a key installation. Too much contingency planning can be counterproductive, but plans that are made should be detailed and tested from time to time.

Contingency plans are of increasing importance for multinational companies which may face expropriation or arbitrary rulings damaging to their business in certain countries. Many such businesses need to have contingency plans to evacuate families and to counter personal attacks on key staff in order to be able to continue in business in turbulent markets.

Supporting plans

Delivery of corporate plans will depend on the supporting plans of subsidiary divisions and strategic business units as well as on key functional plans at both corporate and business unit level. Such functions include marketing, manufacturing, research and development, personnel, purchasing, finance, etc. Marketing planning is of particular importance because of the interface between the company and its customers. Marketing planning is discussed in detail in Chapter 7.

Strategic plans are composed mainly of words out of which a framework of numbers is developed. This framework is usually limited to sales, cost of sales, pre-tax profit, earnings and capital expenditure. From these proforma profit and loss accounts, balance sheets and cashflow (source and application of funds) can be derived. This framework provides indicative figures which can be developed into a budget (and capital budget) for the first year of the plan period. Details of major projects which are current or planned are also brought into the plan and the financial framework.

The role of finance has become increasingly strategic in recent years. The obvious evidence for this is the growth of the treasury function; in many companies this is now managed as a key profit centre. The need to evaluate rapidly the financial implications of strategic options has led to the development of more sophisticated management accounting systems, (e.g. activity-based costing, opportunity costing, etc.). Much of this analysis can very usefully be linked to the mapping of value chains which was examined in Chapter 2. A key text on this subject is Keith Ward's *Strategic Management Accounting* (1992).

Strategic plans may be produced as needed but most organizations plan on a regular cycle because of the need to adjust plans constantly to changing circumstances. The usual pattern is to have an annual planning cycle with a plan period of three to five years. Businesses that have a longer planning horizon (e.g. oil companies) often seek to establish longer-term strategies and make longer-term investments by exploring alternative futures through techniques such as scenario planning. Konosuke Matsushita wrote a 250-year plan for his infant business in 1932 which has never been revealed in detail but the company has become one of the world's giant corporations, and its enormous success in the USA was clearly foreseen in the plan.

Planning cycle

A typical planning cycle will involve a number of steps spread over the year and leading into the next annual cycle. These steps will usually be:

1. Establishing a planning framework by the board of directors
2. Launching the planning process to match that framework
3. Developing bottom-up plans throughout the organization
4. Consolidating these plans
5. Gap analysis to match bottom-up plans to the framework
6. Testing plans for robustness
7. Board approval of plans
8. Developing budgets out of year 1 of the consolidated plan
9. Implementing plans

10. Reviews of progress on strategies and key actions
11. Approval of capital expenditure
12. Adapting plans to new circumstances

1. Planning framework

This will usually be developed from work done by the board and may involve the following steps:

- Analysis of projected results for the current year
- Identifying the critical issues (external and internal) affecting present operations and the new plan period
- Reviewing progress towards longer-term objectives
- Setting objectives for the plan period
- Reviewing major strategies (present and emerging)
- Identifying resource constraints

This process enables the board to reassess present strategies and learn from developments over the past year. The main point of reference is the set of long-term objectives agreed by the board when it set the strategic direction of the business at an earlier date. These themselves need to be tested for relevance but should not be changed unless the nature of the business has changed significantly (e.g. the company is in a different marketplace).

Setting the planning framework is important because it provides the dynamic tension between achieving longer-term objectives as quickly as possible and the ability of the business itself to respond. An unchallenging strategic framework leads to complacency and to underachievement; too demanding a framework may lead to unrealistic plans and disillusionment.

2. Launching the planning process

Strategic planning is the favourite pastime of few people so that the effective launch of the process requires some impulsion. The planning framework needs to be set out fully and clearly and to be accompanied by a memorandum from the managing director to demonstrate the importance attached by the board to effective strategic planning. The content of such a memorandum is, of course, a matter of choice for the managing director, but it may be useful to show appreciation for the work done in the previous year by employees to deliver the strategies of the previous plan and to recognize the commitment which has been shown to making the planning process effective. The commitment of the board should be shown by the quality of the planning framework and by its own involvement in the process at appropriate stages detailed in the timetable accompanying the managing director's memorandum.

3. Developing bottom-up plans

Plans are only as good as the commitment of those who make them. Those who make them should ideally be those who will be expected to deliver them. As a result, any effective planning process needs to involve people in all parts and at virtually all levels of the organization, and that involvement needs to be as open-ended and creative as possible.

There are many planning processes, but most will typically cascade down through the organization, using the planning framework to draw out the issues affecting each part of it and stimulating a creative but structured response to them and to the objectives for the plan period. Many companies find that a teamworking approach to developing plans is useful, particularly where teams are multifunctional and can build bridges across departmental boundaries. Traditionally, plans have been built on a functional or departmental basis; modern practice is beginning to build plans along the lines of key processes or to cover identifiable business units. Each organization needs to experiment to find what pattern will work for it, recognizing the need to produce customer-focused plans and to make accountability clear at all levels. Bottom-up planning is often helped by the infrastructure used for total quality management. This provides a map of interdependencies and a model structure which can be used to generate bottom-up plans. It also provides the linkages and reporting lines to monitor progress against plan objectives and in completing key action programmes.

Most organizations use a limited number of forms, or a basic reporting structure for their bottom-up plans. This is to facilitate comparisons and consolidation. Best practice is to allow a free hand for additional input, expanding on the basic submission and providing deeper insights into the operational area concerned. Where plans have been developed through teamwork it is often useful to allow minority views or even maverick opinions to go forward. These are potentially contributions to the deeper insights referred to above.

4. Consolidating bottom-up plans

This process requires both a consolidation of the framework of numbers derived from the planning process (sales, expenses, pre-tax profits, capital expenditure, etc.) and a review of strategies and key actions to ensure that they are consistent with and complementary to those of other unit plans. Any anomalies need to be resolved rapidly so that the resultant consolidated plan is internally consistent and all unit plans are contributing fully to it.

Within a group particular attention needs to be given to interactive elements in the plans of different businesses. The actions of one company may be dependent on initiatives taken by another. This is particularly the case where groups are run to achieve interactive synergies (e.g. vertical integration between production and sales–Boots Pharmaceuticals and Boots the Chemist) and much less so where businesses are run on a 'stand-alone' basis (e.g. Hanson). It may be necessary for a decision to be taken on which business will lead in developing a particular strategy (e.g. one of territorial expansion), where a firmer bridgehead may be built by one business which has a particular market advantage in the territory targeted, leading to other businesses following up on the advantage secured.

5. Gap analysis

When the plans have been consolidated it will be necessary to match their total outputs against the objectives set in the planning framework for the plan period. These outputs will typically include sales, cashflow, pre-tax profit, market share, etc. with requisite inputs such as expenses, capital expenditure, headcount, etc.

Where the consolidated plans do not deliver the framework objectives a process known as 'gap analysis' is required. In this process the shortfall against each framework objective is studied and possible solutions identified and explored. A shortfall in profits may be due to low sales, narrow margins, high expenses or a combination of these and other factors. Constrained cashflow may be due to distortions in the sales pattern, to inventory build-up, to bunching of investment or to high levels of expense (e.g. advertising) preceding a planned growth in revenue. All these anomalies have to be explored and solutions found, and agreed with those responsible for delivering the plan, before the plans can sensibly be approved.

Gap analysis may also show that the present organization is incapable of delivering the framework objectives, even though action is taken to stretch plans within acceptable limits. If the constraints are due to resources, action may be needed to find new finance or to attract extra talent. If they are due to the inability of the present business activities to deliver the required growth in profits, other solutions such as acquisitions or alliances will need to be built into the plan. Where such solutions are not realistic or cannot be achieved in the required timescale it will be necessary to adjust the framework objectives to match reality.

6. Testing plans for robustness

The consolidated plans also need to be tested for robustness to significant changes in the common assumptions on which they have been built. Most plans are sensitive to certain key factors; it may be the price of key imports, currency exchange rates, or the availability of specific skills. If plans are unduly sensitive to changes in such assumptions the strategies adopted may need to be revised to make them more robust. The process of testing is often called 'what if' analysis, and is a form of modelling which may be taken to varying degrees of sophistication.

Plans need also to be tested for potential market or competitor reaction. Strategies are executed in markets which are dynamic in varying degrees. Plans which assume no reaction to strategies are usually unrealistic. Even where competitive advantage has been seized, competitors will immediately seek to nullify that advantage and may succeed in doing so more quickly than expected. Another factor is the fact that markets are rarely stable so that today's winning product is tomorrow's bore. As Isaac Newton perceived, actions and reactions are equal and opposite–only the timing is left to conjecture.

It is difficult to test plans for emergent strategies, as these are often unforeseeable. Many emergent strategies may, however, be anticipated by intelligent analysis or by intuition. Emergent strategies are frequently shaped by trends and discontinuities which may be discerned by those willing and able to search their environment for new insights. In the same way that fashion is often predictible to those who are attuned to the forces which shape new fashion, the patterns which allow change to emerge in wider markets may be identified and acted upon by those who can find meaning in such patterns. Scenario planning is a powerful tool for exploring 'what makes the difference' in different markets; Shell used it to avoid the overpayment for Britoil, which damaged BP's prospects for many years.

7. Board approval

When plans have been consolidated, stretched, tested and matched against reality it is essential that they should be brought to the board for approval. Some boards (e.g. BTR) are not concerned with the detail of subsidiary plans and run their group as a portfolio of investments from which agreed results are expected. Even in such cases the existence of cogent and cohesive plans underpins the expectations of the investor even though the results will be controlled through a sophisticated monitoring system against budgets, not plans.

Most boards will see themselves as sponsors of the plans of their subsidiaries and as responsible for delivering an overall corporate plan which drives the business towards its long-term objectives. Most boards also recognize that they are accountable to a wide range of stakeholders not only for the results of their business activity but also increasingly for the means of achieving those results. Union Carbide, Exxon, Townsend Thoresen and others have suffered from a failure to ensure that their businesses were mandated to operate correctly. A company's values mould the way it carries out its business; those values must be built into the sinews of its strategic plans and the board must ensure that this is done.

Approval of the corporate plan and of the subsidiary plans of which it is constituted is an important act for the board. Directors are responsible for setting the strategic direction of their company and approval of plans validates their strategic intent and gives a mandate to management to deliver them.

8. Developing budgets

Some companies develop budgets without recourse to strategic planning. Such documents provide a reporting and control framework but lack the strategic direction provided by a plan. Plans also give a framework of reference to enable expenditure against budget to be flexed to meet changing circumstances. Budgets are not a fixed mandate to spend but a structured framework against which to report short-term progress against strategic goals.

It is for this reason that most companies develop their budgets out of the framework of numbers which flows from the strategies and actions in the first year of their strategic plan. Plans are mainly expressed in words and are derived from identifying and exploring options. From these thoughts and words a limited quantity of numbers is derived. If the strategies in the plans are to be delivered effectively those numbers must be broken down to the remotest unit in the company and must be controlled rigorously, not just against the budget framework but, more exactingly, also against the longer-term objectives of the plan. It is for this reason that capital expenditure is only earmarked in the capital budget and has to be approved nearer to the time of implementation, when the need for such expenditure may have disappeared.

9. Implementing plans

When strategic plans have been approved by the board, those who have submitted them will be expected to take the action necessary for their implementation. The mandate given is to achieve the results detailed in the plan and implementation is a process of matching ends with means. The plan will have spelled out the strategies and actions needed to achieve plan objectives, together with the resources needed to ensure delivery. During the course of implementation, while the ends are fixed (plan objectives are not modified without good reason) the means of achieving them may change. Competitor action may cut across agreed strategies and make them ineffective; unforeseen events may present new opportunities to shape better strategies; events may block or open markets–thousands of changes will occur which will test and often change the strategies and actions laid down in the plan. Where plans have been rigorously tested for robustness strategies are more likely to stay on course, and the process of testing will have shaped alternative actions to counter the loss of direction. In the daily battle to move the business forward it is easy to fail to notice strategic drift; it is for this reason that regular reviews of progress are essential. The implementation of marketing plans is examined in Chapters 8 and 9.

10. Reviews of progress with plans

Budgets are used as the basis for monthly reporting to the board on progress in the current year. This reporting is largely tactical and action taken will tend to be tactical for the most part. This process must be supported by a regular examination of the strategic progress of the business, although events may at any time force a strategic reappraisal (e.g. if a bid is made to take over the company). All strategic plans should be subject to formal review at least quarterly. This process should take stock of progress in the year to date against plan objectives, review the effectiveness of strategies (planned or emergent) and examine progress against all items in the Key Action Programme. This is a schedule of actions needed to deliver strategies which has specific deadlines and nominated accountabilities. This review may be part of a board meeting, require a special meeting or extend in scope to a board 'awayday'. Whatever its context, it needs to focus on the lessons of recent trading experience and identify the actions needed to adjust plans to the new reality. Recriminations are, at best, secondary to this focus on learning and action and should themselves be orientated towards action rather than resentment.

Following the review, plans will be adapted through negotiation with those concerned to ensure that winning strategies are reinforced and losing ones scaled down or abandoned. Key Action Programmes should also be adapted to drive the new pattern of strategies.

11. Approval of capital expenditure

Mention was made earlier of the need to separate the budgeting and the approval of capital expenditure. Sums spent on capital may be very substantial, especially in manufacturing businesses, and it is important to have both a rigorous process for allocating funds and a distinct one for approving their disbursement. The lapse of time between the two processes also allows management to reassess the case for expenditure in the light of circumstances that may have changed radically since the budget was prepared.

The process of approving capital expenditure should, therefore, be quite independent of the plan and budgetary procedures. In most businesses the allocation of funds is a competition for scarce resources. When the time comes to approve capital expenditure there will inevitably be new projects to consider which have emerged since the plan and budget were prepared and which may have greater strategic potential than some projects earmarked at an earlier date. The regular reviews of strategic plans may well have discarded certain strategies whose supporting resources may include capital expenditure. The capital expenditure approval process acts as the final check to ensure the exclusion of such projects and that funds are focused on projects which have the greatest relevance to those strategies which are seen to be proving their effectiveness.

12. Adapting plans to new circumstances

Many critics of strategic planning emphasize the danger of 'setting ideas in concrete' and of losing flexibility. They prefer to wait on circumstances and move forward like surfers who catch each chance wave. Flexibility is an essential attribute of successful management but total flexibility leads to confusion, since there is no underlying sense of direction. We have seen earlier that strategies may be planned or emergent, and the experience of most companies is that they move forward in their chosen strategic direction using a varying combination of both types of strategy. Where significant change or progress in a specific direction is needed it is almost inevitable that a planned strategy is needed. President John Kennedy's challenge to put a man on the moon inside ten years could not have been met without a planned strategy. Experience shows that innovation and changing the nature of a business need planned strategies since they require 'thinking outside the box' and a conscious attempt to impose new ideas on an established operation. Within that operation the role of emergent strategies is powerful since the mindset of the business will quickly recognize their potential and act to pursue them. Emergent strategies may also impact in the area of innovation (e.g. by having an alliance proposed by a company outside the present business) but these opportunities are still unusual, even though their frequency is growing.

From this cursory examination of the annual planning cycle it will be evident that there is a sensitive balance to be achieved between the process of planning and the process of implementation. Planning demands thorough analysis and implementation requires constant adjustment. Plans drive the business, budgets provide the means to control the process.

It should also be apparent that planning is highly iterative in its search for robust effectiveness and that the process of implementation provides constant feedback to enable plans to be attuned to a changing reality as it emerges.

Out of the results of one planning cycle the next cycle is born. New plans require the interpretation of the learning provided by building and implementing previous plans. In a harsh competitive world strategic planning provides the Darwinian search for adaptation which enables businesses to survive, and some to prosper.

Hierarchy of plans

Heinecken claims to be the beer that reaches parts that other beers do not. Good planning systems also need to penetrate to all parts of an organization and the architecture of planning systems must fit both the shape and the requirements of the whole operation. The main driver of the wider planning process is the 'bottom-up' process we referred to earlier. Ideally this is as far-reaching as the budgeting process, which is built up, level by level, from the remotest parts of the business. In practice, there are units in many organizations which produce budgets but do not plan, since planning involves more discretion than budgeting. The recent development of total quality management in many organizations has forced the level of discretion further down many structures, and the nodes created for TQM often serve well as discrete units for corporate planning. The growth of process teams and other newly empowered groups has also enriched the fabric of 'bottom-up' planning by ensuring cross-functional integration of plans at the operating level.

Preparing a corporate plan requires the creation of a 'hierarchy of plans' which is headed by the corporate plan itself, directed at corporate objectives and detailing strategies and actions at top level only. This corporate plan is built up from and underpinned by a level-by-level hierarchy of plans for each subsidiary or division, and for each major function. Functional plans are crosslinked to support divisional plans and each strategic business unit within divisions. The 'bottom-up' process starts at the lowest level of discretion within the business, typically a department within a strategic business unit, and is progressively consolidated up to corporate level.

Following gap analysis and corporate decisions on the allocation of resources, plans are realigned and revised to ensure that they reflect at each level the requisite contribution towards meeting corporate objectives. Any proposals which do not serve corporate ends will have been discarded and resources and actions will be focused exclusively on agreed top-level goals. Failure to align lower-level plans rigorously with corporate objectives is, at best, wasteful of effort and resources; at worst, it may be fatal to the business (e.g. Atlantic Computers destroyed British & Commonwealth).

Functional plans are a key part of the hierarchy of plans but must be subordinated not only to corporate objectives but also to those of the divisions and strategic business units which they support. Most businesses have difficulty in balancing the need to support line operations and to develop the excellence needed within functions. Unless space is given in all plans to develop new skills, products and processes, the organization will lack resilience to cope with change. Operational pressures will drive out innovation unless the planning system actively sponsors it and allocates resources to building tomorrow's company. Finding the right balance is one of the hardest challenges which face corporate management, and success in doing so is essential for long-term survival.

The main functional plans include personnel (or human resources), research and development, purchasing, finance and marketing. Each is important–purchasing may dispose of more than half of gross cashflow–but marketing is crucial, as it shapes the interface with customers whose support is the lifeblood of the business. Marketing planning is therefore the essential link between customers and the strategic direction of the business; unfortunately it is rarely as effective as it should be. Marketing planning is examined in detail in Chapter 7.

References

Business International (1991).

The Economist, 'Chaos Theory', 25 June 1994.

Mintzberg, Henry, *The Rise and Fall of Strategic Planning*, Free Press, New York, 1994.

Ward, Keith, *Strategic Management Accounting*, Butterworth-Heinemann, Oxford, 1992.

The marketing concept and the marketing process

CHAPTER

5

The traditional concept of marketing is to identify and satisfy the needs of a customer. This is based on the writings of Drucker, Levitt and others, and remains basically valid despite the passage of time. In the words of Levitt (1975), 'Selling focuses on the needs of the seller, marketing on the needs of the buyer'. Marketing is concerned with long-term relationships, selling often focuses on a single transaction. Marketing might be likened to marriage, selling to seduction.

With the passage of time the marketing concept has spread wider in most organizations and has, in recent years, been reinforced by customer-care programmes and the concept of total quality. Marketing is certainly too important to be left to marketers, as Aubrey Wilson (1991) shows in his book *New Directions in Marketing*. He quotes Hotpoint and English Electric as examples of companies which left marketing to the marketers. Both are no longer independent.

It is very significant that both strategy and marketing operate at two levels in any competitive organization. Strategy is the process which shapes the ability of an organization to compete successfully over time, and, as such, should penetrate all parts of that organization. Strategies are also the specific means by which corporate objectives are achieved. Marketing is the concept of relating to the needs and values of customers and should imbue all plans and actions in the business. Marketing is also a specific profession deploying defined skills in the pursuit of corporate objectives. Both relate to customers, both seek to disarm competitors, and to do so must galvanize the whole organization. Both also provide specific skills and processes to work with other specialists in achieving corporate goals.

The marketing concept is focused primarily on customers. Customers are, however, only one of several 'stakeholders' in any business. Shareholders retain the prime legal rights in any company, the position of employees has strengthened in recent years (despite recent setbacks due to redundancies) and suppliers, local communities, lobbyists and others increasingly claim attention. There has been a growing vogue for 'shareholder value', driven by the increasing concentration of shares into the hands of institutions, pension funds and others who must themselves produce competitive results and who are increasingly exposed to published analysis of their profitability. Lord Hanson openly puts shareholders first, customers second and employees third in his list of priorities. Other practitioners of shareholder value, such as Lloyds Bank, claim that long-term shareholder value can only be built through satisfying customers and staff. A survey of small-business opinion in 1993 placed Lloyds Bank clearly last in the ranking by customer satisfaction.

There is a growing movement today towards employee 'empowerment'. This reflects the increasing complexity of business and the failure of most attempts to drive businesses by command rather than by consensus. This dichotomy is brilliantly explored by Douglas McGregor (1960) in his 'Theory X' and 'Theory Y', and this and other earlier work on motivation has focused increasing attention on employee participation in business enterprise. Such participation and the 'empowerment' it involves can be successful only within a framework of objectives and operating guidelines to give leadership. Empowerment in a vacuum is a formula for disaster.

Models of organizations dedicated to the satisfaction of employees are not hard to find. Much of the public sector has traditionally been employee-orientated rather than committed to customer satisfaction. Even today much of the panoply of customer care in railways, health, social security, local government and elsewhere is only skin-deep. Newly privatized businesses are struggling to change their culture, and only a few, such as British Airways, can confidently project customer-care values. (The recent 'dirty tricks' episode with Virgin Airways has unfortunately removed the gloss for a while!)

Employee ownership shows a mixed picture. Companies like John Lewis and National Freight are very customer-orientated. The history of employee buyouts and cooperatives is tarnished with failures like Triumph motorcycles, with rapid sell-ons like the Henley Forecasting Centre and a long list of liquidations.

All businesses need to establish a dynamic trade-off between their various stakeholders and few will articulate that trade-off openly. It is, however, essential that the trade-off is consistent with the messages sent out by the business if credibility is to be maintained. Customer care is no small part of the message of fraudsters such as Dr Savundra and Peter Clowes; BCCI projected an image of solidity at the very time it was stealing depositors' funds. Less dramatic dichotomies can cause as much damage over time, as the British motor industry's decline has demonstrated.

The evolution of the marketing concept

The marketing concept is not static and its evolution is seen by Professor Johan Arndt (1984) to have had three stages since 1945:

1. The marketing concept
2. The broadened marketing concept
3. The 'new institutional concept'

The marketing concept has been discussed earlier in this chapter and reflects the classical posture of sensitivity to the needs of customers. The broadened marketing concept recognizes that there are internal customers as well as those to whom sales are made. This approach has led to the idea of 'internal marketing' and, more recently, of 'total quality'. The importance of this idea to strategic marketing is fundamental, since it creates the attitudes and disciplines essential to sustain an effective external marketing strategy. We shall revisit this concept frequently in this book.

The 'new institutional concept' (conditioned by Professor Arndt's core discipline as an economist) sees marketing as a combination of exchange, the transaction cost approach in economics and the political economy approach. This seems to hint at a wider system of relationships, perhaps including value chain enhancement and other alliances to which reference will be made later. This is a stage of evolution which has not yet been reached and which may never be fully achieved. More details of this theory of marketing may be found in Professor Arndt's (1984) paper.

Consumerism

Some of the credit for establishing and nurturing the marketing concept must go to the movement known as 'consumerism'. At a time of general shortage, as in the early years following the Second World War, there is no need to be responsive to customers. The selling process is subordinated to the mechanics of allocating products to a host of uncritical recipients. Business at that time was driven by the need to maximize production and overcome shortages of key materials and skills. Because of staff shortages the needs and comfort of employees were paramount and customers were often to be tolerated rather than encouraged.

Even when shortages reduced there was little recognition of the customer as an individual. Using the techniques of mass production to maximize output, businesses pushed for mass consumption through saturation use of media advertising. Later, market forces built planned obsolescence into their products in order to accelerate replacement sales, ignoring quality and offering minimal after-sales service.

This stage is well illustrated in Vance Packard's book *The Waste Makers* (1954) and the environmental impact of mass consumption is evoked in Rachel Carson's *Silent Spring* (1962). President Kennedy enunciated four consumer rights in 1962–the right to safety, the right to be informed, the right to choose and the right to be heard. The first breakthrough for consumerism was, however, Ralph Nader's book *Unsafe at Any Speed* (1965), which forced General Motors to admit to product faults and galvanized consumerism into a cohesive movement.

In the UK consumer interests are principally championed by the Consumers' Association. This body now has over one million members and has moved over time from the position of an 'outsider' lobby to a mainstream organization which seeks to ensure value for money for its members, partly through systematic sampling and testing of products and services. Consumerism has evolved from an 'outsider' in the 1960s to part of the Establishment in the 1990s, mainly due to the switch in focus from product to customer-orientation. Emphasis on the individual and increasing recognition of individual rights now makes the syndicalism of the consumer movement progressively irrelevant. Consumerism faces an increasing challenge from the growing concern to protect the environment and the pressure for curbs on the growth of consumption.

Relationship marketing

In the developed economies mass marketing is becoming less effective as customers become more aware of themselves as individuals and more confident in their individual tastes and of their individual rights. Media advertising has shifted from an emphasis on conformity to stereotypes in the 1960s and 1970s towards a search for individuality. The Guinness advertisements in the last three years have been enormously successful by identifying Guinness with non-conformity. All media now have to be rigorously targeted to achieve acceptable results, and marketing is struggling to reach increasingly segmented audiences without loss of cost effectiveness. The logical end result of this process is a 'one-to-one' relationship. Mass marketing has been moving towards relationship marketing in parallel with the growing focus on the individual. Relationship marketing is not only more challenging than mass marketing but, for those who can master its complexities, the results are more rewarding and sustainable. Relationship marketing is discussed further in Chapter 6.

Marketing and the law

Throughout history there has been a battle of wits between marketers and the law. Artifacts were copied and forged in Roman times and in medieval times markets were subject to charters, and later many goods were hallmarked or the equivalent. In the Wild West vendors moved from town to town selling phoney drugs and defective merchandise and moved on before the law could catch them. In the last hundred years legislation, such as the Sale of Goods Act, has progressively moved the balance in favour of the purchaser and improved communications have narrowed the chances of the purveyors of 'snake oil'. Antitrust legislation has worked to reduce the ability of suppliers to create monopolies and government agencies, such as the Office of Fair Trading, have acted to protect the efficiency of markets.

Despite this progress there remain considerable anomalies which marketers may (and often do) exploit. Trading standards differ between countries and offer outlets to inferior goods. Differing tax laws offer opportunities for arbitrage and court awards differ significantly between countries. This is, however, the lowest common denominator. Developed countries increasingly rely less on the law than on quality standards. Firms seek to differentiate themselves positively by achieving BS 5750 (ISO 9002) or by subscribing to 'charters' or declared sets of values (such as that of the Chartered Institute of Marketing). In times of increasing competition marketing strategists look less at the minimum standards set by the law and increasingly at ways of differentiating themselves positively by setting higher and (ideally) unique standards. In the past, laws set the shape of the marketing process; in the future, it is likely that best practice will shape new laws, increasingly on an international scale, particularly in the wake of the success of the Uruguay Round of GATT.

While the main thrust of legal development is favourable to customers (consumers) there are other developments which have the effect of protecting producers' investment in patents, copyright and branding. These developments are mainly aimed at the suppression of bogus goods, such as the infamous 'Lolex' watches sold in Asia, and at the promotion of inferior products which steal money from consumers. GATT, or its successor the World Trade Organization, will bring increasing pressure to bear on trade piracy, mainly to protect consumers but incidentally to protect producers' investment in intellectual property and brands. As established brands come under increasing attack from retailers' own-label brands, some improvement in the ability of producer brands to protect their position legally in overseas markets will be welcome.

Marketing ethics

Marketing has tended to reflect the values of its time. We have spoken of the drive for mass consumerism in the 1960s and of the cynical promotions of the 1980s which led to a series of well-publicized scandals. These episodes reflect the failure of marketing so far to be true to its true vocation–the building of long-term relationships. In the 1990s there is a growing recognition that businesses can only flourish in the longer term by establishing and maintaining a set of values which can win the support of all stakeholders. Many businesses have spoken of values for years but have failed to live those values in their daily work. Values can only take root, thrive and propagate in a business where they are recognized as an integral part of the shared culture. In their book *A Sense of Mission* (1990), Andrew Campbell, Marion Devine and David Young explore in depth the strategic power of values. A 'Sense of Mission' is not just a mission statement (these are often rather banal) but is a shared purpose for the company; values are the bond between those in the company and external stakeholders.

The importance of values was first recognized by writers such as William Ouchi (1981), who saw them as a governance system. Richard Pascale and Anthony Athos (1981) explored the 'spiritual fabric' which they saw as the secret weapon of many Japanese firms:

> 'What is needed in the West is a non-deified, non-religious spiritualism that enables a firm's superordinate goals to respond truly to the inner meanings that many people seek in their work–or alternatively, seek in their lives and could find in their work if only that were more culturally acceptable. If a person's values are significantly different, he will soon find he is in the wrong place. It is a key responsibility of corporate leadership to set the pattern and tone of this conscience' (Weiss, 1986).

Campbell, Devine and Young (1990) explore the interaction of values and strategy in companies such as Honda and BBA. For them, mission is the product of that interaction, and the 'sense of mission' arises from matching values with those of employees. The real power comes where the pattern of shared values can be extended to include key external stakeholders, of which customers must be the prime target.

Marketing ethics can only really be effective when based on a shared value system. Ethics driven by the 'peur du gendarme' are not stable and cannot create a meaningful marketing relationship. The process of using values to drive marketing is still at its early stages. Some businesses, for example The Body Shop, have been extremely successful in wearing their heart on their sleeve and attracting like-minded people as customers. 'Shared values' is, after all, one mode of the 'Seven S Model' used by McKinley to represent the dynamics of the typical business (Figure 5.1) (Pascale, 1991). Such an emphasis on shared values is more powerful and more sustainable than the use of snobbery or baser human instincts to promote products. The use of shared values as a marketing strategy is a logical next step which awaits recognition by most marketers.

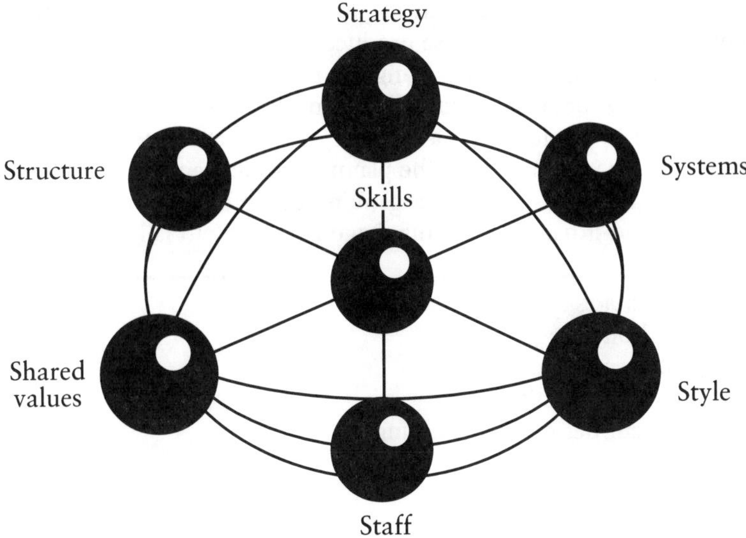

Figure 5.1 The Seven S framework (Pascale, 1991)

The drivers in society

Strategic marketing needs to be driven by issues which the customer finds compelling if it is to be successful on a sustained basis. The key drivers in markets have varied significantly in the last fifty years. Immediately after the Second World War, shortages created a seller's market and the key driver was the buyer's claim to priority. Later, when post-war recovery took hold the key driver became consumption–owning as many household durables as possible and having a clean and well-fed lifestyle. There followed a period where the emphasis was on conspicuous consumption, epitomized by the chromium-plated, gas-guzzling car.

Only as the balance in the marketplace moved in favour of the consumer could modern marketing emerge. The initiative passed to the customer, even though the producer machine still thought it was setting the agenda. Growing competition forced producers to look to their pricing or to drive for differentiation through technology. Harold Wilson's vision of a Britain revolutionized by the 'white heat of technology' was an aberration, leading to technology-driven products like Concorde for which the market revenues will never show a return on the investment made. At the time the real interest of consumers was geared to the stage beyond consumer durables, to entertainment, travel and sport.

Products began to need better packaging and service support, leading to a growing proliferation of 'add-ons' such as that shown in Figure 5.2

(Wilson, (1991). The balance in the marketplace moved increasingly in favour of the customer. Japanese products began to be accepted in certain markets due to their reliability, range of features and relatively attractive prices. Novelty became a key driver in the marketplace with rapid improvement in products and a flow of new products to tempt the buyer. For a while this was more than the planned obsolescence of the US motor industry of the 1960s but was a genuine outpouring of innovation and excitement and it has only recently begun seriously to fail.

---

1. *Design services*
   Physical planning
   Pre-sale service and advice
   Prototype fabrication
   Equipment design and checking
   Facilities advice
   Packaging advice
2. *Product enhancement services*
   Finishing
   Non-destructive testing
   Certification
   Calibration
   Testing
3. *Pre-start-up order services*
   Project co-ordination
   Assembly
   Installation
   Engineering and pre-delivery inspection and testing
   Zero defect
   Start-up
4. *Negotiation services*
   Resolving complaints
   Warranty adjustments, including exchange of product
   Liaison between customers and production department
5. *Education services*
   Guidance on application, use and adaptation of products to customers' needs
   On-site demonstration, instructions, training and in-plant lectures
   Handling and safety advice
   Library service
   Technical literature
   General industrial advice
   Help lines

6. *Visiting services*
   General and specific-purpose visits to customers' plants
   Customer visits to service and production departments
   On-site supervision including the provision of specific facilities, e.g. banking, health monitoring
7. *Maintenance and repair services*
   Periodic testing and adjustment
   Cleaning and repairing
   Rehabilitation and reconditioning
   Loan equipment availability
   Parts stock and repair
8. *Product adaptation services*
   Modifications
   Applications research
   Retro-fit
9. *Emergency services*
10. *Standby services*
11. *Operating services*
    On-line stock and delivery information
    Consumables supplies and stocks
    Waste and packing disposal
12. *Delivery services*
    Stocks
    On-line information
    'Just-in-Time'
    Order fill
    Transit quality control
    Post-delivery inspection
    Groupage
    Consignment (sale-or-return)
    Off-loading
13. *Marketing services*
    Joint promotions
    New product or application development
    Merchandising aids
    Market research
14. *Financial services*
    Credit
    Lease, rent or hire
    Factoring

Discounting

15. *Disposal services*
    Removal
    Trade-in
    Dismantling
    Recycling

Figure 5.2 Summary of services that can comprise a part of a firm's product/service back-up (Wilson, 1991). Reproduced with permission from *New Directives in Marketing* by Aubrey Wilson, published by Kogan Page Ltd, London (1991, 1994)

For many the key driver in the 1980s was greed (but not expressed as such!). The search for the 'free lunch' epitomized that decade and led to a splurge of tasteless marketing and excessive direct mail which damaged the image of marketers. In the rush for quick returns many companies lost their way strategically; some brands such as Pierre Cardin were extended well beyond the frontiers of credibility. Banks, building societies and the financial services businesses bought estate agents as outlets for their products which they subsequently found they could not manage. Was greed the real driver of the 1980s or was it really the search for value? It is interesting to contrast the growth of the personal computer market in the 1980s, driven by increasingly higher specifications and lower prices, with the hype of many brands which sought to drive up profits often at the expense of brand investment. Jaguar was among those that needed rescuing from this situation.

From this analysis it may be deduced that it is difficult to identify the true market drivers at any point in time or for any specific market. Producers were once able to condition markets; since they have lost much of this power in developed markets they have often failed to identify the true market drivers and have fallen victim to their own illusions. *Business Week* in a 1983 article focused on innovation. Despite advances in new product testing techniques and the vast sums of money required to launch a national brand in a major category–$50 milion in 1983–two-thirds of new products still fail, a casualty rate that was 'astonishingly high' (Brooks, 1989). While innovation is a driver in many markets (e.g. fashion, music, etc.) others will be backward-looking (heritage, nostalgia, etc.). As in all markets, the truth will lie in intelligent segmentation so that there may be a number of drivers and repellents the pattern of which may only be discernible by force field analysis (see Appendix 2). Among these drivers and repellents there will at any time be the one which arises from trends in society which each individual may not necessarily share (as the Maastricht Agreement phenomenon so clearly demonstrated).

What may be the drivers of society as we approach the millennium? As societies move up Maslow's (1954) 'hierarchy of needs' from food and shelter towards self-realization it would seem that market drivers will reflect that movement. Crisis and redundancy may cause reversions down the hierarchy but a growing number of potential customers seem to be searching for products and services which give them the ability to enrich their lives (by saving time or by widening their experience) and are also concerned with issues outside themselves. Busy lives need comfort and convenience, and the opportunity to escape from daily pressures (is this why the video entertainment industry has boomed?). Even the busy people in our society take a growing interest in the environment and in the availability of healthcare; while personal charity may have waned, vicarious charity through donations has grown. When we have no time for others it is tempting to expiate our guilt in money!

Hints about the nature of market drivers for the millennium may be found in John Naisbitt's Megatrends (Naisbitt and Aburdene, 1991) which were listed in Chapter 1. Like all futurologists John Naisbitt has to live with his failures as well as his successes; we are nearly halfway through the 1990s without a booming economy and GATT's Uruguay Round will take time to have any significant effect. Bob Beckman (1983) in his book *The Downwave* sees the 1990s as a period of depression! The list of Megatrends shown in Chapter 1 does not highlight the effects of greater longevity, of the growth in crime or of the failure of education in most developed countries. The accelerating pace of change is exhilarating for some but alienating for most people. It will force everyone to adapt as effectively as possible as an individual and to strengthen his or her ability to work effectively in a chosen team. Peter Benton (1990) in his book *Riding the Whirlwind* examines the pattern of turbulence which is emerging in world markets and, despite the risks and setbacks, is optimistic: 'But turbulence is rich in energy, so it must be [human] sympathy with vigour, working with the grain of forces in play, but creative in opportunity–riding the whirlwind and directing the storm.' Out of the ashes of the welfare state and of the dependency culture, will a vigorous individualism and interdependent self-reliance be a key market driver of the future?

References

Arndt, Johan, 'The anthropology of marketing systems: symbols, shared meanings and way of life in interorganisational networks', *Proceedings of International Research Seminar on Industrial Marketing*, Stockholm School of Economics, 1984.

Beckman, R., *The Downwave*, Pan, London, 1983.

Benton, Peter, *Riding the Whirlwind*, Blackwell, Oxford, 1990.

Business Week, 'Marketing: the new priority', 21 November 1983.
Brookes, Richard, *The New Marketing*, Gower, Aldershot, 1989.
Campbell, A., Devine, M. and Young, D., *A Sense of Mission*, Hutchinson, London, 1990.
Carson, Rachel, *Silent Spring*, 1962.
Levitt, T., 'Marketing myopia', *Harvard Business Review*, September/October 1975.
Maslow, A., *Motivation and Personality*, Harper, New York, 1954.
McGregor, Douglas, *The Human Side of Enterprise*, McGraw-Hill, New York, 1960.
Nader, Ralph, *Unsafe at Any Speed*, Grossman, New York, 1965.
Naisbitt, J. and Aburdene, P., *Megatrends 2000*, Futura, London, 1990.
Ouchi, William, *Theory Z: How American business can meet the Japanese challenge*, Addison-Wesley, Reading, MA, 1981.
Packard, Vance, *The Waste Makers*, David McKay, New York, 1954.
Pascale, Richard, *Managing on the Edge*, Penguin, Harmondsworth, 1991.
Pascale, Richard, and Athos, A., *The Art of Japanese Management*, Simon & Schuster, New York, 1981.
Weiss, William, *Journal of Business Ethics*, **5**, 1986.
Wilson, Aubrey, *New Directions in Marketing*, Kogan Page, London, 1991.

CHAPTER

6

Organizing for strategic marketing

In his book *Offensive Marketing* (1987) Hugh Davidson defines offensive marketing as profitable, offensive, integrated, strategic and effectively executed (to be recalled by the mnemonic POISE!). He describes 'offensive' as 'an attitude of mind which decides independently what is best for a company, rather than waiting for competition to make the first move'. In his view, 'winning strategies are rarely developed without intensive analysis and careful consideration of alternatives'. Not for Hugh Davidson the easy path of emergent strategies! His beliefs on organizing for marketing involve the following four principles:

1. Marketing organization should reflect the structure of the marketplace
2. Marketing and sales departments should be integrated
3. New products and new businesses should be handled by separate groups
4. Marketing staff should be integrators, not specialists

Traditional marketing departments have usually been organized around centres of functional excellence–advertising, direct mail, promotions, etc. Latterly there has been a tendency to organize additionally around customer groups–personal clients, business-to-business, etc. An increasing focus on segmenting the marketplace has enabled some businesses to win competitive advantage (e.g. ICL structured around client groups–banks, retailers, etc.). There is now a growing awareness of the total supply chain so that many retailers form buying units with segmented market focus which can interact with the marketing department to communicate right through the supply chain. A case study on strategic procurement at IBM may be found in Chapter 9.

The integration of marketing and sales reflects again the unified supply chain. The marketing function is responsible for creating the best possible conditions to enable sales to be achieved. This requires a very close and interactive partnership, not the rivalry and mutual suspicion which divide too many marketing and sales departments. Both are key parts of the process of winning customers and their task is not achieved until the sale is made and the price is paid. According to an article in *The Economist* (1994), entitled 'Death of the brand manager', two Unilever companies, Lever Brothers and Elida Gibbs, have merged sales and marketing and reorganized them into 'business groups' focused on consumers supported by a 'customer development' team to build relations with retailers and covering all brands marketed by the company.

New products and new businesses are like babies–they need love and attention around the clock! Too many companies see innovation as a filler of spare time rather than as the new generation of the business. Mixing old and new products and businesses is like mixing children of different ages in school. The established businesses see the newer ones as a nuisance, and potentially as a threat; the new businesses are at risk of being bullied or sidelined. New businesses also require highly focused attention so that they not only need to be separated from established businesses but they also require the best brains in order to be able to develop and mature.

Modern organization theory is undergoing seismic change so that the traditional functional and line structure is now in question. With the focus of business re-engineering being on the customer, and its objective being to align all processes to meet customer service standards, many businesses are abandoning functional structures and placing specialists in permanent or semi-permanent process teams. This trend reflects Hugh Davidson's thinking in that the marketing specialists will be integrating internal operations with the needs of customers. A warning against any permanent breakdown of functional structures is sounded by James Womach and David Jones (1994). The authors see functions as the schools to maintain and spread functional expertise, and emphasize the importance of functional staff being able regularly to update and hone their skills and to retain contact with their functional ladder of advancement. The example of Unipart is quoted, as this highly distributed service business has its own 'university' in order to develop and disseminate best practice throughout the group. Motorola has a similar 'university' in the USA. The 'lean enterprise' does rely basically on value-creating process teams and 'the traditional marketing and sales task of specifying the product, taking orders and scheduling delivery become the work of the product development and production teams'. In the lean enterprise 'marketing defines principles of enduring relationships with customers and/or distributors and identifies suitable partners'.

On balance I would prefer to rewrite Hugh Davidson's fourth principle to read 'marketing staff should be integrators, as well as specialists'. The fact that some functions have resisted change in many organizations, initially making matrix management less effective by rationing support for project management (which happened earlier at British Aerospace) and latterly by failing to break down interdepartmental barriers to the natural flow of job processes, does not mean that functional excellence can be discarded or put at risk of atrophy. Much has been written of Britain's poor performance in marketing, so that it is a function which requires greater nurture rather than dispersal. The article in *The Economist* referred to above quotes a study by Coopers & Lybrand as concluding that 'marketing as a discipline is more vital than ever' but that the marketing department was 'critically ill'.

Many marketing departments lost credibility in the recent recession through excessive promotions and price discounting which has helped to undermine brand loyalty. Overpricing, such as by Marlboro, often led to over-reactive price cuts and in a few weeks severely damaged brand loyalties built over years. Recent events have not really sounded the death knell of the marketing department but have discounted the arrogant short-termers and set a premium on the competent long-term players, many of whom, such as Rover Cars, have reorganized totally in order to win the right to survive. Rover studied its target markets to establish the price levels needed to compete and built a business to produce cars for sale profitably at those price levels. A similar strategy was used by Heinz to restore its market share in the pet-food market. This is detailed in an interesting article in *Fortune* (1994).

Failures in marketing performance by some companies do not invalidate the principles of marketing for all, particularly where those principles are regularly tested in the marketplace and are practised on a strategic level rather than solely at a tactical one. These failures in marketing argue for better training, more contact with customers and for perfecting the skills to develop sustainable competitive advantage not for closing the marketing department. All companies need to find a structure which facilitates the development of marketing excellence, either through a strong marketing department or perhaps, as at Unipart, through the establishment of a forum for all functions to nurture and cross-fertilize their skills.

In considering how to organize for strategic marketing we need to identify the key elements required for the task. First, it must be recognized that marketing operates at two levels, both as a set of values built around serving customers which needs to drive the whole business and also as a set of skills which supports that drive. The emphasis on 'customer first' and 'total quality' which is placed on their operations by many companies is testimony to the growing recognition that businesses can only succeed through winning and retaining customers. Any strategic marketing organization must be based on involving the whole company in the marketing process. This can only be made strategic by involving the whole company in the process of shaping and delivering strategic plans (see Chapter 4). 'Customer first' and 'total quality' programmes help to sustain employee involvement in delivering strategies, many of which will be marketing strategies. The strategic plan will be underpinned by a marketing plan (see Chapter 7) which will provide the key link between the deployment of the key values which drive the whole business and the deployment of specific marketing skills which, together with other functional skills, provide the competitive edge for success. It is essential that the whole process is driven by the strategic plan in order to galvanize the whole organization. The model of strategic marketing advanced by Jean-Jacques Lambin in his recent book *Strategic Marketing* (1994) places marketing in the driving role. Marketing has a key part to play in the process, as the interface with customers and marketers, but strategic success must be driven by the whole organization with leadership from the board and not just the marketing department.

Key elements of a strategic marketing organization

The detailed tools of marketing are discussed later (Chapter 7). To use those tools effectively requires a number of specific competences which may or may not be grouped within a marketing department. Much has been made of the fact that Marks & Spencer does not have a formalized marketing department; it does have the marketing competences which we shall now review even though its structure is focused on buying and merchandising.

The following elements would seem to be essential in any marketing organization:

1. Market research
2. Marketing research
3. Trends analysis
4. Information systems
5. Internal marketing/total quality
6. A 'learning' culture
7. Team-building capability
8. Ability to form alliances and make them work
9. Outstanding design capability
10. Skills in product and brand management
11. Effectiveness in 'offensive marketing' (see above)
12. Independent marketing audit

Let us examine each in more detail:

Market research

Market research is one of the key competences in marketing. It is a structured approach to identifying, measuring and exploring specific market areas which can give considerable insight into the shape and dynamics of that market. It requires both a rigorous approach to defining the scope of markets and obtaining as much data as possible about them, combined with the experience and insight to make intelligent guesses at the data which structured research always fails to discover. While actual data and guesses must rigorously be distinguished from each other, the process of 'fitting in the jigsaw' is crucial to turning data into information, i.e. to enable patterns and meaning to be discerned in raw data.

The quality of market research is of prime importance in developing marketing strategy. Many firms prefer to commission important studies from outside professionals in order to maximize the effectiveness of the process and to avoid even unconscious bias. The firm will still need to have well-honed competence in market research in order to be able to test and interpret external research and to pursue focused confidential research into areas of particular promise illuminated in the external study.

A novel approach to market research is the database being developed by Essex University, tracking the lives of some 10 000 individuals. It is planned to revisit these people annually in order to retune the database which is available to market researchers and consumer goods companies. This is an interesting experiment which will probably be the forerunner of other evolving databases.

It is advisable to vary the external firms used for research since regular use of the same researcher can lead to contamination with the prejudices of its client. Research is not an end in itself; it only adds value when it produces information or insights which can lead to action that wins competitive advantage. Fresh eyes are often quicker to spot minor market changes which familiarity might not detect.

Another innovative approach to market research is 'Technical Market Research' or TMR. This process was developed by Goodyear and enables customers to see and experience potential new products in the company's laboratories. The feedback from customers helps to maintain relevance and to speed up the process to market. The TMR process is described in Lauglaug (1993).

Marketing research

Marketing research is the process of matching products to markets and deciding how to use the elements of the 'marketing mix' to facilitate their sale. The 'marketing mix' is a series of marketing tools which can be used selectively and in combination to maximize the effectiveness of bringing a

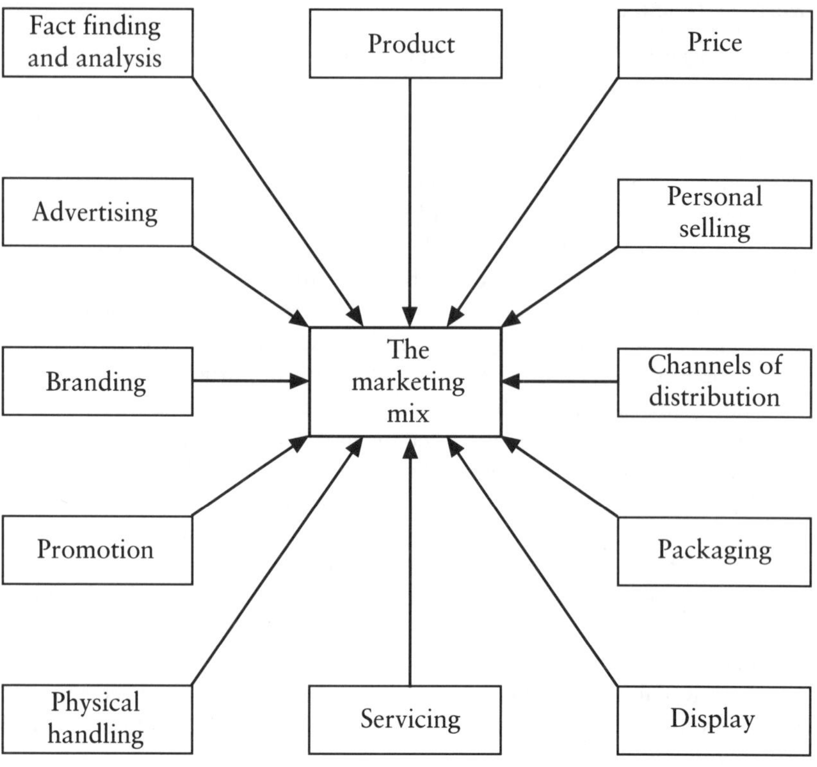

Figure 6.1 The marketing mix (Bordon, 1965)

given product or service to market (see Figure 6.1) (Fifield, 1992). Use of the 'marketing mix' is discussed more fully in Chapter 7 but the role of marketing research is crucial for preparing successful marketing plans.

Skills in marketing research are needed in every company although many businesses use external consultants to advise them either on their choice of media or, after the choice, on how best to use the chosen medium. Without internal skills companies are at the mercy of powerful media salesforces or of consultants who are not always free of bias. Any marketing organization needs sufficient competence in marketing research to be able to make an independent judgement. This level of competence will allow them to use specialist consultants effectively and with confidence.

Trends analysis

Good market research is more than a snapshot of a market at a point in time. Knowledge should be sufficient to trace the history of the market and identify the factors that influence it. From this information will emerge a number of trends that are likely to shape the future development of the market.

It is always tempting to extrapolate identified trends and to assume no change in underlying market conditions. This approach is always fatal, as IBM discovered when the mainframe market went into apparent decline. All marketing organizations need skills to test trends and to explore the assumptions which underpin them. Many have developed models which enable the interaction of key factors in a given market to be tested and evaluated so that the impact of a given change in assumptions may be deduced. These models vary considerably in quality and are rarely large enough to be robust (i.e. they over-react). Some commercial models with large datebases, such as PIMS (Profit Impact of Marketing Strategy) which has over 7000 companies in its system, are able to make their analysis subindustry-specific and of value to each extra client.

There are other tools for trends analysis, such as Delphi and scenario planning which are examined in Appendix 2. Strategic marketing requires the use of tools which can explore as far forward as possible and be as open-ended in their approach as possible. Trends are seductive and the reality of trends analysis is surprise. There are no infallible tools for forecasting the future but tools such as scenario planning enable the possibility of many surprises to be foreseen, and 'forewarned is forearmed'.

Information systems

The growth of IT capability and the decline in the cost of using it has led to increasing interest in database information systems. The need to obtain deeper knowledge of markets and customers to win sustainable competitive advantage and the growing requirement to access such information quickly to give effective customer service is forcing that interest to turn into investment. Many businesses depend on instant information for their survival. In Chapter 8 we examine the creation and growth of Firstdirect, a telephone banking business whose stock-in-trade is 24-hour full-service availability. This can only be achieved by a very sophisticated online database.

Strategic marketing increasingly recognizes the long-term value of continuing customer relationships. 'Relationship marketing' is a major pillar of strategic marketing and itself depends on the existence and maintenance of information systems to service the relationship. For key customers, account management is an essential part of the relationship and account management requires powerful information systems to sustain it. Sophisticated account management systems operate at many levels, from the director to director level at the top, through product or project management interfaces, down to site contacts or deliveries. Each level generates information, even if only the sight of a competitor's lorry at the goods-inwards dock, and all this has to be integrated and interpreted. Chapter 8 includes a case study on relationship marketing at BET.

The quality of information systems will be a key differentiator between competing companies in the medium term. Marketers will need to acquire and perfect their skills in database design and management not least because communication with customers will increasingly be by electronic data interchange and such links will strengthen relationship marketing almost as much as the human contact, which will continue to be essential. Progressive buildup of its consumer database has enabled Heinz to switch the emphasis of its marketing from media advertising to direct mail.

Internal marketing/total quality

We all know many tales of marketing departments that have laboured to create customer bonds and have been betrayed by the inadequacies of other functions. Customers do not distinguish between departments; a promise from any person is a promise from the company. Whether the promise was rash or even misunderstood, the customer looks to the whole company to redeem it.

Failures of this nature made it necessary long ago for marketers to sell themselves internally as well as externally. Various techniques have been used, ranging from newsletters to parties, and results have been mixed. Internal communication remains a 'black science' in most companies; unilateral attempts by marketers to sell themselves internally have rarely succeeded, not least because they often imply that marketing is in some way in a privileged position as the spokesperson for the customer.

Internal marketing is likely to be more successful where it is part of a company-wide operation. Examples of this include the annual planning cycle, but many marketing departments have in the past failed to align their marketing plans with corporate strategies. To be accepted it helps to be seen as a good team player. Internal communication is best structured on a company-wide basis to ensure that messages are not distorted and that they reach all parts of the organization. Examples of good practice in this area may be found in specialist publications such as *Internal Communication Focus*. Teamwork is the order of the day for successful internal communication. Finally, the establishment of total quality systems depends on a company-wide initiative and is driven by teamwork also.

Total quality systems can be of enormous value to marketers as they are customer-focused and should better be able to marshal the resources of the company for effective marketing than any amount of internal marketing by the marketing function alone. There is a danger that the concept of internal customers and suppliers, on which the total quality process is built, may make individuals inward-looking. The whole object of total quality is to maximize service to the external customer–'he who pays the bills'–and a key function of marketers in total quality-driven companies must be to ensure that the end game of customer delight is kept uppermost in the minds of all players so that it can consistently be won. The lesson that quality is 'in the eye of the customer' has taken most businesses too long to learn. Quality pioneers like Motorola have saved large sums through quality improvement ($700 million in five years for Motorola) but have only recently begun to study their customers' quality needs. It is likely that savings from such a refocusing of quality effort may be considerably larger.

A key element of total quality is effective customer service. Growing emphasis on service in recent years, and the introduction of customer charters by public bodies, have led to a steady increase in customer expectations. Customer satisfaction is now barely adequate; customer delight is needed to obtain a competitive advantage. Digital Equipment, the computer services company, has developed with John Humble a new approach to delivering service, identifiable by the acronym PROMPT:

1. Prioritizing customer needs (customers determine what is important)
2. Reliability is critical (quality, reliability, speed of delivery, courtesy)
3. Organizing for customers (the customer, not your organization, is the business)
4. Personal training (training in customer service is not a standard product)
5. Technology focusing (technology provides new opportunities to serve customers better)

John Humble's process involves three stages:

1. Determining how customers currently perceive your service
2. Clarifying your vision of the future service to be provided
3. Developing an action plan to realize that vision

The whole process is well described in an article by Michael Quinn and John Humble (1993).

Delivering effective service is not only a matter of culture; it requires great care in setting standards which will enthuse customers and in maintaining or beating those standards. Severn Trent, the water and waste management company, sets great store by agreeing and delivering clearly defined standards of service. Its concept 'service as an exact science' is a powerful recognition that values must be measured to be meaningful.

A 'learning' culture

Businesses are like a living organism, they must continuously adapt to changing conditions or they will die. Adaptation is achieved by a process known as 'learning', which is essentially Darwinian in nature. Learning can only be achieved by encouraging innovation and risk and by allowing people to make mistakes within controlled limits. The experience generated by the learning process develops competence and helps to force the adaptation which enables companies to remain competitive. Companies need therefore to create and foster a culture which encourages learning and which recognizes that rapid adaptation is a key competitive advantage. Learning is both a personal and a communal phenomenon. We each need to enlarge our competences to compete with each other; we need each other to develop shared learning which enables the company to survive and prosper.

A key part of the learning process is the ability to listen carefully to customers. In the words of Dr Fernando Flores (1993):

> 'Listening is a good deal more than the information gathering of traditional market research. Listening is primarily about establishing and building rapport. To be less than careful in this regard is to court failure.'

Listening requires a structured response through meeting a customer's needs and obtaining confirmation of his or her satisfaction. According to Dr Flores again:

> 'The organization that is listening, that organizes for completion and that builds on learning will gain a decisive competitive advantage into the next century. It will be a leader in observing and adapting to the new ways of doing business in the new world that is rapidly unfolding before us every day.'

Because they operate directly in markets and need to handle customers and cope with competitors, marketers need particularly strong learning skills. As the company's window on the external world, marketers and others will find the need to bring learning back into the organization. Skills in teaching will need to complement skills in learning if the company is to adapt effectively to a world where change seems to accelerate year by year.

Team-building capability

This combination of teaching and learning skills should help marketers to be effective in building teams for specific tasks. The competences needed to do this include:

1. An understanding of team dynamics
2. The ability to pick individuals with the right combination of characteristics
3. To ensure that the task is properly defined
4. To oversee the working of the team and help to solve problems

Team dynamics is a complex issue which has been studied in particular by Meredith Belbin (1981) of Henley Management College for many years. From his experiments and observations Belbin has identified a number of discrete personality types (see Table 6.1). Teams which are composed solely of one type (like many company boards in the 1950s) fail totally; those with an imbalance in their membership are inadequate in varying degrees. Successful teams usually have a full range of personality types and few duplications. Identifying the personality type of each individual is, therefore, crucial to success in team building.

Defining the team tasks is important and should not be left to the team's discretion or interpretation. Their energies should be committed to deciding how to carry out the task and what resources they need to do so.

Overseeing the working of the team requires briefing beforehand and at regular intervals, checking that bonding between individuals is achieved or dealing with disputes if the team cannot resolve them itself. Leadership should come from within the team and coaching from outside should be limited to the level essential to maintain reasonable progress. Too much interference inhibits the learning process within the team; the availability of support is all that is necessary in most cases, and it may well not be called upon.

Ability to form alliances and make them work

Most companies today operate in global markets even if they are small and highly local in their focus. The small sweet-manufacturer in Boston, Lincolnshire, competes with the might of Nestlé whether he knows it or not. As trade barriers increasingly fall, smaller companies will have to face this reality and find strategies to cope with it.

One of the strategies which has become increasingly favoured by both large and small businesses is the formation of alliances. This recognizes the

Table 6.1 Useful people to have in teams

Type	*Symbol*	*Typical features*	*Positive qualities*	*Allowable weaknesses*
Company Worker	CW	Conservative, dutiful, predictable	Organizing ability, practical common sense, hard-working, self-discipline	Lack of flexibility, unresponsiveness to unproven ideas
Chairman	CH	Calm, self-confident controlled	A capacity for treating and welcoming all potential contributors on their merits and without prejudice. A strong sense of objectives.	No more than ordinary in terms of intellect or creative ability
Shaper	SH	Highly strung, outgoing, dynamic	Drive and a readiness to challenge inertia, ineffectiveness, complacency or self-deception	Proneness to provocation, irritation and impatience
Plant	PL	Individualistic, serious-minded, unorthodox	Genius, imagination, intellect, knowledge	Up in the clouds, inclined to disregard practical details or protocol
Resource Investigator	RI	Extroverted, enthusiastic, curious, communicative	A capacity for contacting people and exploring anything new. An ability to respond to challenge	Liable to lose interest once the initial fascination has passed
Monitor-Evaluator	ME	Sober, unemotional, prudent	Judgement, discretion, hard-headedness	Lacks inspiration or the ability to motivate others
Team Worker	TW	Socially orientated, rather mild, sensitive	An ability to respond to people and to situations, and to promote team spirit	Indecisiveness at moments of crisis
Completer-Finisher	CF	Painstaking, orderly, conscientious, anxious	A capacity for follow-through. Perfectionism	A tendency to worry about small things. A reluctance to 'let go'

From Belbin (1981)

reality that few companies have the resources to achieve global coverage in their own right, and that even those who are well endowed with resources find it helpful to share operations in some markets in order either to reduce risk or to win local competitive advantage. Alliances are at differing levels of commitment, varying from joint companies, through marketing agreements to informal tactical cooperation.

Marketing skills lie at the heart of alliances, since the case for making them will be based on market and marketing research and marketing plans will drive much of their activity. Marketers will need to be more strategic in their thinking if they are to provide leadership in this area. Too often marketers see external companies as actual or potential competitors, not reasoning that circumstances may make a competitor an ally against a common threat from a larger group. There is an old Arab saying that 'my enemy's enemy is my friend'. This may not be the foundation for a long-term alliance but many successful strategies have been built on no more.

Making alliances work requires constant attention to maintain both trust and momentum. Much of the bonding in this process must come from the marketing function and it will require great care to ensure that both parties fulfil the terms of their alliance. Usually the mutual contributions will be complementary since the alliance will be built on continuing individual advantages. Both parties will, however, have a common set of target customers so that, even if one party has a clear sole responsibility for the alliance's marketing, the marketing function of the other partner will wish to ensure their competence to do so before the alliance is made and maintain a watching brief as the alliance develops.

Outstanding design capability

Design is not just a concern for designers. It is an integral part of the total package offered to the customer and must be cohesive with it. Any marketing organization needs to have the skills required to understand the role of design in the marketing mix, i.e. as a part of Product, and to be able to shape design to maximize customer acceptance. Where a company is in a fashion-driven business, design is paramount and may well be consciously short term in its appeal. This does not make design any less strategic, since a fashion house like Dior seeks to establish a long-term reputation for setting trends rather than to achieve an occasional short-term triumph. Many designs are themselves strategic; the original Volkswagen design created the small-car industry in Germany and Olivetti's Lettera 22 typewriter design set an office machinery standard for decades. With such designs it is possible to win a clear competitive advantage and, through an interplay of branding and design evolution, maintain it for a considerable period. Jaguar is a company that has pursued this strategy with notable success.

Successful design requires not just aesthetic sense but an awareness of 'fitness for purpose' which matches customer needs that may not even have been articulated. The Sony Walkman was not the product of market research but of intelligent perception of an unfulfilled need. Akio Morita is, in any case, an unusual phenomenon in that he combines brilliance in design with technical innovation and perceptive marketing in one person. He is, however, no bad model for the aspiring strategic marketer to seek to emulate.

Design has been underappreciated in the UK for too long. The decline of the Design Council is symptomatic of a failure of manufacturers to build a bridge through good design between their technical competence and the markets which they too rarely understand. Christopher Lorenz (1990) has been leading a crusade in favour of better design for some years. His book *The Design Dimension* is a classic on the issue. Despite his work and the efforts of others, design remains the weakest element in the strategic marketing mix of most companies.

Skills in product and brand management

One of the basic dilemmas of marketing is that it seeks to respond to customers' needs and can usually do so only by creating a product. Customers seek solutions to their problems and answers to their needs; these are rarely matched by products (or even services) which depend on compromise in order to be marketed profitably. History is littered with the corpses of companies which were blinded by love of their products to changes in the marketplace. The whole British motorcycle industry is a striking example, but even today companies allow themselves to indulge in product-led strategies—IBM yesterday, Microsoft today.

Marketers need constantly to be on their guard against product-led thinking and should seek every opportunity to 'open the windows' and bring fresh thinking into the business. Products are, however, a key investment for the company and need to compete with each other for development, manufacturing and marketing resources and the longer-term investment needed to fulfil their potential. Many companies adopt a matrix organization to reflect this interaction of functions and products and appoint product managers to build market share and develop the potential of their product.

In many companies product managers are part of the marketing department which helps to ensure that market awareness is not lost. In some cases product groups are large enough to be self-standing units with their own development, manufacturing and marketing resources. Whatever the structure, there remains a constant challenge to relate to the realities of the marketplace.

Brand management has developed on the back of product management but brands have mostly been built by sustained promotion through the media and at point of sale. Building brands depends on providing meaningful information to buyers and developing their trust. Brand management is essentially a marketing phenomenon, although investment in brands is a substantial cost to the whole business. Distribution and selling costs were $23^1/_2$ per cent of sales for Unilever in 1993 and a significant part of that expenditure will have been made to underpin the brands which are far better known than the name of their owner. The value of brands is reflected in the goodwill paid for acquiring the companies that own them. This sum is now so significant that a number of companies capitalize the value of brands (e.g. Reckitt & Colman). Brands can also be fragile; a failure of quality led to a disastrous loss of market share by Perrier from which it has only just begun to recover.

Brand management is, therefore, a key strategic focus for many businesses, particularly those in fast-moving consumer goods (FMCG). Many FMCG companies have created brands wildly both as vehicles for new product development and to fit individual geographic or other market segment tastes. For many this proliferation of brands has become counter-productive and there is a move to rationalize individual brands under 'umbrella brands'. At Proctor & Gamble the management focus is now on categories of product and these are grouped under umbrella brands rather than being separately branded. It may be significant that many FMCG groups are beginning to raise awareness of the corporate image which will in time provide the ultimate in brand power. Nestlé has led the way in this trend.

Effectiveness in 'offensive marketing'

I referred earlier to Hugh Davidson's (1987) concept of 'offensive marketing'. This has five characteristics (which make the word POISE):

1. Profitable
2. Offensive
3. Integrated
4. Strategic
5. Effectively executed

Hugh Davidson emphasizes that the key objective of marketing is to increase profit. Recent panic by some marketers during the recession in piling on coupon schemes and discounted promotions shows how easily this principle can be betrayed. Good marketing adds value for the customer and marketers should never take their eyes off the prize of higher margins and increased profits.

Offensive marketing requires seizing the initiative from competitors and responding massively when *they* have taken an initiative. It is not the rashness of taking action without consideration of likely responses and of subsequent moves. A good chess player thinks several moves in advance, a good general will also have thought through the consequences of his initial move. Occasionally, it may pay to allow a competitor to make the first move, (for example, in pioneering a new product) and to position yourself to seize the benefit of your competitor's investment. Usually, however, the benefit of surprise creates a competitive advantage which can be held for some time. Midland Bank won a sustained increase in market share of current accounts by being the first to offer 'free banking' for accounts in credit.

Integrating marketing throughout the business has been shown to be essential for success. The example of Unipart shows how integrating all functions is beneficial; integrating marketing, as the interface with the customer, will be the most beneficial move to create and sustain competitive advantage.

Strategic direction is essential for the sustained success of any company. This has to be built on extensive market analysis and the identification and evaluation of alternative strategies. Strong strategic direction provides the leadership which can sustain a business in the face of adversity. Strategic marketing is both a key contribution to the creation of strategic direction and a major element of its implementation.

Effective execution is, therefore, the ultimate test of strategic marketing. It depends not only on intelligent and thorough preparation but also on teamwork between the marketing function and all other parts of the business. We have seen how the drivers of this teamwork are effective strategic planning and a total commitment to meeting customer needs.

Independent marketing audit

All functions and processes need regular review and marketing is no exception. Such a review is more effective if it is done (or at least overseen) by independent parties. The auditing of company finances is now a well-established principle and yet few companies audit the functions, processes and systems which drive their business. More detailed consideration of the marketing audit is given in Chapter 10.

Conclusion

It will be seen that organizing for strategic marketing requires great care and commitment. The process will be driven by the strategic planning system for the whole company which will be supported by the marketing function both in the provision of market and competitor data and by the building of a marketing plan to support delivery of corporate strategies.

The marketing function will need to be structured to enable it to deliver its commitments to the corporate strategic plan. It will need the skills which we have examined and for some companies, other specific skills (e.g. defence companies need political skills to deal with Whitehall). The exact structure of the marketing department will depend on the tasks it needs to fulfil. Not all companies require strong brand management although all will need to maintain and enhance their corporate image. There is a tendency for corporate communication to be established as a distinct function although its links with marketing will need to be close. Sometimes there is a separate government relations function, particularly where businesses are subject to legislation or regulation; this function also interacts closely with marketing.

These trends may be seen in some ways as a criticism of marketing. Recent attempts to re-engineer business processes have placed marketing in the path of the bulldozers of radical thinking, and the creation of process teams, as we have seen above, threatens the maintenance of functional excellence in the businesses concerned. Marketing has too often been arrogant, self-preoccupied and tactical in its thinking and actions. Its survival as an effective force will increasingly depend on its ability to take the offensive and to operate effectively at a strategic level.

References

Belbin, Meredith, *Management Teams–Why They Succeed or Fail*, Heinemann, London, 1981.

Bordon, N. H., 'The concept of the marketing mix', in Schwartz, G. (ed.), *Science in Marketing*, Wiley, Chichester, 1965.

Davidson, Hugh, *Offensive Marketing*, Penguin, Harmondsworth, 1987.

The Economist, 'Death of the brand manager', 9 April 1994.

Fifield, Paul, *Marketing Strategy*, Butterworth-Heinemann, Oxford, 1992.

Flores, Fernando, 'Innovation by listening carefully to customers', *Long Range Planning*, June 1993.

Fortune, 'How to escape a price war', 13 June 1994.

Lambin, J.-J., *Strategic Marketing*, McGraw-Hill, New York, 1994.

Lauglaug, Antonio S., 'Technical market research–get customers to collaborate in developing products', *Long Range Planning*, April 1993.

Lorenz, Christopher, *The Design Dimension*, Blackwell, Oxford, 1990.

Quinn, M. and Humble, J., 'Using service to gain a competitive edge–the PROMPT approach', *Long Range Planning*, April 1993.

Womach, J. and Jones, D., 'From lean production to the lean enterprise', *Harvard Business Review*, March/April 1994.

Marketing planning

CHAPTER 7

In Chapter 4 the first reference was made to marketing planning, as one of a number of functional plans, and it was stated that it is rarely as effective as it should be. Professor Malcolm McDonald (1989) of the Cranfield School of Management, a leading guru on the subject, sees it as 'one of the most baffling of all management problems' and yet 'the actual process of marketing planning is simple in outline'. Marketing planning as a process does not differ significantly from that of corporate planning; it involves the setting of objectives, the elaboration of strategies to meet them and the quantification of resources needed for their achievement. The part of the process of developing marketing plans which creates bafflement is to differentiate between strategic marketing planning and operational or tactical marketing planning. As Malcolm McDonald says: 'Few practising marketers understand the real significance of a strategic marketing plan as opposed to a tactical marketing or operational marketing plan.' The key difference between the two lies in the generation of options and the process of evaluating and eliminating them. This is the very heart of strategic planning, and marketing planning, at its best, is an extension of that process which we examined in Chapter 4.

The strategic marketing planning process is seen by Malcolm McDonald to have nine stages, which I will use as a template for developing my own views on marketing planning:

1. Corporate objectives
2. Marketing audit
3. SWOT analysis
4. Assumptions
5. Marketing objectives and strategies
6. Estimate expected results
7. Identify alternative plans and mixes (and iterate)
8. Programmes
9. Measurement and review

Corporate objectives

The corporate objectives will have been included in the document issued by the board at the beginning of the planning cycle in order to set a framework for all plans. Each has to contribute to achieving these objectives and must be rigorously aligned with them to be acceptable and effective. The subject of corporate objectives has been discussed in Chapter 2.

Marketing audit

Malcolm McDonald uses the term 'audit' to answer the question 'where are we now?' in the given context. A marketing audit would be part of a wider review of the company's environment and internal operations. The use of this term conflicts with its stricter sense, which indicates a check on conformity to given norms. In the strict sense a marketing audit is a process of ensuring compliance by the marketing function with the policies, procedures, processes and systems approved for marketing operations. I prefer the term 'marketing review' or 'marketing appraisal' which catches the qualitative nature of the process.

The marketing review will normally take stock of both the external and internal situation in which the company finds itself. Each part of the business will contribute to the total review which was examined in detail in Chapter 3. The marketing plan will make a larger contribution to the external review than most other functions due to its largely external orientation.

The marketing review can often best be carried out by non-attributable interviews of selected customers and other departments in the company, producing a set of issues which can be explored and evaluated in a workshop.

SWOT analysis

Analysis of strengths, weaknesses, opportunities and threats ('SWOT analysis') is a key step in the development of strategy at group, divisional or functional level. Although the analysis is aimed at the particular unit concerned, it needs to be made from the standpoint of the unit's customers if it is to be meaningful. With the advent of total quality these customers will increasingly be internal but, in the case of the marketing plan, the ultimate focus must be on external customers. As the corporate plan will also be focused on external customers, the analysis in the marketing plan is often a valuable input into the corporate plan and great care needs to be given to it.

SWOT analysis focuses on identifying and evaluating the strengths and weaknesses of the business unit as a customer might see them. It requires utter rigour if the myths which develop in a company and the echoes of promotional propaganda are to be set aside. SWOT analysis has to strip the image of the business unit down to reality. Only by doing this can the concomitant opportunities and threats be clearly discussed and realistically evaluated.

Raw material for the SWOT analysis will usually emerge from the marketing review or it may be generated by non-attributable interviews which will bring to the surface the key issues facing the business unit. The value of the interviews may be enhanced by using outside interviewers to handle the process; on a non-attributable basis the author has found this approach to yield powerful results. Unless this process is frank and open, it will not touch the issues that are crucial for the future competitiveness of the business.

The process of SWOT analysis is usually handled in a workshop, often using an external facilitator to finesse internal sensitivities, and involving all staff members who need to have ownership of the outcome. It is often helpful to include some 'young Turks' or mavericks who will not be afraid to comment on the Emperor's lack of clothes! Comments which cannot immediately be substantiated may be debated or even researched after the event.

The workshop will seek to draw out from participants the strengths and weaknesses of the business, both from the evidence of the review or interviews and from their knowledge of the business, its customers and competitors. It is useful to compare and contrast the business with its competitors in identifying strengths and weaknesses from the viewpoint of customers. A strengths and weaknesses profile of key competitors can be built up as a subset of the process, and this can often produce new insights into potential competitive advantage or disadvantage and help to shape effective strategies.

In the process of identifying the strengths and weaknesses of the business unit the facilitator will need to draw out the critical factors for success in dealing with its customers. These are factors such as quality, customer service, speed of delivery, price, etc., and the impact of this picture is strengthened by attempting to rank these factors from the standpoint of the customer. This ranking will vary from market to market but it is critical to achieve as close a fit with the perception of the customers of the specific business as possible. Customers of Sainsbury may rank choice above price; those of Aldi will not. The ranking of critical success factors should, where possible, be validated subsequently by customer interviews or by the use of customer-focus groups.

When strengths and weaknesses have been identified, the workshop needs to attempt to rank them, or at least the top half-dozen. This ensures that attention is focused on the 'factors that make the difference' and will need to correlate to the critical success factor ranking.

At this point the workshop needs to focus on opportunities and threats. Many of these will read directly across from the identified strengths and weaknesses. If, for instance, innovation has been identified as a strength there will be an opportunity to market new products. If financial controls have been identified as a weakness, there will be a threat of systems failure. The workshop will also need to look beyond the obvious opportunities and threats to those that emerge from combining strengths and weaknesses. For example, if there is too narrow a product line and spare cash in the business there may be potential for an acquisition or at least to invest in new products.

Strengths and weaknesses should not be taken at face value but need to be fully debated. Being 'well established' may be seen as a strength but some may detect the seeds of failure waiting to be watered by complacency. One person's strength may be another's weakness; the value of the process lies in the debate which goes behind the surface of each factor.

At the end of the process there will be a clearer appreciation of how others see the business. Many companies stimulate that process by including customers, suppliers and even competitors in the interview schedule which precedes the workshop. The conclusions of the workshop should be validated by customer contact afterwards, as indicated earlier. In my experience this openness is rarely abused and often produces insights which a wholly internal process cannot.

Assumptions

All plans are only as good as the validity of the assumptions about external factors on which they are built. Marketing plans are particularly sensitive to sound assumptions as so many factors affecting the market place are qualitative and difficult to measure. In most planning systems assumptions will partly be provided from the corporate level in order to avoid confusion. It would, for example, be confusing if the marketing department assumed a base rate of 4 per cent and other parts of the business assumed rates varying between 6 per cent and 8 per cent! The only assumptions needed for planning are those which would, if changed, significantly alter the potential outcome of the plan. An umbrella manufacturer would have to make assumptions about rainfall which would be redundant in many other plans!

Many of the key assumptions needed for planning will come from the marketing function. These will typically include movements in market prices, buying patterns, the timing of competitive product launches, etc. Many of these will be critical for the results of the whole company. Further comments on assumptions are made later in this chapter (see 'Estimate expected results').

Marketing objectives

Marketing objectives are of fundamental importance to delivering the corporate plan since they define the products to be sold and the markets in which to sell them. Despite the growth in importance of corporate treasurers in recent years, the major part of the cashflow and profits of a typical company will be generated by successful implementation of the marketing plan. Setting marketing objectives that deliver results in line with corporate objectives is therefore crucial.

Marketing objectives will be built up from the following:

1. The sale of existing products to established customers
2. The sale of existing products to new customers
3. The sale of new products to established customers
4. The sale of new products to new customers

While a company may have very long-term objectives which are not measurable but are ones 'which you know you have achieved when you get there', plans with a horizon of five years or less must have specifically quantified objectives to serve as clear milestones towards the long-term objectives on the distant horizon. To say that the company intends to become market leader in a specific market segment is precise enough as a long-term objective because it is impossible to foretell whether market leadership requires 80 per cent, 50 per cent or 30 per cent market share at that future time. To move in that direction it is essential to set a market share of 10 per cent in five years if you presently have 2 per cent.

Marketing objectives should never be derived by extrapolating the present pattern of sales. Marketing planning, as a process, demands new thinking at every stage, and it would be of little value to engage in lively SWOT analysis and then ignore its implications at the next stage of the process. Yet this is what too many companies still do, because setting objectives requires total commitment. If the SWOT analysis reveals new opportunities do we dare to commit ourselves to realizing them? If there are threats in the SWOT analysis can we really show a downturn in sales while we cope with them? Surely we shall muddle through somehow...

The objectives to be adopted in the plan must be as solidly established as possible, and qualified where necessary by assumptions, but they must reflect the analysis done in the planning process and justify the resources which will be required. If the objectives do not match those at corporate level it will be necessary to engage in gap analysis (see Chapter 4) in which the provision of resources from the centre will be contingent on finding new products and for markets to close the gap between corporate and marketing objectives.

Marketing objectives may be stated in terms of turnover, product volume, market share, distributor sell-in or whatever may be appropriate for the business. The measure chosen should be clear, quantifiable and verifiable. It often helps to adopt measures common to a particular industry (e.g. passenger kilometres for airlines) in order to facilitate competitor comparisons against a shared benchmark.

Marketing strategies

Marketing strategies are the means of meeting marketing objectives. In general terms most marketing strategies may be subsumed in McCarthy's (1975) famous four Ps formula:

1. Product–what to sell
2. Price–what to charge
3. Place–how to distribute/deliver
4. Promotion–how to encourage purchase

As Baker and Hart (1989) point out, the formula does not allow choice of customer, which is a key choice in most marketing strategies. The interplay of McCarthy's four Ps is termed a 'marketing mix' (see Figure 7.1) (Fifield, 1992). There are a number of factors under each heading which need to be considered in structuring any marketing strategy. The original 'marketing mix' was developed by Neil Borden at the Harvard Business School in the 1960s. He identified the following twelve elements which differ little from McCarthy's model:

1. Product planning
2. Pricing
3. Branding
4. Channels of distribution
5. Personal selling
6. Advertising
7. Promotions

8. Packaging
9. Display
10. Servicing
11. Physical handling
12. Fact finding and analysis

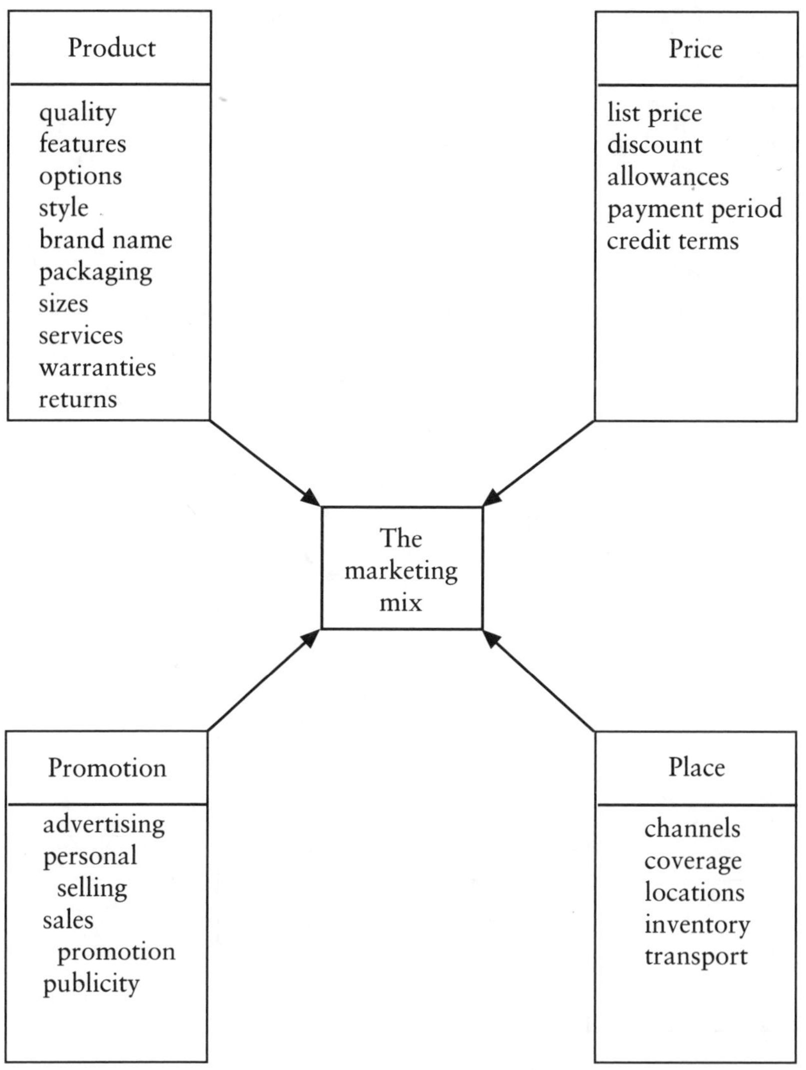

Figure 7.1 McCarthy's developed marketing mix (McCarthy, 1975).

The Bordon and McCarthy models still have considerable use but are being modified by new thinking. For instance, the four Ps model has been modified into a seven Ps model by Booms and Bitner (1981) (Figure 7.2) (Fifield, 1992). In this model 'People' recognizes the personal nature of service marketing, 'Process' reflects the personal involvement of the customer in delivering the product and 'Physical evidence' the importance of trying to make services tangible even if only by token (e.g. the flowers in a hotel room).

Martin Christopher, Adrian Payne and David Ballantyne of the Cranfield School of Management in their book *Relationship Marketing* (1991) point out that the models mentioned above are appropriate for 'transaction marketing' rather than the strategy of 'relationship marketing' which they have evolved. This gives a major clue to the nature of marketing strategies as compared with corporate strategies.

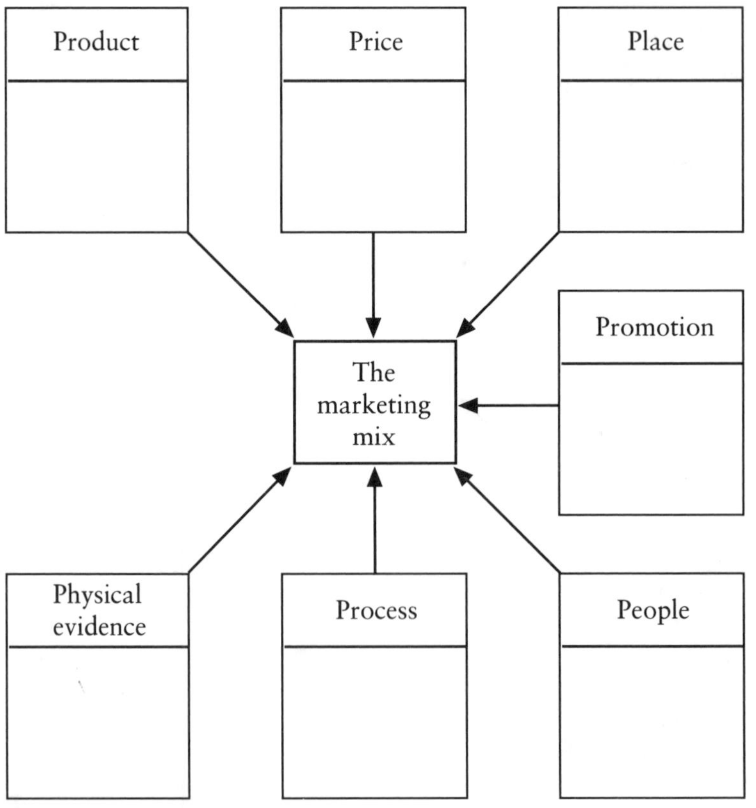

Figure 7.2 Booms and Bitner's version of the marketing mix (Booms and Bitner, 1981)

Marketing strategies relate directly to the marketplace and build a bridge between the business and its actual and potential customers. Only by crossing this bridge can the corporate strategies be effectively realized. If the corporate strategy is to open up the Asian market, the bridgehead will be won by marketing strategies which exploit targeted market segments. The synergy between corporate and marketing strategies, as shown by this example, should be very powerful. That synergy depends, however, on strict alignment of corporate and marketing strategies. We have all seen examples of the 'ivory tower' corporate strategy which is out of touch with market realities (at BP, for example, where strategies were based on the assumption of an oil price of $30 per barrel) but more insidious is the tendency of marketers to create strategies which serve no corporate strategic purpose. Fewer of these examples hit the headlines but they are often very damaging. Frequently marketing people react to apparent opportunities without rigorous assessment of the strategic needs of the business (e.g. the mortgage insurance rush of the late 1980s). Such emergent strategies will evolve as circumstances change and businesses need to react to them, but this reaction must be governed by the strategic objectives of the business, not opportunistic impulses.

It is dangerous to categorize marketing strategies too exactly since they have to be a response to customer needs which is appropriate and flexible. Customer needs will change, perhaps quite often, whereas corporate objectives should be more stable. The ends are fixed, the means are variable. It is possible, however, to identify certain types of marketing strategy which are distinctive (Table 7.1).

Table 7.1

Strategy	*Characteristics*	*Examples*
Transactional	One-off deals. Maximize return on sole transaction. (This is ironically the classical economic model!)	Distress sales
Relationship	Looking to generate repeat sales	Services
Value based	Seeking to add value (and profit) to basic product	Extended warranty for cars
Quality-driven	Customizing product/service as much as possible	Tailored suit
Emergent	Reactive, opportunistic	Fashions
Innovative	Creative, finding unrequited needs	Theatre
Word of mouth	Delighting customers so much that they have to seek actively to recommend you to others	Phoning customers on their birthday

All marketing strategies are shaped with a clear customer focus and use appropriate elements from the marketing mix. Too many marketers see the marketing mix as the building blocks of strategy rather than as the support elements for delivering strategies developed through the total corporate planning process.

In examining marketing strategy it should be recognized that strategies will vary considerably between those for developed and those for less developed markets. In approaching the latter it may often be more sensible to adopt strategies appropriate for Western markets of the 1950s–product-orientated 'push' rather than 'pull' promotions, and ready availability of supply. A valuable insight into approaching such markets is given in Joanna Kinsey's book *Marketing in Developing Countries* (1988).

Estimate expected results

Planning is a process for matching a range of optional means to a desired end. In marketing planning the various strategies available need to be assessed in terms of their potential contribution to meeting company objectives, within an acceptable pattern of risk. Where multiple strategies are used, the sum of their projected outputs is related to company objectives and the robustness of those outputs tested against different eventualities, such as a competitor reaction, fiscal changes, distributor resistance, etc. The possible impact of one strategy on another has to be tested. For example, if a cheaper line of products is introduced will it dilute the profitability of established products?

Estimating the results of strategies requires a rigorous approach to assumptions. These must be realistic, as comprehensive as possible and mutually consistent. Assumptions are made about factors which may have a material impact on the company's business. They must be carefully recorded and agreed by all concerned. Testing the strategies requires that the assumptions be changed one at a time, with the others remaining constant, so that the impact of each change can be individually assessed. Typical assumptions for planning purposes include:

1. Interest rates
2. Inflation rates
3. GDP growth
4. Exchange rates (currencies)
5. Price of key materials/parts
6. Labour costs

7. Distribution costs
8. Tax rates (including VAT)
9. Weather
10. Profit margins by product
11. Volume of products
12. Mix of products
13. Overhead recovery

etc.

Assumptions need to be made about all factors which significantly affect the effectiveness of possible strategies, as well as on the impact of other risks (e.g. bad debts, exchange losses) and the cost of hedging these and other risks.

Identify alternative plans and mixes (and iterate)

When the different possible strategies are evaluated and tested against changes in assumptions some will emerge as more robust to changed assumptions and risk potential than others. Usually there will be a pattern in which some strategies are patently incapable of achieving the goals set for them even with an increase in resources or with help from other strategies. Another set of strategies will be found to be both effective and robust to changed assumptions and risk profile. A third set will lie between the two extremes. This process is not unlike that of triage practised in hospitals, where patients are sorted into those who are likely to recover, those whose recovery is uncertain and those who have no realistic chance of recovery. In the same manner, strategies that are ineffective when tested can be discarded, those that are likely to be successful can be reinforced and those that are adequate can be tuned up to be more effective or discarded if they cannot respond to changes in resources or support from other strategies.

This process demands a good deal of creativity and time to test strategies thoroughly and to reiterate the process until the optimal mix of strategies is achieved to meet plan objectives. Usually there will be a gap between the results achieved by workable strategies and plan objectives. This will require careful 'gap analysis' to find ways to bridge the differences (see Chapter 4).

In deciding which strategies to adopt and which to discard, great rigour is required. Each strategy should be tested against a full and mutually consistent set of assumptions and changes in these assumptions should be properly documented and tested for consistency. Clear reasons need to be given for discarding strategies and they should be archived in such a way that they may be retrieved if circumstances force a change of assumptions. Equally, those strategies that are adopted should have clear reasons given for their adoption so that they may be discontinued if the reasons for their adoption become invalid.

The process of evaluating strategies is best carried out as a team exercise. This is both to avoid conscious or unconscious bias and to ensure that the benefit of a range of talents is obtained. Most importantly, participation in the decision process gives ownership of the result among those involved and is likely to achieve a more effective implementation of the chosen strategies.

Programmes

Malcolm McDonald (1989) defines a programme as

> 'a term used in marketing planning to denote the stages or tasks to be undertaken by marketing, field sales or other functions within an organization to implement the chosen strategies and to accomplish the objectives set forth in the marketing plan. Typically descriptions of programmes include a statement of objectives as well as a definition of the persons or units responsible and a schedule for completion of the steps for which the person or unit is responsible'.

Programmes are closely linked to budgets and, like budgets, are focused on the immediate year ahead. Strategic programmes and projects may, however, be focused beyond the immediate year in order to support longer-term strategies. Programmes are commitments to action; budgets provide the resources to support them.

Programmes are usually developed in a manner similar to the Key Action Plans which support strategic plans. They will usually be classified under the relevant corporate objectives (see above) and under the specific strategies to deliver those objectives which they are intended to support. In the same way that strategies need to be carefully evaluated to ensure that they will deliver the various objectives of the company, programmes have to be broken down into the individual actions needed to implement the various strategies and built up within realistic time frames to ensure that the sum of the actions committed will deliver the relevant strategies on time. Building realistic programmes is frequently the main weakness of marketing plans, leaving strategies under-supported or lacking effective timing. Equally, an over-rigid set of programmes can lead to difficulty in adapting to tactical changes and opportunities as they emerge during implementation. In John Lennon's words: 'Life is what happens to you while you're making other plans'. All good planning systems have to be flexible enough to cope with real life!

Measurement and review

Implementation is the Achilles' heel of the planning process. Great attention is lavished on developing ambitious plans and their implementation is often almost left to chance. There is an old management saying, 'if you can't measure it, it won't get done'. This is the hub of the implementation issue; there is a need for quantified objectives to drive the process and for results to be measured in identical terms. If the objectives lack precision the results will not be able to be measured meaningfully. Measurements do not only need to be precise but they must also be agreed with those responsible for achieving specific results as meaningful and sensible, especially if rewards are linked to performance, as is increasingly the case.

Given the predilection of British business for financial figures, most measurements have tended to be in monetary terms. Accounting systems are well bedded into most companies so that they provide the obvious and ready basis for measurements affecting the business. Financial measures are not, however, the only ones needed by a business; most businesses are alert to market share as a measure but few have accurate ways of measuring it. Increasingly, intangible factors, such as customer satisfaction, product quality and brand loyalty, are becoming important to businesses. Measuring such factors is a new challenge faced by marketers, and some agreed measure is essential in order to know that results have been delivered. Often the only way of measuring such factors is by proxy; for example, customer satisfaction might be deduced from measuring the ratio of repeat orders to new orders. Attempts to measure customer satisfaction by the volume of letters of complaint or praise are usually meaningless, since few customers complain or applaud in the UK market. As so often happens, it is the silent majority that it is crucial to understand, and this body rarely speaks openly.

Review of marketing strategies needs to operate on both a constant feedback basis and a regular formal basis. Staff who are responsible for delivering strategies need to be constantly alert to reactions from the markeplace which may change their effectiveness. This feedback needs constantly to be interpreted and the assumptions supporting the strategy changed.

If necessary, the strategy will need to be modified to meet the new reality which has emerged. Regular formal reviews enable management control to be exercised where operating staff have not picked up signals which call for strategies to be adapted. Marketing is a pragmatic art and needs to adjust constantly to a pattern of reality which is often very elusive but which is usually driven by the changing needs of customers.

Marketing planning remains for most companies a process which focuses on the 'marketing mix' and tactical issues, rather than on the achievement of strategic objectives. Malcolm McDonald (1989) distinguishes between strategic marketing planning and operational marketing planning, but too few companies show sufficient patience to generate, analyse and prioritize strategic options. The focus on strategic marketing has been sharpened by the publication of Jean-Jacques Lambin's book *Strategic Marketing* (1994), which develops in detail the processes of market segmentation, analysis and option generation which face strategic marketing planning. Jean-Jacques Lambin seeks

> 'to introduce up-front the strategic dimension of marketing while most introductory marketing text books tend to treat marketing management as a stand-alone business function and to overlook the hidden part of the marketing iceberg, i.e. the strategic choices on which marketing management decisions must be based. Similarly, most strategic marketing texts examine strategic decisions that are made at corporate level but devote only scant attention to how these decisions are implemented at operational level for individual brands or products.'

Lambin seeks to integrate strategic and operational marketing, avoiding the emphasis on marketing solely as an operational activity and focusing on 'the underlying business philosophy without which marketing is simply a set of short-term selling tools'. Lambin makes a significant contribution to integrating strategic and operational marketing planning but fails to focus clearly on the nexus between corporate and business unit strategic planning and strategic marketing planning. This book attempts to fill that gap.

References

Baker, Michael and Hart, Susan, *Marketing and Competitive Success*, Philip Allan, Deddington, 1989.

Booms, B. H. and Bitner, M. J., 'Marketing strategy and organization structures for service firms', in Donnelly, J. and George, W. R., *Marketing of Services*, American Marketing Association, New York, 1981.

Christopher, M., Payne, A. and Ballantyne, D., *Relationship Marketing*, Butterworth-Heinemann, Oxford, 1991.

Fifield, Paul, *Marketing Strategy*, Butterworth-Heinemann, Oxford, 1992.

Kinsey, Joanna, *Marketing in Developing Countries*, Macmillan, London, 1988.

Lambin, J.-J., *Strategic Marketing*, McGraw-Hill, New York, 1994.
McCarthy, E. J., *Basic Marketing*, Irwin, Homewood, IL, 1975.
McDonald, Malcolm, *Marketing Plans*, Heinemann, London, 1989.

CHAPTER 8

Marketing implementation, practice and controls: 1

In his book *The Mind of the Strategist* (1982), Kenichi Ohmae discusses the search for the perfect strategy. In his view 'the key to victory lies in developing a market strategy that will give you an edge–even a slight edge–on the competition and then putting it into effect at exactly the right moment'. Too often the urge to find a flawless strategy leads to the Hamlet syndrome–'and enterprises of great pith and moment ... lose the name of action'. Both Napoleon and Hitler laid plans to invade Britain and lost the favourable moment because of doubts about their strategy. In theory the more time that is spent on developing options and choosing strategies, the more likely they are to succeed. Too often, however, strategists forget that strategies have no value until translated into action, and bureaucratic delays permit competitors to steal the promised prize. The failure of most large telephone companies in the mobile telephone market is a case in point for this phenomenon.

Another interesting approach to the problem of balancing strategies and implementation is shown in an article by Amar Bhide in the *Harvard Business Review* (1994). His research into winning entrepreneurs shows that the idea that they do not plan is misleading:

> 'Appearances to the contrary, successful entrepreneurs don't take risks blindly. Rather they use a quick cheap approach that represents a middle ground between planning paralysis and no planning at all. They don't expect perfection–even the most astute entrepreneurs have their share of false starts. Compared to typical corporate practice, however, the entrepreneurial approach is more economical and timely.'

In examining such a model, however, it must be remembered that entrepreneurs answer typically almost only to themselves; most company directors need to find a style of leadership which involves other constituencies, and strategic planning is as much about ownership as analysis. Bhide's entrepreneurial model seems to have three key elements:

1. Screen opportunities quickly to weed out unpromising ventures
2. Analyse ideas parsimoniously–focus on a few important issues

3. Integrate action and analysis–don't wait for all the answers and be prepared to change course.

The dangers of such an approach, particularly in areas of high risk are obvious, but the research does underline the basic reality that many planners in a more bureaucratic environment tend to forget–strategies are of no value until they have been made to work.

In this chapter our focus is on effective implementation of strategies in the marketplace. Markets are rarely static and implementation has to be achieved in the midst of change. Strategies may need to be modified, adapted or even abandoned in order to keep moving the company towards its strategic objectives. Those who succeed in implementing strategies have usually set themselves clear strategic objectives and properly benchmarked shorter-term goals. They also have effective controls to calibrate their operations constantly against those goals. Thomas Bonoma in a 1984 article is quoted by Richard Brookes in *The New Marketing* (1988):

> 'The marketing literature is replete with research and analysis to help managers devise marketing strategies tailored to the marketplace. Yet when it comes to implementing those strategies, the literature is silent and the self-help books ring hollow.'

Brookes focuses on imaginative implementation rather than formal strategic planning. He sees pragmatism, aggression and risk taking as being characteristic of the 'new marketing'. Among the new approaches which he examines are:

1. Changing the rules
2. Looking for leverages in R&D, production and operations
3. Collaborative marketing
4. Leveraging trade marketing
5. Recognizing the end of the mass market
6. Leveraging by marketing 'value'
7. Customer servicing (the fifth 'P')

Richard Brookes is highly critical of what he sees as unimaginative implementation which he traces to a sameness in marketing education, training and practice. Too many 'me-too' strategies brought the level of marketing competence in the 1980s to low and often risible levels–'a toaster given away free to every new customer opening a bank account would be topped by a free microwave oven being offered by the bank across the street'. He quotes Lee Iaccocca (1984):

> 'If I have to sum up in one word the qualities that make a good manager, I'd say that it all comes down to decisiveness. You can use the fanciest computers in the world and you can gather all the charts and numbers, but in the end you have to bring all your information together, set up a timetable, and act . . . To a certain extent, I've always operated by gut feeling. I like to be in the trenches. I never was one of those guys who could just sit around and strategize endlessly.'

This quotation implies that strategy and action are mutually exclusive, an implication which many critics of strategic planning have exploited. Others have seen the whole process as tentative: L. E. Lindblom (1980) wrote an article entitled 'The science of muddling through'! As John Kay states in his recent book *Foundations of Corporate Success* (1993): 'Strategy is necessarily incremental and adaptive, but that does not in any way imply that its evolution cannot be, or should not be analysed, managed and controlled.' For him 'the world is full of adapting incremental processes where the adaptation is subject to partial, but imperfect, control processes, ranging from travelling in space to boiling an egg'. Implementation is just such a process.

The subject of implementation can best be illustrated by the use of case studies. Conscious of the need to cast light on issues which are likely to be shared by many companies seeking to be effective in strategic marketing, the case studies have been chosen and researched in the following areas:

1. Changing the rules–Firstdirect, Girobank and Telesure
2. Leveraging value (and values)–Merrydown Wine
3. Leveraging differentiation–BET
4. Leveraging information–branding and own-label
5. Leveraging control–Exel Logistics
6. Leveraging reach–National Starch
7. Leveraging alliances–IBM

These case studies will be examined in this and the next chapter and conclusions drawn about their overall message.

Changing the rules

Changing the rules has always been one of the most fruitful strategies even before Hannibal crossed the Alps to take the Romans by surprise. The benefits of this strategy lie not only in the key element of surprise but also in forcing others to change their strategies and to have to catch up on the lead which you have seized. A striking example of this strategy in use is provided by the development of Firstdirect, the telephone bank.

The origin of 'Firstdirect' lies in a report written by David Mills in June 1981 which led to a strategy of opening special branches of Forward Trust (part of Midland Bank) as 'Forward Trust and Savings' outlets. The idea was developed from the consumer credit movement in the USA.

The concept was to attract upmarket customers to a convenient and friendly source of personal service for both savings and loans. The target customers were A, B, C1/C2, aged between 18 and 44 years, and with bank accounts. Such customers are usually good credit risks and do not use the full services of their bank because most banks lack empathy. Strong customer empathy was guaranteed both by highly targeted training and by creating a culture of super-service in the business. Great care was taken to support the operation with highly developed systems for marketing information, business processing and control.

The strategy was to offer a limited line of transparent products (many bank products are not understood even by the staff) promoted by direct and indirect marketing, including off-page press advertising, targeted mailshots, etc. and priced differentially for risk. For the strategy to succeed it was recognized that dedicated resources were essential, that a long-term perspective was needed and that strong and lasting commitment was fundamental.

When David Mills returned to Midland Bank, in charge of the marketing function and then as a Regional Director and later as Information Technology Director, he continued to work with selected colleagues on a more radical formula. A proposal to the group board to establish a direct banking operation was approved in January 1989 and Firstdirect began operations in its Leeds 'factory' in October 1989.

Firstdirect operates entirely by telephone, using a sophisticated automatic call distribution system available for 24 hours of every day in the year. The telephones are shift-worked and highly selective recruitment and training of staff ensures that callers are in immediate personal rapport with their respondent. Firstdirect has a most sophisticated interlocking set of systems which enables all information to be captured once in all systems and adjustments made instantly. All parts of the management information system (a megadatabase) and the business system are instantly available to respondents who can deal with any situation purposefully and politely.

Cross-selling opportunities can be developed although aggressive marketing is not allowed. Customers direct the conversation, although the respondent needs to establish key facts in a systematic way and confirm customer instructions politely.

Firstdirect has shaped its services as a result of constant market research which focuses on the needs of its potential client base and the gap between expectation and reality in the financial services sector. Although Firstdirect targets A, B, C1 and C2 individuals and has a clientele heavily skewed towards the AB groupings, David Mills insists that he offers a 'Ford, not a Jaguar service'. The style of Firstdirect is deliberately classless to reflect the upward mobility of many of its customers. The long-term vision of David Mills is to create the world's best personal bank–a vision remote from Merrill Lynch's famous cash management account but grounded in meeting the needs of busy people, many of whom travel a great deal and may telephone from Australia to buy or sell shares. The latest research shows that client satisfaction for banks is 50 per cent, for building societies 69 per cent and for Firstdirect 81 per cent, and 89 per cent of its customers recommend Firstdirect to their friends.

At present, Firstdirect has some 500 000 accounts, growing at 6000 per month. As 12 per cent of clients change bank each year, there is enormous potential and growth is limited by the availability of resources rather than demand. Firstdirect has 1700 staff at present, started to increase its payroll substantially from 1992 onwards and opened a second site in 1994. Great importance is attached to psychometric testing in order to ensure that new staff are friendly, articulate and equable. Customers are always addressed by name and, if a specific service is asked for (e.g. mortgages), they are passed to a named person. Although telephone receptionists work shifts so that customers cannot ask for them by name, the training given is such that customers recognize a friendly style rather than an individual voice and feel 'at home'. Only 5 per cent of Firstdirect's staff have previously worked for a bank.

Firstdirect offers a full financial services product range but avoids hard selling. Its customer list is not available to other organizations, as David Mills believes in old-fashioned banking secrecy. Only one in four Firstdirect clients is or was a Midland Bank customer and most of them are beyond postgraduate age, since research shows that customers are only profitable to banks from about the age of 25 years. No attempt has yet been made, therefore, to 'catch them young', although this may be done at a later stage. Market segmentation by lifestyle and product medium has been started but much more remains to be done.

Firstdirect is an example of strategic marketing where a competitive advantage has been seized by changing the rules. Traditional banks are tied to expensive buildings and are only now achieving economies of scale in back-office processing. Firstdirect has put all its investment in people and systems and has deliberately created a culture that is different from that of banks and building societies. The present chief executive, Kevin Newman, emphasizes the egalitarian culture of Firstdirect by sitting among the telephone sales staff rather than in an office. Firstdirect's approach is also strategic in that it is following a long-run planned programme of development with full support from the Midland Group. Firstdirect is ahead of plan in its development and no other clearing bank has been able to catch up on its pre-emptive move. This is due partly to the other preoccupations of banks following the recession and the difficulty of finding a top-level champion to expend a sizeable amount of capital on a new formula. It is also the result of the long learning curve from conception to action (seven years in the case of Firstdirect) and the further learning curve from investment to profitability. The other banks are intensely interested in the Firstdirect formula, TSB in particular, and some have been sufficiently hurt to be forced to retaliate. Meanwhile, Firstdirect forges ahead and raises the stakes for its belated competitors.

Another approach ...

Founded in 1968, Girobank is now a major UK clearing bank. It has 1.5 million active personal account holders and a significant number of business customers. If the 3 million personal accounts of Girobank's new parent, the Alliance & Leicester Building Society, are added in, the total makes the group a major force in UK personal banking. Girobank has no conventional branches and has no face-to-face relationship with its clients. Given the present largely negative view of bank managers held by much of the public, this is no problem. The savings on infrastructure can be used to develop new and flexible services delivered to meet real public needs.

Girobank operates through four key media–the mail, the telephone, the 20 000 Post Office Counters network and the 5500 LINK cash machines. Girobank pioneered telephone banking and its 300 telephone staff handle over 100 000 calls per week. A client-orientated database enables the full pattern of relationship to be seen and facilitates cross-selling. Girobank has developed a sophisticated credit-scoring process to assess new account applications. This is now tuned to the point where it believes that it has a higher reject rate than the high street banks but a significantly lower rate of loss on loans to individuals. This is partly due, of course, to the £10 000 loan limit imposed by the Building Societies Commission. Girobank customers cover a wide spectrum, with a significant content of pensioners and married women. Nearly 20 per cent of accounts are ABs and the average balance in the Key Way interest-paying current account reflects a higher-earning clientele. Although many Girobank customers are busy professionals, the economic justification for a 24-hour telephone service was not found until early 1994. Ninety-five per cent of calls are answered within 15 seconds or less.

Girobank was not strongly promoted in its first twenty years and is now seeking to differentiate itself positively from the high street banks and to develop a more distinctive brand image. To many it is seen as 'the people's bank', identified with its former parent, the Post Office. Many of its potential clients are people who save in building societies and use banks for current transactions. The easy accessibility of the Girobank telephone service and the availability of 20 000 Post Office branches makes a switch of banking arrangements both tempting and culturally more agreeable.

For a long time Girobank has been seen as a sleeping giant due to the constraints of the public sector. Now, subject to certain limitations under the Building Societies Act, it has the potential to shape a major new force in financial services free of the infrastructure and historical burden which hamper its established rivals.

Revolutionizing motor insurance

Mention of the subject of selling motor insurance by telephone brings to the mind of most people the phenomenon of Direct Line. This high-profile company has imprinted its name on the public consciousness and has built a 9 per cent market share of UK motor insurance through heavy advertising and careful selection of low-risk clients. The dazzle of Direct Line has, however, obscured the different market approach of AA Autoquote, whose clientele is more broadly based and who acts as agent for several insurers, widening choice and spreading risk, but so far gaining a market share only about one tenth of that of Direct Line.

A quick examination of the UK motor insurance market shows that 75 per cent of the business is written by high street agents, small shops operating with little investment and relying on personal contact to maintain business. At present, direct telesales writers (Direct Line, Churchill Insurance Services and insurers' telephone operations) have 15 per cent of the market. The balance is held by agents with multiple outlets (AA Swinton, Safeguard, etc.) and a new breed of 'telebroker' of which Telesure is the precursor. The total UK motor insurance market is some £3.5 billion per year, growing at 5–8 per cent per annum. Direct sales are increasing at 35 per cent per annum and between-writers and brokers now have a 25 per cent market share. In the USA direct insurance has 60 per cent market share, in Australia 90 per cent. UK market share by the year 2000 is estimated to double to 50 per cent.

The rapid growth of telephone selling of insurance shows considerable client dissatisfaction with present arrangements. Motor insurance is seen to be unnecessarily expensive, its marketing is frequently opaque and claims processing is often slow and confrontational. Cheap motor insurance is tainted with memories of Dr Savundra, notorious for the collapse of Auto and General, and other scam-masters. The multiple agents offering a telephone service (AA, Swinton, etc.) do not offer a free choice of product as they are committed to particular groups of insurers. Nor is their telephone service professionally manned as calls are channelled to their high street shops whose staff are not trained in telephone broking. Such use of the telephone without changing the underlying realities of the business leaves an opportunity therefore to make motor insurance no longer a distress purchase but to create a bond of trust which has mainly been lacking in this market. To do so requires good products, excellent distribution and outstanding service.

Direct Line moved the motor insurance business away from the 'Dark Ages' by cutting out brokers and offering keen prices without delay to low-risk applicants. Its operation is backed by a large online database, enabling risk to be assessed and policies written quickly. One location can cover the whole country, as with Firstdirect's telephone banking. Keen pricing and quick response has made Direct Line a significant threat to the big insurers, some fourteen of whom have countered its strategy by establishing their own telephone insurance operations.

Direct Line offers no choice to its potential clients. AA Autoquote offers 'the best price', which it obtains usually from its own product range provided by a small panel of insurers. It has tried to develop electronic data interchange (EDI) but there are only five brokers with EDI capability at present. The key to an improved service to clients lies in maximizing EDI between insurers and the commercial outlet.

The establishment of Telesure in January 1992 marks the next step in the evolution of the marketing of motor insurancce. Telesure was the first 'telebroker' creating a formula geared to the client's interest rather than to that of any particular insurer. By using 'next generation' computer technology, based on intelligent personal computing networks and wide-area networks involving an extensive range of insurers and partners, Telesure offers the widest choice in the market at a speed no competition can match.

Telesure has established proprietary software which optimizes its effectiveness as a broker, giving flexibility and choice, and has so far developed a 60 per cent EDI capability with insurers, with 90 per cent targeted. This software, with growing EDI links, coupled with a growing range of products developed in conjunction with most of the major insurers, enables Telesure to offer all that Direct Line can, plus a range of choice of 172 products. EDI gives Telesure a growing competitive advantage against AA Autoquote and the provision of a 24-hour recovery service by Mondial Assistance rounds off the total product offer.

As a result of this unique formula Telesure has now won a firm client base which is growing at an accelerating rate. Great care is taken to diagnose the needs of clients, using a set of seventy questions while other brokers use only some fifteen. The extra time taken is more than compensated by lower error rates and a lower incidence of claims. Telesure has a high conversion rate on quotations and all its key operating ratios are in the top 10 per cent of the broking market.

Telesure expects to have significantly grown its client base by the end of 1994 and to grow exponentially thereafter towards being a leading player in the market by the year 2000. Business will mainly be won from the high street agents, most of whom will not be able to match the growing demand for service and price competitiveness. Telesure's own branded products have EDI priority at present which is steadily building brand awareness and loyalty, and putting Telesure into a position where its volume will begin to be significant for insurers. To cope with this growth Telesure is having to double its operational staff every year and will continue to do so up to the year 2000. Demanding standards are set in the selection of staff; a significant number of graduates are in key roles such as team leaders and their associates are expected to have good knowledge and experience of the insurance market. The quality of staff is seen to be a key competitive advantage and great care is taken both in selection and in developing shared learning (e.g. by evening debriefing sessions and team analysis of business opportunities).

The breaking down of barriers in the financial services market has swept away the semi-cartels and restrictive practices which used to characterize the insurance market. Customers are now more aware of their needs and more demanding in having them met. For years real product choice, flexible distribution and effective service have been missing in the insurance market. New, aggressive and professional, entrants are looking at the market with fresh minds and setting new standards which many of the old participants will find difficult to match. Direct Line started a revolution which has been advanced further by the new formula devised by Telesure. Seven new telebrokers have now entered the market since Telesure was established but Telesure is maintaining its lead both in range of choice and technology. Telesure and its imitators are bringing choice and real value into the motor insurance market and making a distress purchase into a cause for customer delight.

Leveraging value (and values)

Value-based marketing is becoming a key instrument of strategy. Value is defined by the customer and the strategy is aimed at increasing the perceived value of the company's products or services over time. 'Value' in this context may operate at two levels: it must, as a minimum, offer better 'value for money'. If 'value' can be elevated to the level of shared values (i.e. that the offering creates a bond between supplier and customer) the strategic impact can be much higher. The example of Merrydown Wine operates on both levels.

It is no coincidence that Richard Purdey, chairman and managing director of Merrydown Wine plc, is a Member of the Chartered Institute of

Marketing. Marketing is the key driving force of a business which is totally customer-orientated and lives the values of quality, integrity and fun.

Merrydown Wine was conceived in fun. Its founders, Ian Howie, John Kellond-Knight and Jack Ward, had known each other from kindergarten and Howie and Ward had discovered Apfelwein as students visiting Germany. The urge to produce a top-quality fruit wine started there and grew through early experiments, often in Ward's garage at his house 'Merrydown' near Rotherfield in Sussex, to the point where a partnership was established over a bottle of whitecurrant wine in 1946.

Although Jack Ward preferred to make fruit wine, after the Second World War there was a limited supply of fruit other than dessert and cooking apples. On the Kent/Sussex border apples were readily available and most of the early production was cider, with a smaller quantity of redcurrant wine. Second-hand hock bottles were used for the latter; 'vintage cider' was bottled in recycled champagne bottles, largely because nobody else could clean and re-use them. The concept of vintage cider, with dates from 1946 onwards, bottled in champagne bottles rapidly proved successful. It won fame among hard drinkers, who found a new challenge and among students and partygoers, who sought novelty. Jack Ward even had to queue at 'The Mill' in Cambridge one evening to buy a glass of his own cider!

In 1947 the company moved to Horam Manor, which offered space for expansion without uprooting the business. In 1950 a supply deal with Kent cider makers Church Farm (long defunct) enabled Merrydown to increase the availability of product. Sales had been started on the basis of direct retail supply, both to protect margins and to maximize market feedback. Ian Howie had led the marketing side of the company from the start and proved to be a shrewd innovator and able to place product in locations which gave it an increasing reputation. A constant theme of Merrydown marketing was, and remains, the understanding of customers' values and the alignment of the company's values with those of the target client base. This client base does not include the hard drinkers but is focused on clients with a healthy and discerning lifestyle.

New products now began to emerge–Pompost, an organic apple compost, cider vinegar, honey, mead, English wine and in 1969 a cooperative to allow growers of English grapes to have their produce skilfully turned into wine. In the same way that loyalty and support had earlier been built among apple growers, Merrydown now had growing relationships with the expanding new vineyards of southern England. The individual interests of the grape growers meant, however, that this altruistic scheme could not endure. In 1981 the new managing director, Richard Purdey, took the company back to its roots and towards sustainable profitability.

Ian Howie had foreseen earlier the need to reduce unit costs and had overseen a programme of installing more productive capacity and a juice-concentration plant to optimize storage. This not only enabled fruit juice to be sent to other users, thus increasing cashflow, but also allowed a second generation of new products to emerge. To escape excise duty a new lower-proof vintage cider which was slightly carbonated was test marketed in 1975. Despite great precautions in bottling, secondary fermentation occasionally caused bottles to explode. Quick action and process redesign enabled the trade to share the fun of the explosive launch, the stabilized product became well established and other products were added to complete an unique range.

Through the 1980s Merrydown continued to build its leadership position in the top niche of the cider market. To many its product is no more 'cider' than Rolls-Royce is a car. Its market positioning enables its drinkers to make a statement about themselves, not unlike that of Guinness' 'Man in Black' except that Merrydown is also a well-regarded ladies' drink. The volume cider producers, Bulmers, Gaymers (Whiteways, Coates) and Taunton expanded massively in the 1960s and had escaped the tax imposition in 1956 on higher-strength ciders and perrys which slowed the progress of Merrydown (a higher-proof drink). In 1963 the total UK market for cider was 18 million gallons. By 1972 it was 35 million gallons and by 1983 64 million gallons. The volume sold in 1992 exceeded 84 million gallons and the industry is set to produce 100 million gallons by the millennium.

The major manufacturers all now have standard, middle and premium products (e.g. Bulmer's Woodpecker and Strongbow). Merrydown has a super-standard product in its Traditional Cider and super-premium products in Vintage Gold and Vintage Dry. A premium keg draught cider rounds out the super-standard range. Acquisition of Shloer apple and grape juice drinks, PLJ lemon juice and Piermont have also positioned Merrydown in the high-margin non-alcoholic drinks market which represents a new high-growth sector for the company. Cider has also increased its share of the 'beer' market from 4 per cent to 7 per cent in the last ten years. Merrydown's innovations have led to the recognition of a fast-growing premium sector of the cider market into which Taunton Cider moved with its Diamond White brand, and was followed as recession hit their established markets by all the other cider makers, so that there are now thirty products competing in the premium sector. Skilful brand building by Merrydown and careful market positioning have ensured that the Merrydown cider brand (in particular, Merrydown Vintage) retains a super-premium rating and the resultant strength in margins was able for a while to fuel the wider growth of the business. This growth was in premium cider, own label cider and adult soft drinks and the company also has a sizeable natural foods business, Martlet Natural Foods Ltd, which grew out of its earlier speciality vinegars and honeys. The Dorothy

Carter preserves brand rounds out a prestigious range of high-quality natural food products.

In the early 1990s pressure grew on the operating margins of Merrydown due both to competitive activity and to changes in patterns of consumption. In addition to the established competitors there were new entrepreneurial entrants into the market sector which Merrydown had created and developed, often producing tertiary or economy brands. Products resembling Merrydown Vintage were sold at less than half the established price of the real Vintage product. Early in 1994 Merrydown plc felt obliged to issue a profits warning which was echoed by its main competitors.

Results for the year to the end of March 1994 showed a pre-tax loss of £2.79 million even though sales rose by 33 per cent to £25.6 million. During the year Merrydown had restructured its business to reduce its cost base by £1.5 million, incurring exceptional costs of £2.99 million. A decision was also taken to sell Martlet Natural Foods and to focus on the core drinks business.

Merrydown is once again at a strategic crossroads. After the struggles of the 1960s it expanded without sufficient vision in the 1970s and created a fast-growing niche market within the UK in the 1980s. Now the vision of the future of Merrydown has clarified; it is to become a global premium branded drinks business focused on value for money. Careful nurturing of the Merrydown brand over forty-seven years has ensured that there is a powerful platform from which to launch Merrydown into wider markets as the next century approaches. Once again the values of the company and of its clientele have been brought firmly back into alignment by recognizing that quality implies value for money. Merrydown's current gearing is around 88 per cent, and this is destined to reduce to 50 per cent by early 1995 and further over the next three years despite the setback to profits in 1993. Further expansion will be financed by a combination of cashflow, equity and medium-term debt, although there is no immediate need for a rights issue. In which direction will Merrydown now go?

Exports are currently £1.2 million and the scope for expansion is significant. Joint distribution deals and reciprocal marketing arrangements offer scope for selling strong branded products like Merrydown on a larger scale. A recent agreement with Tooheys in Sydney to launch Merrydown Premium cider in Australia is a typical example. Strong brands lend themselves to franchising but require rigorous quality control. Merrydown was built on shared values and teamwork and Richard Purdey has patiently developed a new team capable of providing the impetus and skills needed to move Merrydown from being a British company towards a global market positioning. New marketing skills are being deployed to segment the cider market by age and by lifestyle and to reassess Merrydown's new positioning in the non-alcoholic drinks market, particularly with the premium Shloer brand. Companies do not have to be big to succeed in global marketing, as Dunhill has shown. They do need to protect their image of quality rigorously, to offer complete integrity in their dealings and to add value to the lifestyle ambitions of their clients. Merrydown always seeks something extra; their latest brand evolution, Merrydown Original in unique new bottles, is enabling younger drinkers to rediscover the fun element in Merrydown. You can build a great business on quality, integrity and fun.

Leveraging differentiation

Differentiation is one of Michael Porter's generic strategies. Where there is no clear differentiation products can command no premium over those of competitors and become mere commodities, differentiated solely by the price on the day. For businesses providing routine products and services, differentiation has to be the only way in which they can attract interest and command an above-average price. Many companies differentiate their products and services by branding, others by attaching features known to be of interest to their customers. A company which has used branding, product differentiation and relationship marketing to gain leverage is BET.

BET plc is a constituent of the FTSE 100 Index and one of the UK's largest services companies. In the 1980s BET grew strongly through acquisitions and entered a wide range of services businesses, most of which had little or no interrelationship. BET plc operated as a financial holding company, in a manner not dissimilar to BTR or Hanson. Each subsidiary was managed independently within a financial framework and was a portfolio investment in the eyes of corporate management.

Following a change of executive management in 1991, BET plc has begun to pursue a different strategy. First, it has recognized that a sprawling portfolio of services businesses lacks focus and has begun to develop a sharper definition of its mission. As a result, non-core businesses such as BIFFA, the waste business, have been divested, mostly at a significant profit. Second, BET has recognized that many of its businesses are commodities unless it can find the means to differentiate them from those of competitors. Contract cleaning is an obvious example. Third, BET has faced up to the reality that there are few economies of scale in services and that size may often produce disadvantages in reactivity and cost structure compared with small local competitors.

As a result of this analysis BET is now seeking to identify the businesses in its portfolio which it can expect to steer into a sustainable competitive advantage. To do this will usually require a constant pressure to lower their cost base, while enhancing quality and differentiating them strongly from their competitors.

This cannot be done without a clear understanding of value in the eyes of current and potential customers and a sustained drive to shape each business accordingly. Careful analysis is also needed to understand each business as a platform for higher added-value services (e.g. the cleaning business gives entry to the service of maintaining flowers and plants).

The key to successful differentiation lies, in the view of John Allan the former group marketing director (now Chief Executive of Ocean plc), in asking customers the right questions. For example, Shorrock now recognizes that false alarms are highly irritating to customers. Reducing Shorrock's false alarm rates to consistently below those of competitors has given it a clear competitive edge. By a rapid follow-up with new installations to head off potential faults, Shorrock is seen to be serious about low false alarm rates which wins confidence. Such visits also accelerate payment for the new installation.

BET is doing considerable work on the issue of customer satisfaction, which is difficult to measure in most businesses. John Allan's approach is to identify the key drivers of customers. This process involves 'sitting in the customer's chair' not only at operating levels but, with larger customers, also at a number of levels right up to top management. In this way it is possible, for instance, for Initial to provide a towel service at factory level and for that relationship to place BET at top level in a position to propose a total facilities management service. Auditing the costs of non-core services for customers is a powerful marketing tool, as these services are often lacking the professional focus needed to make them cost effective. BET is developing its own approach to value chain analysis which will make cost audit an increasingly valuable tool.

John Allan sees BET Group adding value for subsidiaries in various ways. These include a close relationship with major customers, a clearing house for market intelligence across the group, the development of new tools for subsidiaries and the improvement of marketing processes throughout BET. The process of sharpening focus should lead to increased responsiveness and generate innovation. John Allan sees the prospect of creating a virtuous circle through such processes. For example, clear focus on adding value helps to avoid quoting for commodity work. When customers know you can add value there is often the opportunity to influence the specification of a given project. It is also advantageous to identify key skills needed to add value; BET has invested in quantity surveyors to sharpen its bids and to enhance its management of claims.

BET's strategic planning has been financially driven in the past. John Allan now hopes to see a strategic planning process which will be driven by corporate issues and priorities, and objectives which are not solely financial. Such a process would need to allow more time to develop and explore options, particularly for corporate self-renewal, since services markets mature at a frightening rate. Greater attention will be given to identifying core competences and the systems needs of a fast-changing business. Branding will be a key issue to be addressed although much of the marketing thrust will need to be in the business-to-business area. The key marketing issue facing BET in the next few years is to establish a sustainable competitive advantage in businesses with low entry costs and small economies of scale. The key differentiation in services businesses is the human factor. Learning will be one of the key drivers for the future and the issues of personal responsibility and involvement right through the business will be paramount.

References

Bhide, Amar, 'How entrepreneurs craft strategies that work', *Harvard Business Review*, March/April 1994.

Brookes, Richard, *The New Marketing*, Gower, Aldershot, 1988.

Iaccocca, Lee, *An Autobiography*, Bantam, New York, 1984.

Kay, John, *Foundations of Corporate Success*, Oxford University Press, Oxford, 1993.

Lindblom, L. E., 'The science of muddling through', *Public Administration Review*, 1980.

Ohmae, Kenichi, *The Mind of the Strategist*, McGraw-Hill, New York, 1982.

Marketing implementation, practice and controls: 2

CHAPTER 9

In Chapter 8 we looked at the practical issues of implementing marketing strategies and some case studies focused on creative strategies. This chapter continues the process of identifying creative strategies and exploring specific examples.

Leveraging information

Information is one of the key elements of competitive advantage. At one time the main emphasis of information was to transmit it through media advertising; more recently there has been a growing emphasis on seeking information from prospective customers in order to serve them better. In the retailing sector, information used to be collected by firms such as Nielsen and sold on a syndicated basis to manufacturers and retailers. With the growing concentration of power among retailers, and the huge investment in automated checkouts and IT systems needed to control their business, the balance of advantage in terms of online information about sales patterns moved sharply towards the bigger retailers. This information has enabled them both to drive down buying prices and to develop own-label brands as a counterweight to manufacturers' branding and pricing strengths and as a means of widening their own margins.

In the eighteenth century few people were rich enough to make discretionary purchases and those that did knew clearly what they wanted, or had advisers who guided their decisions. Little of the finest English furniture of the time has even the discreetest label since the identity of the cabinet-maker was of no consequence. The marking, or branding, of products is only necessary when the prospective purchasers lack knowledge or confidence. This situation developed on a significant scale only in the late nineteenth century.

Branding developed to assist product recognition and to give assurance of quality. Initially, branding and company names were usually synonymous, but over time, mergers and acquisitions created a dichotomy between holding company names and those of their subsidiaries or of the products of subsidiaries. This forced a choice between promoting an 'umbrella' name or of promoting product names. Groups like Boots have promoted the 'Boots' brand; Unilever has promoted Persil, Lipton, Timotei and other product brands. Branding has enabled skilful marketers to differentiate their products from those of competitors and in most cases to command a premium over them. In the case of Marlboro cigarettes a premium of 70 per cent over undifferentiated products was achieved prior to the recent price war. Such premiums are of great value but require large and sustained investment to win and protect. It is for this reason that substantial 'goodwill' is paid for acquiring established brands and that companies seek to capitalize at least some of the value of their acquired brands.

Because of the consumer preference which branding can achieve in varying degrees, manufacturers of branded products became increasingly powerful in the marketplace up to the mid-1980s. They were able to impose their will on distributors and retail outlets and their brand promotion exercised 'pull' by consumers in favour of their products. In most cases such 'pull' was more powerful than the 'push' which retailers sought to exercise in favour of lesser brands or cheaper products by promotions or discounting.

Around the mid-1980s the growth and concentration of retailing, in particular of food, began to act as a countervailing force to the power of branded manufacturers. Initially, this power was used to reduce buying prices of branded products, but this strategy rapidly met resistance. Retailers had been spending heavily on their own corporate image which began to attract consumer loyalty in its own right. It was only one short step to develop and promote selected products under the retailer's brand.

Own-label manufacturing has been established for many years. Migros in Switzerland has long been 100 per cent own-label and Cooperative Retail Services in the UK has always made and sold under its own brand.

Own-label goods are quite distinct from unbranded or generic products. In earlier times shops stocked goods in sacks, hoppers or trays and most of them were unmarked. Tea and butter could be seen and identified; their quality was implicitly guaranteed by the vendor. It is a short step from such an approach to merchandising to packeting the tea and labelling it 'tea'. This basic approach to marketing products persists in certain 'cut-price' retail outlets and must be the cheapest way to merchandise most products. It is interesting and revealing that many of the customers for generic products are in the AB social categories—a return to the self-assurance of the eighteenth-century cognoscenti.

In recent years the balance of power in many markets has moved from the manufacturer towards the retailer. This resulted in a steady growth of retailer brands and increased competition for manufacturers' brands to find retail shelf space. Marks & Spencer is entirely own-label; John Lewis has strongly developed the 'Jonelle' brand in recent years. In groceries Sainsbury, Tesco and others have built up an increasingly comprehensive range of own-label merchandise and are winning brand acceptance and, according to the Census Association, brand preference. Euromonitor estimates that by 1992 own-label had 10 per cent of all retail sales in Western Europe (27 per cent in the UK). This strategic shift of power is now threatened by the rise of discounters and by a growing counterattack from manufacturers.

The move to discounting has been accelerated by two major factors: the strategic shift upmarket of the major retailing groups in order to widen margins, and the recession which hit the USA and the UK in the late 1980s and moved later into Europe. With the move upmarket, retailers have positioned their own-label brands closer to the market stance of manufacturers' brands, opening up a lower market segment into which discounters have moved strongly. As a result, experts such as Philippe Kaas, of O. C. and C. Strategy Consultants, see retailers developing two (at least) propositions: one driven by value and the other driven by cost. The shape of this strategy is beginning to emerge with an increase in marketing effort by key retailers such as Sainsbury to ensure that their house-label really adds value for the customer. At the same time, a growing number of retailers are launching non-house brands (e.g. Sainsbury's 'Novon') which have enabled them to capture increased market share. Others are positioned as a 'fighting brand' ('premier prix') to counter the growing market share of discounters like Aldi, which itself is over 90 per cent own-label. Growth in many retail markets has been achieved by heavy investment in prime sites and information technology. There is now an excess of retail capacity in most markets and margins are under heavy pressure. Own-label will no longer be a means of switching premium-priced sales from branded goods but will have to demonstrate clear added value to its customers.

Discounters have long been an established segment of the retail market. Their market share moves to reflect market changes (e.g. Comet grew out of the end of resale price maintenance). Historically they were seen as 'downmarket'–a factor which has fuelled Tesco's drive to catch up with Sainsbury in perception as well as profitability. In recent times discounters have been less encumbered by class distinctions but seen as what they mostly are–highly professional, price-driven retailers selling both to those who are trying to stretch a limited budget and to a growing number of self-assured professional people who see no point in subsidizing media advertising. The European discounters are estimated to have between 25 per cent and 30 per cent of the grocery market and many discounters (e.g. Kwik Save) are more profitable than the industry average. Supplying the larger discounters has so far produced reasonable returns for most manufacturers but the pressures of retail competition will make that situation increasingly untenable for many of them. At present, discounters are more firmly established on the Continent than in the UK, but the recent recession has begun to move market share towards them. A large percentage of Continental discounters sell over 90 per cent of their products as controlled labels, i.e. own labels. More recently the American 'warehouse clubs', such as Costco, have begun to cross the Atlantic. Whether their rudimentary sites and limited product range will appeal in Europe remains to be seen.

What will be the future pattern of manufacturers' branding and own-label? Certain trends seem clear; the future of manufacturers who do not have No. 1 or No. 2 market shares will increasingly be problematical. The growth of retail sales seen in the 1980s is unlikely to be sustained in the 1990s. Even to hold retailing's share of disposable income it will be essential both to innovate continuously and rapidly and to value analyse existing products ruthlessly. The vogue for business re-engineering which has hit manufacturing in competitive areas such as engineering will move rapidly into other areas of production and services. Only by radical change will many of today's major firms be able to survive, as Ford learned in the early 1980s.

The threat to established brands was dramatized by the recent 40 cents price cut for Marlboro cigarettes in the USA. Major brand leaders like Unilever lost 20 per cent of their market value as a result, even though much of that has since been restored. Branding can no longer be a media-driven threat to the uninformed public that it was in the past. The promise of value, or the implication that alternatives are not to be trusted, will no longer 'wash' for Persil or for any other brand, although the negative effect of issues such as quality is more damaging for branded products, as the controversy over Persil Power has shown. On the other hand, people are finding that Novon offers a wide range of high-quality cleaning products, professional products brought to the general market–an example of the kind of innovation needed to survive and prosper in the competitive 1990s.

Other new formulae are emerging, many in the USA. Loblaw's has launched 'President's Choice', a formula backed personally by David Nichol with the offer of personal contact with him to comment on the product ('write to me personally'). Sam Walton has launched 'Sam's Choice' as WalMart's flagship brand. Many US retailers are developing ranges of 'green' products to appeal to the environmentally conscious customer.

Own-label can be expected to increase its market share progressively in developed markets where customers are becoming more discerning and concerned to buy with individuality from a growing range of competing products. In most markets producers continue to exert economic power over consumers in conditions of imperfect competition. Such markets may be expected to change, and such change will be fuelled by the successful conclusion to the GATT Uraguay Round. In the competitive world of the

1990s the outmoded distinction between branded and own-label products will disappear as producers and distributors seek to appeal to consumers as individuals. This will require far more sensitive and sophisticated marketing techniques than most companies have deployed to date. The old social groups segmentation has become virtually useless; lifestyle segmentation is increasingly being used but this will need to be refined towards a more individual study of customers. A newer segmentation model (Laing Henry) is shown in Chapter 11. The investment made to capture and analyse the pattern of sales through information technology in recent years will need to be matched by even more sensitive analysis of customer motivation in order to achieve a degree of focus which even direct marketing has so far failed to deliver.

Leveraging control

In the previous case study we saw how online information can, in the hands of retailers who have direct end-user interfaces and who integrate supplies for different manufacturers, be a source of competitive advantage. When all major retailers are equally well equipped this advantage is, of course, eroded.

Information is also a key means of exerting control, particularly in complex situations which require instant response. Logistics has always been a key differentiator–Napoleon went to great lengths to ensure his supply lines ('an army marches on its stomach')–and competitive markets in recent years have increasingly made logistics crucial for success. Michael Porter's analysis of the supply chain has made companies focus on the total supply process and has led to an integration of storage, transport, wholesaling and other disparate elements of the supply chain into total logistics systems. Modern logistics systems, such as that of Exel Logistics, leverage control powerfully in support of their wide range of clients.

Bordon's basic marketing mix comprises the 'four Ps'–product, price, place and promotion. Each requires careful consideration but for too many companies the weak link is 'place'.

Logistics is the term now used to cover the concept of 'place'. The science of logistics, like strategy, was first developed by the military and given growing importance as the skills of warfare increasingly called for rapid movement, sudden concentration, surprise and follow-through. The German offensive in the Ardennes in 1944 failed for lack of fuel resources; today the best-prepared marketing strategies can fail due to faulty logistics. The need to have the right product in the right place at the right time seems simple, but its achievement depends either on an excessive commitment of resources to cover all possible contingencies (often by having excess stocks in the supply chain) or by skilful analysis of the probable pattern of needs and achieving pinpoint accuracy with 'just-in-time' supply.

The growing importance of logistics as a source of competitive advantage has led to growing specialization in this area. One of the key players in the logistics market is Exel Logistics, part of NFC plc, formerly the National Freight Corporation, which has grown to UK market leadership in logistics in the last four years. Exel Logistics employs nearly 16 500 staff in the UK, Europe and North America and operates 3700 vehicles, 1.6 million square metres of warehousing and nearly 1 million cubic metres of cold storage capacity. Sales in 1992/3 exceeded £700 million and pre-tax profit approached £65 million. Logistics is not only fast growing but also appears to be very profitable.

The focus of Exel Logistics' strategy is on the whole supply chain comprising:

1. All information flows between the different but interdependent parties in the chain
2. All physical movements and storage of new materials, supplies, parts and finished goods
3. Flows into and out of manufacturing locations
4. Storage of finished goods
5. Delivery to customers, including home delivery where needed

The mission of the business is to add value for its customers, by effective and reliable management of the supply chain in terms of both cost and timing. Logistics skills depend on responsiveness and control; to win competitive advantage as a logistics provider these have to be sharpened in order to create sustained confidence in the working of one supply chain and preference for using it rather than that of other contractors. Given the increasing cost of changing distribution arrangements, logistics systems are of growing strategic importance and key (if invisible) differentiators in the marketplace.

Logistics is now a very substantial business. The ILDM Survey for 1991/2 put average distribution costs at 4.7 per cent of industry sector sales, with smaller companies suffering a competitive disadvantage. The cost trend is downwards, forcing users to find more efficient solutions. Strategically, however, such solutions are untenable and all businesses are being forced to make choices between core operations which they will retain and peripheral ones which they will increasingly contract out to specialists. The growing size of investment needed to establish and run effective logistics systems makes the contracting out of this function increasingly likely for a majority of businesses. Growing emphasis on real-time IT systems, automation and optimum warehouse location will begin to make life untenable for smaller logistics operations in the next few years. The operating assets of Exel Logistics at the end of 1993 were some £224 million and the need for a rapid growth in investment is partly driving the call for £263 million of new equity capital by NFC in 1994.

The nature of logistics is changing rapidly. Earlier transport and storage were seen as separate functions and not as part of a total system. Competitive pressures have led to a sustained search for cost savings throughout the supply chain, forcing some companies to take over and integrate logistics for themselves but persuading an increasing number to seek a total service from an external supplier under a long-term performance-based contract.

In parallel with the contracting out of logistics has come the contracting out of information services to firms such as International Network Services. Some transport contractors use such services to assist them to compete with total logistics contractors like Exel Logistics, whose sophistication in the use of databases, EDI and real-time computing provides a very real competitive advantage. Logistics is now so embedded in the operational core of most businesses that contractors' staff are seen as colleagues, not as outsiders, and are expected to have loyalty to their client company no less than to their employer. This new pattern is wholly consistent with Charles Handy's vision of the future pattern of work in which lifetime company employees will be the exception, not the rule.

In order to succeed in winning and holding UK market leadership and to drive its business into overseas markets, Exel Logistics needed to follow the classical marketing formula of segmentation. Some new businesses (e.g. the book distributors DMS) were acquired with a strongly focused market position and gave a basis on which to build; others such as EL Grocery and EL Industrial had to be built in 1989 out of previously unfocused elements within the old NFC or, as EL Chillflow, evolve out of an existing business (frozen food distribution). Segmentation also shaped the Newsflow, Fashionflow (Marks & Spencer), Storeflow (Storehouse) and Media Services businesses.

By 1990 Exel Logistics had established the basic segmentation of its business activities and had significant UK market shares in most segments. It had to make the strategic choice either to enter new market segments in the UK (e.g. pharmaceuticals) or develop new services in existing markets (e.g. food) or to return to its initial vision of being an international group. The emphasis of business development shifted towards overseas markets.

In 1986 NFC had bought Dauphin Distribution Services, a large US warehousing and distribution business serving the food and grocery trades. By 1990 25 per cent of NFC's profits came from the USA and a target of 40–50 per cent of profits from overseas was set for 1995. An objective was set to become the US market leader in warehousing and logistics via services to global clients. At the same time, Exel Logistics sought to exploit the 1993 opening of Europe as a single market by initially targeting the food distribution business, which was a strong element of its success in achieving market leadership in the UK.

Exel Logistics sought to accelerate the realization of its strategic ambitions in the USA by a series of focused acquisitions which gave coverage in its five key regions (North-East, Mid-West, South-East, Texas and West Coast). This strategy also enabled three operational units to be formed in 1991 specializing in grocery services, dedicated distribution for multinationals and dedicated delivery systems for a variety of clients including vehicle manufacturers and banks, with a presence in over thirty states.

For Europe an acquisition strategy was also chosen, focused on grocery distribution, initially in Spain, Germany, France and Holland. Unlike the integrated approach in the USA, the European strategy recognized the cultural differences to be accommodated in each country and sought to create local identities with national staff beneath the Exel Logistics umbrella.

Considerable impetus to the growth of Exel Logistics has been given by the rising trend towards outsourcing in major markets. Initially, this developed strongly in the UK grocery retail market and has now reached a 70 per cent level of contracting out. This phenomenon also affects manufacturers (e.g. Unilever). Exel Logistics has been able to benefit from the development of this trend in Europe, using the skills developed for the demanding market in the UK. In the USA the established pattern is different, involving either public or dedicated warehousing with shared load trucking contracted separately. Exel Logistics has adapted to this pattern–for example, subcontracting secondary transport and forming a strategic alliance with an inbound free truck load carrier, Schneider.

Growing competition in key markets will force companies to seek lower costs and greater effectiveness in their operations. The supply chain is a crucial part of those operations and will require greater professionalism in order to sustain the competitiveness of suppliers and end users. The critical success factors in logistics are reliability, reactiveness and cost. Reassurance of clients is of crucial importance; this is achieved largely by performance but sustained by detailed communication. Exel Logistics has invested heavily, for example, in database information systems technology and works as closely as possible with client staff to build and maintain confidence. It is a measure of the dedication of Exel Logistics' staff that they often feel that they work for Tesco rather than their employer. That commitment to the customers' needs is the cutting edge of modern logistics.

Leveraging reach

The previous two cases showed the power of information and control in national markets. Increasingly, companies need to operate globally if they are to achieve economies of scale or fully exploit valuable niches. Pharmaceuticals companies need global markets to recover their fearsome expenditure on research and development; operations like Hard Rock Café need to franchise globally to retain the support of their widely travelling clientele. Operating globally is dependent on information and control but also requires length of reach, that is, the ability to integrate worldwide without managing in detail from the centre. There are many different models for doing this; some companies, such as Reckitt & Colman, line manage globally by geography, others, like Proctor & Gamble, focus control through product groups. The example of National Starch & Chemical, a globally managed subsidiary of Unilever, shows how reach can be leveraged effectively.

Of all major marketing strategies, that of creating Marshall McLuhan's 'global village' is one of the hardest to achieve. 'Global village' implies a span of competence, from effective global competitiveness down to total integration at local level. Such a stretch demands effective linkage at all intermediate points as well.

A few companies can approach this ideal through powerful branding. Coca-Cola is one of the world's most powerful brands and trades in nearly 200 countries, holding up to some 45 per cent market share in carbonated drinks. Powerful brands, though, demand enormous investment to sustain themselves and the steady advance of own-label retailers, especially in recession, shows that building brands is not a one-way investment.

Few businesses could be more remote from Coca-Cola than National Starch & Chemical. In 1995 it will celebrate its centenary, having started as National Gum & Mica Company. Still a world force in the adhesives business, National Starch is now also a world leader in speciality chemicals, resins, electronic materials, speciality industrial starches and speciality food starches. National Starch has its roots in New York and New Jersey and for many years saw itself as an American company. Even though National Starch had been active in the UK and Canada for more than fifty years, international expansion took off only in the late 1960s and early 1970s with a focus primarily on continental Europe, Japan and Mexico. The move into less well-known markets was made largely by joint ventures, many of whom were subsequently bought out. Expansion was driven by a wealth of new products and new processes developed by National Starch at its research centre. Emphasis was on added value and commodity products like particle board and adhesive tapes were discarded. Research also became increasingly customer-led, for example, with researchers working with senior development executives in multinational companies in order to understand their problems. National Starch also has a long-standing commitment to the environment and has continued to develop environmentally friendly products, processes and packaging systems since well before 'green' issues became so important to business.

National Starch has developed its business on relationships rather than branding. Largely unknown to 'the man in the street', National Starch has a growing number of loyal customers in world markets. It is seen as a highly competent specialist, with a strong innovative culture and a willingness to work closely with its customers. More than that, National Starch, having built its international business from local roots, is seen by its customers largely to be 'part of the network' rather than an interloper. This local focus is not yet complete in all the markets where National Starch presently trades; R&D remains largely driven still by US needs, for example. However, National Starch's more than 125 facilities in thirty-five countries spanning five continents presents a sound foundation on which to build a global business.

The dictum 'think globally, act locally' ignores one of the basic truths of global business in the twentieth century. We have now moved from the trading-company model on which many international businesses were built to an integrated customer-driven industrial model for the twenty-first century. Even today no global company can be built and sustained without a strong regional pivot on which global ambitions and local needs can interact. Most companies which may make any claim to be 'global' have built their businesses from a national base in a 'home' country, have expanded into overseas markets (initially to trade and sometimes to manufacture as well) and have become multinational by trading goods from their different factories in various countries into other national markets in which they have a presence. Such a system becomes anarchic unless it is tightly controlled; almost inevitably, control is exercised from 'headquarters' in the 'home' country and can only be effective by being intrusive. By being intrusive it undermines the authority and effectiveness of local management.

The importance of the strong regional pivot begins to become apparent as businesses struggle to be both global and local. Headquarters begins to recognize the need to give greater autonomy to operating businesses but does not wish to lose control of its total activity pattern. Individual businesses want more autonomy but need the benefits of group membership to leverage their competitiveness. The regional pivot enables both to optimize their position, but enormous care must be taken to ensure that its costs are more than offset by clearly demonstrable benefits.

The first clear benefit of the regional pivot is that it matches the structure which global customers are building. Multilevel marketing requires companies to have person-to-person interfaces with customers at all levels, from managing director down to stores clerk. On the same principle, global companies will need to match global customers at all levels from global through regional to local (and down to the stores clerk!). This hierarchy of interfaces ensures that any customer issue at any level can be dealt with promptly and appropriately.

The second benefit of a regional pivot is that it relates to the growing reality of what Kenichi Ohmae (1990) calls the 'interlinked economy', the triad of the Americas, Europe and Asia. The forces which are shaping this triad are complex but they are real. Even after the success of the GATT Uraguay Round there will be political and cultural pressures to shape these major regional groupings and businesses with global ambitions will need to adapt to them.

The third benefit of a regional pivot is that key 'corporate' functions can be moved closer to individual customers without undue loss of scale or control. An obvious example is R&D, which is often concentrated in the 'home' market for historical or control reasons. Emergent markets need close contact with R&D and this can often be more effective by being decentralized to regional or even lower level. The regional pivot can also be effective in concentrating functions which cannot be run optimally at local level (e.g. information technology and human resources management).

The term 'regional pivot' has been used rather than 'regional headquarters'. In his book *The Borderless World* (1990) Kenichi Ohmae talks of 'decomposing the centre'. He points out that Nissan, Yamaha, Sony, Honda, Omron and Matsushita, among others, have decentralized responsibility for strategy and operations to each of the triad markets, keeping only corporate service and resource allocation at the centre:

> Decomposing the corporate center into several regional headquarters is becoming an essential part of every successful company's transition to global competitor status ... the strength of a global corporation derives in no small measure from its ability, as a fully fledged insider, to understand local customers' needs. At the same time, it can deploy human financial and technological resources on a global scale.'

Ohmae talks of 'regional headquarters'–National Starch prides itself on having moved beyond Ohmae's prescription to the point where it has virtually decomposed its regional headquarters in Europe.

National Starch recognizes that Europe is not and is unlikely ever to be a totally homogeneous market. Cultural differences and local preferences will continue to shape each individual market, as will pricing differences, distribution patterns and the nature of competition. However, National Starch sees a gradual convergence, which is being driven by customers, as the interdependence of European markets breaks in upon national patterns and as customers take a more European or even global view of their needs. National Starch's regional/local structure is important here, ensuring that the company is able to serve each market in a manner ideally suited to its needs. Consequently, National Starch has encouraged the development of pan-European divisions, managing international markets as pan-European issues on a regional basis. On the other hand, local markets are managed by the local organization. As a result, National Starch continues to support the individual culture of each of its European businesses, giving them some autonomy and encouraging them to take a high profile in their communities. Each business is expected to deal with local issues independently within the framework of its division's regional strategy. Staff interfacing with customers are nationals in order to maximize cultural acceptance. At the same time, key managers are encouraged to widen their European experience by working in different countries. Since major customers are doing the same, the interface at top level remains intimate as the growing number of Euro-executives find common ground beyond their native roots.

Ultimately, this regional pivot system provides an additional level of focus and communication that allows the local organizations to influence and share the regional strategy and, at the same time, allows the region to influence and share the global strategy. As such, it has proved successful for National Starch in allowing it to meet the various needs of its global customers at local, regional and global level.

National Starch has a small headquarters for Europe based in High Wycombe, not far from London Airport. Although ten permanent regional staff are located at High Wycombe, a total of more than forty-five officially work out of High Wycombe, including a Management Information System group and a Safety and Environmental Affairs Group which may be devolved later. The role of the group of ten based at High Wycombe is to act as parent to thirty-eight facilities in Europe, employing some 1900 people. Parenting involves directing cashflow, treasury management, and human resource planning, and acting as the interface, where appropriate, between its divisions and the corporate centre in New Jersey. Communication is the key to adding value from High Wycombe; increasingly that communication involves the integration of global, regional and local marketing strategies.

The present group vice-president, European Operations, Douglas Corbishley, took on the task of building a European business in 1986. He saw clearly that the regional pivot was essential both in order to maximize the effectiveness of National Starch's businesses in Europe and to create the leverage, together with other regional pivots, to allow the group to be a competitive world player. A regional pivot is also being established in the Asia-Pacific region, under the leadership of Leonard Berlik. America is run largely as a US-focused operation and a separate unit to manage the American businesses independently from the group headquarters in New Jersey will be essential in order to move these businesses nearer to local and regional customers. When the focus of group headquarters is on global customers rather than US operations, National Starch will begin to obtain the full benefit of its globalization strategy. Then, perhaps, it will be their turn to achieve what Akio Morita of Sony called 'global localization' and Kenichi Ohmae's vision of 'decomposing the centre' will become a reality.

Leveraging alliances

Following the example of National Starch, it is interesting to examine the radical re-engineering which has transformed IBM into a 'new-look' global company. Like many companies which grew on the back of technological success, IBM has been forced to redefine its mission to meet more competitive times and to dispose of those parts of its business which are not 'core' elements for fulfilling that mission. The 'new-look' global company also recognizes that the cost of new technology, and the concomitant risks, make it necessary to share certain research and development costs, often with competitors. Creating alliances can be very powerful, and produce some interesting surprises, as the following case study shows.

There was once a saying 'whatever is good for General Motors is good for America'. Producer power was seen to be the arbiter of international competitiveness; that producer power was based on totally integrated manufacture, total control of all processes and, until antitrust legislation had full effect, control of markets. IBM was created in such an environment and built its dominance of the computer industry by allowing its earlier competitors to overreach themselves through innovation while methodically laying siege to key accounts to sell solid and reliable computer systems. All key parts of such systems were designed and built by IBM and users were effectively colonized by IBM since there was no other source of training and support services to develop and maintain the systems carried on IBM equipment. All units, spare parts and consumable materials could only be obtained from IBM and most were manufactured by IBM.

In later years IBM expanded its world market share to over 70 per cent and became less responsive to market changes. The emergence of the minicomputer, spearheaded by Digital Equipment, took IBM by surprise and the increasing use of microcomputers for business was also unforeseen. In the latter case IBM reacted with unaccustomed vigour and established a project team outside the framework of the group which was able rapidly to bring to market the personal computer and rapidly establish it as the industry standard. Most of the parts and software for the PC were procured outside IBM, most notably the MS–DOS operating system from Microsoft.

At this time IBM was beginning to come to terms with the customer-led demand for 'open systems', which would enable users to develop systems using equipment from various manufacturers. This meant adopting industry standards and opening the door to relevant technology for companies that are actual or potential competitors. The producer was no longer in control of markets; users were demanding more and more from their IT systems and favouring the suppliers who cooperated with them. The market was no longer led by the manufacture of hardware but by the ability of software to facilitate increasingly ambitious applications of IT. Systems integration became the key to market success, not sophisticated machinery.

Coincidentally with these changes the rapid growth rate of some 15 per cent per annum experienced in the 1970s and 1980s declined to yearly rates of less than 5 per cent. The market for mainframe computers which had been the foundation-stone of IBM's dominance declined rapidly in favour of dispersed systems. Customer pressure had been pushing PC performance to levels equivalent to that of a 1970s mainframe computer and prices which had been declining relative to performance for several years fell in real terms. Most other computer firms recognized the danger signals earlier than IBM, largely because they were hit by market changes earlier. Cost and staffing cuts were savage in most of them; IBM had a tradition of lifetime employment and even in the late 1980s was producing some 70 per cent of input costs internally. Like Ford in the early 1980s, IBM hit the buffers in the late 1980s.

Much has been written about the two attempts by IBM's chairman, John Akers, to introduce change-management programmes at IBM. These have been characterized as 'too little, too late' and Akers has been replaced by Lou Gerstner, formerly of American Express and R. J. R. Nabisco. From a peak of 400 000 employees in 1986, IBM's workforce has already declined to 250 000 and Gerstner has targeted cuts of another 115 000 by the end of 1994. Change management has now moved to 'rightsizing', driven not by vision but by the need to survive in areas of the computer market where shareholder value can be rebuilt.

Behind the walls of red ink washing over IBM, significant progress has been made in many areas and black ink is appearing again. One of the most interesting of these areas is strategic procurement. This is led by nine strategists, five in the USA and four in Europe, few of whom are purchasing specialists. The regional procurement manager for Northern Europe, John Gillett, was based in Havant and had a purchase budget of some £4 billion per year. He has subsequently moved to Paris to head the European procurement function. In the three years since the new procurement division was set up, the ratio of made-in costs to bought-out costs has inverted from 70:30 to 30:70 and continues to fall. This has been achieved by rigorous examination of all activities and seeking outside supply of all goods and services which are not 'strategic'. Even R&D is no longer wholly carried out in-house.

The definition of 'strategic' is largely led by John Gillett's activities. To set an example, he has placed most of his routine purchasing in the hands of outside professionals. The main focus of his work is to query all activities on a zero-based budgeting basis but with a keen eye for customer need. By the end of 1992 the UK operation had reduced its cost base by £700 million (£200 million from resources, £150 million from 'belt tightening', £150 million from product costs, £100 million from purchasing strategies, and so on). IBM Europe started to attack costs seriously a year after the UK and the US operation started at much the same time.

One of the most significant parts of the new procurement activity is managing strategic relationships. Some of these are with former IBM units which have been bought out as a result of the process of cutting the business back to its essential core. The basis of this strategy is to create a limited number of 'self-supporting' suppliers, having the following criteria:

1. Fully evaluated and approved to standards creating a competitive advantage
2. Has the management structure/attitude to meet IBM's demands
3. Is a key part of IBM's long-term sourcing strategy
4. Has new product demand sourced today and planned for tomorrow
5. Is suitable for generic sourcing
6. Has the capacity to achieve all IBM's targets:
   - 100 per cent defect-free deliveries
   - 100 per cent on-time deliveries
   - 100 per cent ability to work with continuous flow manufacture (just-in-time deliveries)
   - Zero administration referrals
   - Intervention-free receipts
7. Has flexibility
8. Has the capacity to plan for continuity of production protection.

The relationship which IBM seeks to build with 'self-supporting' suppliers requires:

1. Thinking long term

2. Developing the stakeholder approach (rather than an adversarial one)
3. Building teamwork through finding joint ventures and activities that enhance both sides' ability to respond to the market–sharing resources where appropriate
4. Making mutual commitment and sharing risk and reward

These strategic relationships operate at many levels. At the most complex level is the strategy for developing memory chips which are a key element of computer design but which, like microprocessors, are subject to accelerating obsolescence as competition drives for enhanced memory at ever lower prices per byte. The development and tooling costs of new chips have escalated as rapidly as their obsolescence rate. A new memory chip line now costs of $1 billion, which has driven all but a few manufacturers out of business. IBM has established partnerships with Siemens and Toshiba in which each company develops, tools and manufactures future memory chips by taking turns with each successive new design. As product life cycles overlap, the impact of negative cashflow successively on each manufacturer is mitigated by continued sales of earlier chips.

Several of the new relationships between IBM and its suppliers have evolved into new businesses. An example of this is the business which developed from IBM's decision to contract out its 'customer call' service. From a number of potential partners, IBM selected Manpower and agreed with them specific cost and output targets. In three years the cost per call has been reduced by 18 per cent, customer satisfaction has risen from 85 per cent to 98 per cent and productivity has increased by 22 per cent. The relationship is based on equality of the partners, full cost visibility and rewards for innovation. The dramatic progress which has been achieved in this partnership has set new standards for enquiry service operations and IBM and Manpower have established a joint venture to market their competence to other current and potential users of enquiry services. In this and other ways, IBM is redefining its business and, having broken down its former bureaucratic structure, is ensuring that the company is reshaped in a flexible and responsive mould to cope with the discontinuities which increasingly impact on the IT business.

It may be asked what this process has to do with procurement. In reality, the process which John Gillett managed is one of fundamental strategic change which, because of IBM's high incidence of in-house costs, needed to be led by accelerated procurement in order to break the mould. Few of John Gillett's key staff are lifetime buyers, though he is keen on them qualifying for membership of the Chartered Institute of Purchasing and Supply. All are highly qualified in a variety of professions, 70 per cent have degrees and twelve are MBAs. The average age of John's staff is thirty-one and staff move in and out of the procurement unit rapidly. John insists that his operation is not a consultancy. Its success is based on the ability to ask penetrating questions and to work with others as a catalyst for changes which other people develop and own. Teamworking is a core skill and great care is taken in selecting and training staff for the procurement operation and equal care in rotating them to avoid the development of 'cosy' relationships or any blunting of the sharp cutting edge on which progress depends.

The headcount of IBM (UK) was 18 000 in 1989 and 11 000 in 1993. It will continue to shrink back to the basic core of design, sales, customer support and manufacturing. At the same time, IBM's 'complementary workforce' has risen from 2500 to 4000 and outsourcing headcount from 100 to 3000. Outsourcing routine purchasing has enabled attention to be focused on the key suppliers and attention has now switched to managing those more actively and selecting carefully those with whom a strategic relationship can be developed. This process requires time to work with suppliers, to help them gear up to meet IBM's stringent standards and to transfer to them some of the zeal which is transforming IBM itself.

A key part of the new procurement role is the development and integration of activities around the world. For example, the development of IBM's newest multi-gigabyte storage file needed to be achieved in fifteen months rather than the three years taken by its predecessor. It needed also to be two times faster, 75 per cent cheaper and five times more reliable. This required a concurrent engineering approach, using a common interactive database, shared by suppliers all around the world in order to design in real time. Suppliers also had full access to IBM's latest design and modelling tools in order to achieve the targets.

What will be the future of IBM's strategic procurement? John Gillett sees the need for continuous challenge to maintain the competitive advantage achieved so far. This will require the process of changing and developing new staff to be continued and for the appetite for endless change to be maintained. No return to the old self-contained IBM could be tolerated; any expansion in future will be carried by developing the capacity of suppliers and of strategic partnerships. IBM itself will concentrate on customers and markets and on anticipating their needs before they are even articulated. The process of working more closely with suppliers will not only support this but will also provide an essential element of the marketing insight needed to anticipate needs. Ninety-five per cent of IBM's suppliers are also customers for its products, creating a strategic bond which few other companies are likely to enjoy!

Conclusions

It will have emerged from the case studies developed in this and the previous chapter that effective marketing strategies need to be clearly differentiated. Too many strategies are imitative or pedestrian and do not attract the attention, let alone the support, of the customer. 'Me-too' strategies are rarely sustainable and some, like price-cutting, can be positively damaging.

The strategies that we have examined may be distinguished either by achieving surprise, and a sustainable shift in the market rules in favour of the initiator, or by focusing on a key factor and using that focus to leverage the outcome. The strategies of surprise and concentration are, of course, key parts of military strategy which may be successfully adapted to business use.

Outcomes are rarely the same as were expected when a strategy was adopted. Some of the case studies show the pattern of action and reaction which characterizes the implementation of strategy. The strategy of food retailers for moving upmarket and using own-label products to open up their margins has created space for discounters to attack the lower end of the market. The story of Merrydown shows how the outcome for the business differs from the vision of the founders, and yet the business has been successful and has nurtured its values through the vicissitudes which it has faced.

The case studies show that the implementation of marketing strategies is a process of learning which takes businesses through experiences not all of which could have been foreseen. Where implementation is successful it is usually because the objectives to be achieved remain clear and unchanged even though the means of reaching them may need to be adapted considerably in order to achieve success. Rather like white-water rafters, the businesses reach their goal but may have had to adapt frenziedly to do so!

Reference

Ohmae, Kenichi, *The Borderless World*, Fontana, London, 1990.

Marketing audit and corporate self-renewal

CHAPTER 10

Reference was made earlier to marketing audit. Malcolm McDonald uses this term for the second stage in marketing planning, that is, for the review of the effectiveness of earlier marketing plans and their implementation. Audit is a term which, in a business context, implies the use of independent and/or external persons to examine the workings of a given process or processes. The most obvious model is the financial audit required by the Companies Act in order to give reassurance to shareholders that the finances of their company are in good order. Such an audit must be carried out by an external firm of accountants, licensed to do such work by the Department of Trade and Industry. A growing number of companies also have an audit committee of the board; the existence of such a committee is a basic requirement for registration at the New York Stock Exchange and is now recommended for UK companies in the Cadbury Report. Such a committee is controlled by non-executive directors who should bring an external view and independence to bear on their scrutiny of the accounting and other processes in the company. In my book *Strategic Leadership* (1991) I call for the creation of a strategy committee of the board similarly constituted, which would ensure that the strategic health of the company was not put at risk due to inadequate strategic processes, overemphasis on short-term results or to manipulation by executive directors or others for personal gain. The failure of the British & Commonwealth Group to exercise effective due diligence in acquiring Atlantic Computers was an error at a strategic as well as at an operating level. The inability of the London International Group to foresee the possibility of a resurgence in the condom market due to AIDS was compounded by a series of poor acquisitions and product innovations. In so many of these cases the non-executive directors have no real access to opinions and facts other than those presented by their executive colleagues on the board.

Marketing audit fits into this area of concern, since marketing is often both the source of external information to shape strategic plans and also the key function in implementing them. The growth of interest in quality, and the development of quality standards and certification (BS 5750, ISO 9002) has also encouraged a greater focus on marketing quality. One firm which offers a quality system focused on marketing is Marketing

Quality Assurance (MQA). Such systems have a role to play in ensuring that internal procedures are properly established, documented and maintained. They do not, however, focus on the effectiveness of the marketing function or on the professional quality of its advice.

The professional input into the strategic marketing process is shaped by the marketing plan. The marketing review stage of the planning process assesses the external and internal environment of the business, evaluates the success of marketing operations and draws inferences for future marketing plans. The quality of this work may or may not be enhanced by using external input or by obtaining customer feedback through research in focus groups. An example of external evaluation of competitive intelligence which showed up blind spots in assessing competitors' capabilities, intentions and possible reactions is shown in an article in *Long Range Planning* by Gilad, Gordon and Sudit (1993). Without some external intervention the process of marketing review can become self-feeding and perpetuate marketing strategies which do not fit with corporate strategy or even with the realities of the wider world. The marketing strategy developed by Midland Bank some years ago to develop and sell lifestyle-based service packages with evocative names (Meridian, Orchard, etc.) succeeded brilliantly in promotional terms but failed to arrange for proper training of branch staff to sell it and did not have the back-office capacity to handle the changes required. Marketing strategies must be driven by corporate strategy and integrated with the plans of all parts of the business. Mismatches may be identified by corporate planners but it is useful to recognize the value of some external intervention from time to time to review the professional tone of the marketing function. Such a process is a real marketing audit.

Who should carry out the marketing audit? It may be sensible to give the task to an external peer group, either the marketing faculty from a business school or recognized marketing consultants. Such people should have the credibility to gain the respect of the marketing staff in the company. Their brief should be discussed with the internal staff and agreed previously so that any element of inquisition can be set aside and a sensible professional dialogue can be achieved. External reviewers should bring appropriate techniques to bear–structured interviews, workshops, modelling, issues diagnosis, benchmarking, etc. Ideally, the review should be a challenging learning process for the internal staff, carried out in the context of their own business, and should not seek culpability but should see weaknesses as an opportunity to work out shared solutions together. External review removes the direct challenge of internal politics from the process, concentrating the challenge on an open-learning opportunity.

External facilitation should also help to improve the process for the environmental audit. The importance of this process is emphasized by Paul Fifield in his recent book *Marketing Strategy* (1992): 'Auditing the environment in which the organisation must operate is arguably the most important and most significant data gathering activity that any business, firm, service or even government department, can undertake.' The environmental audit comprises at least five elements–the political, economic, technological, sociological and international forces which impinge on the business. The key factor which makes this audit crucial is the fact that these elements are matters over which the business can have little or no control. It must understand them and their dynamics in order to make the best use of factors which may be favourable and mitigate the effect of those which may become damaging. Many marketers find this process to be tedious but its value, if well done, is immense as the basis for building competitive advantage. Paul Fifield rightly warns, however, about the danger of empire building in this key area of management information; the search for knowledge knows no limits and environmental audit must be focused firmly on the real strategic needs of the business. External review can often warn of incipient overgrowth in this area, which is not easy to control.

Another possible approach to marketing audit is to use non- executive directors to carry out periodic reviews. Such an approach has the double benefit of improving the company knowledge of the directors concerned, thus making their future contribution likely to be more effective. This role could be part of the task of the strategy committee of the board, since marketing effectiveness is a key part of the input and delivery of strategic plans. In approaching this task the committee might ask itself the questions posed by Gary Hamel and C. K. Pralahad in their article in the *Harvard Business Review* (1994) and shown in Table 10.1. The questions are the same; trouble almost certainly lies ahead if the answers are not significantly different!

The development of the use of teams to undertake cross-functional tasks might offer another way of exposing the marketing process to non-marketing peer assessment. Project teams, for example, need to plan and work as a small, short-lived business. Marketing staff involved in project teams will need to bring their skills to bear on planning the development of the project and possibly the marketing of the products generated by it. These skills will often be deployed in open meetings and will be subject to scrutiny by colleagues who will be keen to make the project successful. The intensive learning pressures in such situations may well be a catalyst for improving marketing competence, particularly if there is external professional facilitation to bring new techniques to be tested.

The importance of marketing audit has grown in recent years because of the role of marketing as the 'window on the world' of most companies. The role of purchasing is similar in this respect in some companies, not least in the retailing business, and we have seen the marketing role of purchasing in the case study on IBM in Chapter 9. As the external environment has

Table 10.1 Competing for the future

Today	*In the future*
Which customers do you serve today?	Which customers will you serve in the future?
Through which channels do you reach your customers today?	Through which channels will you reach your customers in the future?
Who are your competitors today?	Who will your competitors be in the future?
What is the basis for your competitive advantage today?	What will be the basis for your competitive advantage in the future?
Where do your margins come from today?	Where will your margins come from in the future?
What skills or capabilities make you unique today?	What skills or capabilities will make you unique in the future?

From Hamel and Pralahad (1994)

become more unstable and the ability of the individual firm to control its environment has lessened, the importance of the quality of the research and analysis done by marketing for the business has escalated. The risks of faulty analysis to the company have grown substantially as the chances of predicting outcomes have worsened in a world which is daily more complex and more unstable. Strategic marketing has now become too important to leave solely to marketing people.

Corporate self-renewal

In my book *Strategic Leadership* (1991) I focus strongly on the issue of corporate self-renewal:

> 'One of the greatest challenges facing any Board is that of corporate renewal. Any organization has an inbuilt tendency to conservatism and to bureaucratic sclerosis. The proud history of many a company is given as the justification for failing to take the risk of innovation and change and a board room which was once thriving with purposeful activity becomes a museum of past glories.'

Patrick Haggerty, former CEO of Texas Instruments, was fanatical about corporate renewal. He laid down the board's responsibility as follows:

'1) Assuring that the corporate structure, policies and practices are realistic, sufficiently elastic and yet powerful enough to cope not just with the external national and international environment as it now exists but as it will be through future years and over the entire corporate span of interests;

2) Assuring that the corporation's products and services are truly innovative and really are contributing in a major way to constructive change in the world around it;

3) Assuring that an innovative, aggressive, properly educated and experienced staff of professional managers, scientists, engineers and other specialists is available and being generated in sufficient depth and talent to meet the corporation's long-range goals' (Haggerty, 1980).

Haggerty also sought to move towards having executive directors whose principal occupation would be to advance corporate renewal:

> 'This would ensure our having high-level, capable people who have the time to study, to think quietly about and to comprehend the impact of the rapidly changing internal and external environment and the relationship of both to our corporate self-renewal. These directors would have no operating responsibilities. Their duties would relate entirely to their functions as directors and advisors to the Board.'

Corporate self-renewal is concerned with building tomorrow's company while managing today's business. The shape of tomorrow's company will need to be individually tailored but the Interim Report of the Royal Society of Arts (1994) seeks to identify the forces which will mould companies for the future. The report recognizes that the pressures of international competition will force companies to take a more informal and inclusive view of their total environment–'tomorrow's company will understand and measure the value which it derives from all its key relationships, and thereby be able to make informed decisions when it has to balance and trade off the conflicting claims of customers, suppliers, employees, investors and the communities in which it operates'. It will, in addition, need to select and develop its future managers, plan its finances and, most importantly, generate the new products and services needed to meet the future needs of its customers.

In the 1960s and the 1980s many companies sought to achieve growth through acquisition. Most of that activity was, in reality, focused on improving short-term results but much of it was rationalized in terms of strategic development. The reasons for General Motors to acquire EDS included a search for more dynamic markets for the future. Even today EDS remains a misfit with the established culture of General Motors, and its founder, Ross Perot, has left to exploit his new freedom. More than ten years and a crisis were needed to enable Sir Colin Marshall to integrate BEA and BOAC into British Airways. Corporate self-renewal through acquisition is a risky process and can lead to severe damage to the core business. The acquisition by Daimler-Benz of Deutsche Aerospace and its investment in Cap Gemini Sogeti are attempts to move into markets with a more sparkling future than cars and trucks. Like General Motors, there is no evidence yet that such moves promote real self-renewal and may well detract from the effort needed to re-engineer the core business.

Corporate self-renewal is, therefore, a commitment which is usually best met by organic development. Firms such as Minnosota Mining and Manufacture (3M) and, more recently, Morgan Crucible have developed a culture of innovation which is very powerful. At 3M all employees are encouraged to spend part of their time in creating and developing new products and have some budgetary support in doing so. Morgan Crucible focuses firmly on emergent customer needs and has a record of anticipating and steering market trends in subsystems. Merck has a powerful culture of innovation in pharmaceutical products, allowing considerable scope for personal initiative in fundamental research, thus increasing the options for potential product development. Firms are finding the need to sharpen their project management processes, not only to pick and pursue the best investment prospects but also to train and develop their future top managers. Dupont was an early pioneer in this area but some quite significant self-renewal projects have been recorded, not least the IBM project to produce their PC. This project not only involved some of the best brains in the corporation but was also set up outside the framework of the business to give it cultural freedom and total flexibility in sourcing parts and services.

The current vogue for business re-engineering presents a significant challenge to strategic self-renewal. Business re- engineering has been sold to many companies as a strategic process but, in practice, most companies focus on cost reduction rather than strategic repositioning. Too often the re-engineering is carried out to fit the company for today's (or even yesterday's) challenges and not to compete successfully in the future. No better example of this can be given than Xerox Corporation, which reduced costs and stabilized its market share but failed to bring to market a whole range of new products which would have saved it from being a one-product company.

Successful corporate self-renewal depends fundamentally on good marketing. The IBM team launching the PC had to be free to address and understand a market which corporate culture dismissed as unimportant. Hewlett-Packard sought for many years to market proprietary protocol-based computers and its printer business was expected to follow. The management of the Printers and Plotters Division was convinced by research that the market future lay in open-systems architecture and designed its equipment to meet this. Hewlett-Packard is now market leader in laser printers worldwide.

Corporate self-renewal is not easily achieved and it seems that the average life of any company is no more than forty years! This appears to be due to a phenomenon which Joseph Schumpeter, the economist, called the 'creative destruction' of capitalism. This is a cycle of birth and death which releases resources to a new generation of entrepreneurs who will use them more effectively. A few companies have, however, managed to survive for hundreds of years (Table 10.2 shows some British examples) and some of these remain in the control of the same family that founded them (e.g. Durtnell). Some long-lived businesses are small, some large, such as Stora Kopparbergs.

What are the factors which have ensured self-renewal of these businesses? Some have remained in their chosen business (e.g. Monte dei Paschi); others, such as Stora Kopperbergs, started in one business (copper mining) and are now in another (forestry). One factor which they must all share is a prudent management with a sense of succession. Many proud businesses, such as BSA, have been destroyed by hubris; others, such as Vickers, had lost their way strategically and are seeking to re-establish themselves. The businesses which have concentrated on self-renewal have managed to avoid mortgaging their future, unlike Banesto,

Table 10.2 Britain's oldest companies

Established	
1136	Aberdeen Harbour Board
1534	Cambridge University Press
1586	Oxford University Press
1591	Durtnell (Kent builders)
1608	Old Bushmills Whiskey Distillery, County Antrim
1635	The Post Office
1650	Alldays Peacock (industrial fans), West Bromwich
1651	Hays (business services), Guildford
1660	Vandome and Hart (weighing machines), London
1670	James Gibbons Format (locksmiths and metal foundry), Wolverhampton
1671	Mocatta and Goldsmid (gold and silver bullion merchants), London
1677	Firmin and Sons (military accessories), Birmingham
1688	Lloyds of London (insurance market)
1689	Ede and Ravenscroft (wig and gown makers), London
1690	Barclays Bank
1692	Coutts (bankers)
1694	Bank of England
1695	Bank of Scotland
1698	Shepherd Neame (Kent brewers)
1699	Wilton Royal Carpet Factory, near Salisbury
1699	The Folkes Group (open die forging), Stourbridge

Financial Times, 29 December 1992

and have built from generation to generation. Theirs was never 'my business' but 'our business'.

In his recent book *The Empty Raincoat* (1994) Charles Handy explores 'a sense of continuity'. This is seen to be important as a means of making sense of a world which is increasingly unstable and paradoxical. He quotes Mitsui Corporation as a continuing success after 600 years–'still going strong and thinking far. You only look ahead as far as you can look back.' Handy sees some hope for change: 'In the marketplace, fashion, that god of the merchandisers, may be losing some adherents, or rather the new fashion may be ... to choose what suits you ... home made, second- hand, good not flashy quality, the stuff that lasts, may become the style.' The insight that the ability to look back conditions the quality of foresight is precious. Much of the success of Winston Churchill has been attributed by some of his contemporaries to his highly developed sense of history; Henry Ford is supposed to have dismissed history as 'bunk'. May I suggest that both are right, since history can often act to prevent innovation and be the excuse for inaction. A sense of history does, however, act as a bond with earlier generations and as an incentive to build for later generations. Those who are responsible for corporate self-renewal should see themselves as a bridge between the past and the future, as (to paraphrase Charles Handy) Ram was the link between Adam and King David.

References

Davies, Adrian, *Strategic Leadership*, Woodhead Faulkner, Cambridge, 1991.

Fifield, Paul, *Marketing Strategy*, Butterworth-Heinemann, Oxford, 1992.

Gilad, B., Gordon G. and Sudit, E., 'Identifying gaps and blind spots in competitive intelligence', *Long Range Planning*, December 1993.

Haggerty, Patrick, 'Corporate self-renewal', *Long Range Planning*, 1980.

Hamel, A. and Pralahad, C. K., 'Competing for the future', *Harvard Business Review*, July/August 1994.

Handy, Charles, *The Empty Raincoat*, Hutchinson, London, 1994.

Royal Society of Arts, *Tomorrow's Company: the role of business in a changing world*, 1994.

Strategic marketing beyond the second millennium

CHAPTER 11

In Chapter 1 I referred to the Megatrends foreseen by John Naisbitt and Patricia Aburdene (1991) beyond the second millennium. These reflect the breakdown of the socialist state, globalization balanced by cultural nationalism, the enfranchisement of women and, above all, the triumph of the individual. These Megatrends and possible alternative scenarios from my fertile imagination are shown in Table 11.1. Who is to say which is more likely to occur?

In his more recent book, *Global Paradox* (1994) John Naisbitt pursues further the dichotomy between globalization and nationalism, and examines the paradox that as the world economy grows larger it is the smaller companies which become more powerful. European Union is seen as unlikely to be achieved, though free trade will be sustained. Freddie Heineken, the brewer, sees Europe as a grouping of seventy-five states,

Table 11.1 Scenarios for the future

Megatrends 2000	*Alternative scenarios*
1. The booming global economy of the 1990s	1. The competitive global economy of the 1990s
2. The renaissance of the arts	2. The era of global sports
3. The emergence of free-market socialism	3. The fascist revival
4. Global lifestyles and cultural nationalism	4. The return of tribalism
5. The privatisation of the welfare state	5. The growth of the workfare state
6. The rise of the Pacific Rim	6. The taming of the tigers
7. The decade of women in leadership	7. The decade of women with choice
8. The age of biology	8. The genetic nightmare
9. The religious revival of the new millennium	9. The defeat of Christianity
10. The triumph of the individual	10. The return of the family

Adapted from Naisbitt and Aburdene (1991)

each with a population of no more than 10 million, and each a viable political unit. Economies of scale in economic terms are to be achieved by alliances and treaties. Global communications and information systems (e.g. Internet) already make boundaries obsolete; global tourism and the free flow of capital combine with global communications to open the world to every individual. In the words of John Naisbitt (1994):

> 'With the end of communism, the decline of the nation state, the building of a single market world economy, the spread of democracy throughout the world, and the new revolution in telecommunication, the opportunities, the possibilities, for individuals, families, companies, and institutions are far, far greater than they have ever been in any of our lifetimes. The Global Paradox tells us that the opportunities for each of us as individuals are far greater than at any time in human history'.

Each individual is a customer of someone. What are the implications of these trends for strategic marketing? Clearly, all marketing activity will in future need to be focused on the individual; this implies that 'mass marketing' is unlikely to be successful and that greater efforts will need to be made to segment markets, ideally down to the individual customer. An example of a more modern approach to segmentation is Laing Henry's (1991) twelve groupings, based on an analysis of 24 000 individual adults (Table 11.2).

We also need to recognize that people buy emotionally and not logically. In the words of Paul Fifield (1992):

> 'Customers are not machines. Customers, whether consumer or industrial, do not make logical, rational decisions about what they buy. People are emotive and even the most important purchase decisions tend to be primarily emotion-based even though they may have the veneer of rationality placed on them later ... To sell we have to approach people emotionally—to understand we have also to understand emotionally.'

Paul Fifield recounts how he has needed to train marketers to develop right-brain characteristics such as emotion, feeling and intuition, and has helped them to unlearn the left-brain approaches of analysis and scientific method in order to unlock the right side of the brain. Presumably both sides of the brain should then be able to function in balance!

If the focus of marketing is increasingly to be on the individual, the task of reaching out to individuals will become a major challenge. The growing emphasis on database marketing seen in recent years and codified in books such as Arthur Hughes' *Strategic Database Marketing* (1994) will provide some improvement over the use of special-interest group listings which has characterized direct marketing until recently. Quite apart from the difficulty of marketing to people who are already dead, the lack of focus

Table 11.2 The Capps, Kids and Grazers

According to the Laing Henry system, the six biggest categories to target are:

1. *Mainstream Media Rejectors* (15.7%) southern graduates, light users of television and newspapers, into healthy foods.
2. *Soaps and Sun* (14.1%) more interested in *Neighbours* than politics, buy *The Sun, News of the World* and magazines such as *Woman's Own* and *True Romance*, use junk food.
3. *Andy Capps* (12.3%) prefer the *Daily Mirror*, don't go to the cinema, watch a lot of televised sport, *That's Life, Songs of Praise.*
4. *Armchair Adventurers* (10.6%) read *Daily Express* or *Daily Mail*, watch a moderate amount of television, go for gardening, *Panorama, Tomorrow's World.*
5. *Thatcher's Orphans* (10%) read the tabloids for entertainment, not news, watch many ITV programmes, dip into Channel 4, like TV ads, want a satellite dish.
6. *Chart Show Kids* (9.9%) medium for ITV/C4, heavy for cinema and satellite; watch *Chart Show, Top of the Pops, Neighbours*, read pop music and car magazines. Next come:

   Genteel Media Grazers (6.2%) watch lots of TV, especially game shows; houseproud, gardeners, don't use credit cards.

   Telly Dawn to Dusk (5.9%) 55-plus, heavy viewers of ITV, Channel 4, satellite/ cable; dislike foreign food/travel.

   Other categories: *Avant Guardians; Thirtysomethings; High Arts, High Finance, National Trustees.*

provided by most lists leads both to wastage and resentment. How can this situation be improved?

Recently I was involved in facilitating a workshop for a major insurance company and stimulated a battle between the in-house sales people and outside marketers. I challenged the workshop to define the changes needed to enable potential clients to design their own tailored insurance policies. From incredulity we moved towards a recognition that this challenge would need to be met over time even though a complete change in culture was required and the costs of doing so would need to be carefully assessed and recovered.

This incident may provide a crude model of a new approach to consumer marketing, in which the prospective client is involved in designing his or her own product. Industrial marketing has long involved a process of interaction in designing the product required and has been supported by economies of scale. The growing sophistication of communication, with increased possibilities of interaction, together with vast expansion of computer power, increasingly make the interaction of the industrial marketing model more readily applicable to consumer marketing. The implications of this change, for media advertising and agencies in particular, would seem to be sombre. World advertising has plateaued at some $200 billion and a growing proportion seems to be handled in-house by marketing departments.

The growing power and self-awareness of the individual will also make it increasingly difficult to manipulate customers. Bodies like the Consumers' Association have lobbied for years for greater consumer protection, and they have achieved considerable success. The press has also become increasingly vociferous about marketing scandals, most recently in respect of the forced sale of personal pensions to employees with employer-supported schemes. There remains the problem for individuals of the cost of litigation and this hinders progress towards balanced markets. Despite the legislation in place, 'caveat emptor' remains the only safe advice for consumers faced with powerful companies desperate to achieve the sale of their products. Marketing will never fulfil its promise until it becomes an open and even-handed process between consenting parties.

What may be the strands from which strategic marketing will be woven in the new millennium? I believe that these are likely to include:

1. Aspirational marketing
2. Relationship marketing
3. Societal marketing
4. Time-based marketing
5. Global marketing

Let us examine each of these in turn.

Aspirational marketing

We have already focused on the growth of individualism and some of its implications for marketing. The process of marketing to individuals is likely to expand as people globally move up Maslow's 'hierarchy of needs'. There will still be a need to market the daily necessities of life but these will be supplemented by an expanding range of discretionary purchases to meet needs many of which are as yet unknown. Such purchases will in part be driven by the process of 'redesigning life' explored in Charles Handy's book *The Empty Raincoat* (1994):

> 'The demise of the traditional job, the re-scheduling of time and the new areas of choice for would-be parents combined with longer and healthier lifespans, mean that the traditional sequence of events in life–school, job, house, children, retirement–is no longer fixed. Flexilife is now the mode.'

With greater time and flexibility is coming a growing range of opportunities for self-fulfilment. Howard Gardner of Harvard University has identified 'seven intelligences' of the individual:

1. Linguistic
2. Musical
3. Logical/mathematical
4. Spatial
5. Kinaesthetic (balancing the mind and bodily movement)
6. Interpersonal intelligence
7. Self-knowledge and self-awareness

Really talented persons are able to develop all these intelligences in varying degrees and increasing self-awareness should lead to a wealth of marketing opportunities. Learning, as a process of combining knowledge and experience, is likely to be a very significant market even before the year 2000.

Growth of the aspirations market will also be fuelled by greater interest in the arts, in heritage and a wide range of collecting interests. The recent rush of television companies to develop sports channels may prove to be overdone. As people become more self-aware, participation in sports is likely to be more satisfying than the role of a spectator.

Among the aspirations which will create significant markets in the coming years will be self-employment. Writers such as Handy and Naisbitt see a steady shift away from large towards small business. Even in large businesses people will need greater empowerment to be fulfilled. While an increasing number of people will wish, (and, in some cases, find themselves compelled) to work for themselves, others will be happy to work in a framework of support, through franchises, part-ownership arrangements and formulae yet to emerge. Even after the debacle at Lloyd's it is unlikely that individuals will abandon their instincts to make money, nor should they. In the words of Samuel Johnson, 'There are few ways in which a man can be more innocently employed than in getting money'. Whatever their prime occupation people will continue to respond to the opportunity to play in financial markets or indulge in other speculative activities. The whole future of the National Heritage Fund hangs on the aspirations of millions of punters in the National Lottery!

Relationship marketing

We have already seen the growth of relationship marketing as a strategic weapon. At present, it is imperfectly developed but new possibilities such as electronic data interchange (EDI) will make the communication interface, which is essential for relationship marketing, much stronger. It is likely that the one-way approach to relationship marketing now adopted, one of binding customers to your organization for all time, will evolve into more flexible patterns. In the same way that large groups are breaking up and floating off non-core activities, it will become necessary to review relationships with customers in the light of changing circumstances. The growth of alliances, as an alternative to growth by acquisition, reflects the greater uncertainty of future markets, particularly when most will in time become global.

Relationship marketing will probably become wider in scope, and will be aimed at positioning the company with a growing range of stakeholders, not just customers. The need to optimize relations with opinion formers and others who influence customers will make relationship marketing more complex. Relationship marketing will increasingly depend on ever more sophisticated databases and on new techniques such as neural nets. Success in relationship marketing will become harder to achieve, particularly as the individuals in the interface are replaced increasingly frequently and as the pressure of competition impinges on the relationship. At such a time the insights to enable you to anticipate the needs within a virtually symbiotic relationship will be tested against the realities of commercial seduction and unlimited promises.

Societal marketing

The pressure of issues such as health, safety and the environment were recognized in Philip Kotler's (1979) 'societal marketing concept': 'The societal marketing concept holds that the organization's task is to determine the needs, wants and interests of target markets and to deliver the desired satisfactions more effectively and efficiently than competitors in a way that preserves and enhances the consumer's and society's well-being.' Jean-Jacques Lambin (1994) identifies two key ideas which distinguish the concept of societal marketing from that of classical marketing:

'a) marketing must be concerned with the well-being of buyers and not simply with the satisfaction of their short term needs

b) the firm must pay attention to the side-effects of its economic and industrial activity in order to ensure the long term well-being of society as a whole and not only that of individual consumers'

Societal marketing is, therefore, essentially a strategic concept since it is concerned with the long-term effects of its actions on both buyer and society. It must be questioned whether, for example, the skilful marketing of cigarettes can fit into the framework of societal marketing. The societal approach to marketing calls into question the whole concept of free markets and *laissez-faire* trading. It mixes politics with trading and raises enormous challenges to companies which are law-abiding and of honest intent but at risk of societal disfavour for reasons often outside their control. The pressure placed on companies can be considerable. The price of South African gold shares has for years been at a discount to that of other gold shares, in terms of the implicit value per ounce of their discovered reserves. A growing number of market funds refuse to buy shares in 'pariah companies' such as defence equipment manufacturers. A judgement is made that such businesses are fomenting war, forgetting the inconvenient truth that the balance of deterrence achieved since 1945 has brought the longest period of relative peace in the history of mankind.

Despite the dangers of societal marketing it appears to be here to stay. The demise of socialism in its classical form and the growth of individualism presents a challenge to the preservation of an orderly society. Marketing has rarely given evidence of great responsibility in its recent history and its philosophy has largely been transaction-based. At a time when the role of business is in question, as in the RSA report on *Tomorrow's Company*, marketing may need to look not for the immediate profit to meet this year's budget but for a sustainable stream of profits over the coming years. Societal marketing will no doubt be a growing part of the mix of strategies employed by companies in the future.

Time-based marketing

It was the Japanese who taught the West the value of time. By the use of 'just-in-time' supply systems they reduced their inventories and speed of manufacture; with 'continuous engineering', they were able to reduce the time from conception to market. In total, these techniques have telescoped the end-to-end marketing process so that identified product opportunities can be turned into profits faster and more reliably.

In the 1980s a new car model would take five to six years from conception to market; today some cars emerge in less than two years. The key marketing advantage is the ability to be first to market with a product that meets a requirement that may be ephemeral. Benetton is able to react to unpredictable changes in demand for different colours by manufacturing its knitwear in white wool and dyeing to order. The speed with which the London 'rag trade' can copy couturier clothes is legendary. Even where the market is less ephemeral, extension of the 'time-to-market' process can lead to the manufacture of yesterday's products (e.g. the Ford Edsel). Having been frequently late to market, Philips reorganized their new product development function and gave designers an integrating role rather than one just of stylist. This process is well described in Christopher Lorenz's book *The Design Dimension* (1986) and illustrates some of the challenges faced in the quest for speed to market. A more specific focus on new product development is provided by Donald Reinertsen and Preston Smith (1991). This analysis uncovers, for example, the wasted time at the 'fuzzy front end' of projects, before they are commissioned, which typically can be 50 per cent of the actual development time.

Time pressures are likely to increase as competition increases globally. Time-based strategies will become more important particularly when facing low-cost competitors. Innovation can, in most markets, command a premium but this is usually short-lived as 'me-too' products rush into the market. Product life cycles seem to be shortening but regular and sustained product enhancement as developed by the Japanese has enabled extensions to be achieved. Here again the process is very time sensitive.

Global marketing

In his book *The Marketing Imagination* (1986) Ted Levitt sees globalization of markets in the following terms:

> 'A powerful force now drives the world towards a single converging commonality, and that force is technology. It has proletarianized communication, transport and travel, making them easily and cheaply accessible to the world's most isolated places and impoverished multitudes. Suddenly no place and nobody is insulated from the alluring attractions of modernity. Almost everybody everywhere wants all the things they have heard about, seen or experienced via the new technological facilities that drive their wants or wishes. And it drives these increasingly into global commonality, thus homogenizing markets everywhere'.

Kenichi Ohmae (1991) sees a slightly different picture:

> 'People vary in how they want to live. There is no universal style, nor even a style that holds firmly at national level. We all know this. What has changed in the past few years is the ability of the interlinked economy [of the world] to accommodate that variation and that multiplicity of styles. By definition, such an economy is pluralist.'

Few products have yet fulfilled the vision of Ted Levitt; Coca-Cola, Levi's and Pepsi-Cola come close, others like Hard Rock Café are trying hard but universality is rare. McDonald's hamburgers are unlikely to appeal in India nor Guinness's beer in Saudi Arabia (at least not in the open!). There does appear to be some sense in the New Age mantra 'think globally, act locally'. This is the basis of the case study on National Starch in Chapter 9.

John Naisbitt (1994) sees the growing emergence of 'tribalism' and the breakdown of large units in government and business. With the globalization of the world economy comes a countervailing concern to protect tribal identity and culture. He sees lifestyles to be globalizing but culture to be localizing. In sum, he reverses the New Age mantra into 'think locally, act globally'!

Although in *Megatrends 2000* the next millennium is seen as the 'Triumph of the Individual', we face the dilemma of individuals merging themselves into tribes, dressing alike, eating and drinking alike and watching the same sports. Few individuals are not, in some measure, subject to peer pressure but it is to be hoped that the worst excesses of tribal pressure, such as that which supports the IRA, will disappear as individuals are increasingly enfranchised.

Global marketing will become an essential skill as markets become global. Even small companies are increasingly forced to market globally. Lingrain, a grain marketing cooperative in East Anglia, trades in world markets and more than half of its business is in imports and exports. Small specialist UK dealers in art, antiques, philately and other collectibles are part of a growing global market. Even businesses which see themselves as local–builders, taxi firms, florists–will, over time, face the pressure of outside competition. This may come in the form of international franchises or from larger groups entering their business, as Tesco has recently done with flowers. Such firms will need to find ways of marketing their own skills on a wider scale, through alliances, franchises or organic growth to counter the pressures from which there will be 'no hiding place'. Greater care than ever will need to be taken to contain exploitative formulae such as 'network marketing' and pyramid selling.

What will be the future of the marketing department as we enter the new millennium? Paul Fifield (1992) sees a need to return to the marketing concept after thirty years in which 'marketing as a business discipline has almost become respectable'. He doubts, however, that the change from 'the creative, flamboyant, uncontrollable types of people' to a marketing department full of people with 'a more systematic, controlled and scientific approach' will meet the challenges now facing marketing.

The return to the marketing concept will require a wider sharing of responsibility for marketing. The marketing department will need to be integrators, as Hugh Davidson recommends, and involve everybody else in the marketing process. Robert Waterman (1994) tells how R&D researchers at Proctor & Gamble are trained to be fully competent in market research. This enables them to identify the qualities sought in a product by customers and to translate them effectively into technical specifications. The same book focuses on the self-directed teams which are becoming increasingly usual in American factories. All such teams are customer focused and all members are involved in the practicalities of marketing. This emphasis on autonomy and the encouragement of learning that goes with it are important drivers to spread the marketing concept throughout the company. In his recent book Philip Sadler (1993) unveils three subcultures in a range of companies which he had researched. These subcultures were the 'managerial' (focused on efficiency, profit, growth, competitiveness, quality and service), the 'sales and marketing' (focused on competitiveness, growth and individual achievement) and the 'professional, technical and scientific' (focused on professional goals rather than those of the employer). In each company one subculture tends to dominate but will change as the balance of power is shifted by personalities or events. Philip Sadler sees the successful companies in the future as being those, like Hewlett-Packard, who manage to balance the three subcultures and extract the maximum value from each.

In a hard hitting article in *Marketing Business* about a report for the Chartered Institute of Marketing by Cranfield's Centre for Advanced Research in Marketing, Malcolm McDonald (1994) recognizes that 'marketing's contribution to business success has never been under greater scrutiny'. The fault lies partly with British companies: 'The failure of British business lies in its views of marketing as a practical tactical function rather than a corporate philosphy.' Malcolm McDonald considers the challenges to marketing to be internationalization, customer sophistication and power, low market growth and margins, as well as process thinking and time-based competition. He sees the future focus of marketing at three levels:

- 'at a corporate culture and pervasive philosophical level
- at a strategic level
- at a tactical level'

The present emphasis on business process re-engineering is seen as 'an excellent platform on which to introduce the marketing philosophy'. Malcolm McDonald regards marketing as a key contributor to business strategy–'the essence of the contribution that marketing makes to business strategy is to provide a keen understanding of the dynamics of the marketplace and an external reference point, and ultimately to be the custodian of the customer'. Marketing is 'part of an overall business philosophy' and a driver for involving customer-facing staff in the process of strategy formulation.

If these changes can be achieved we may yet see the realization of

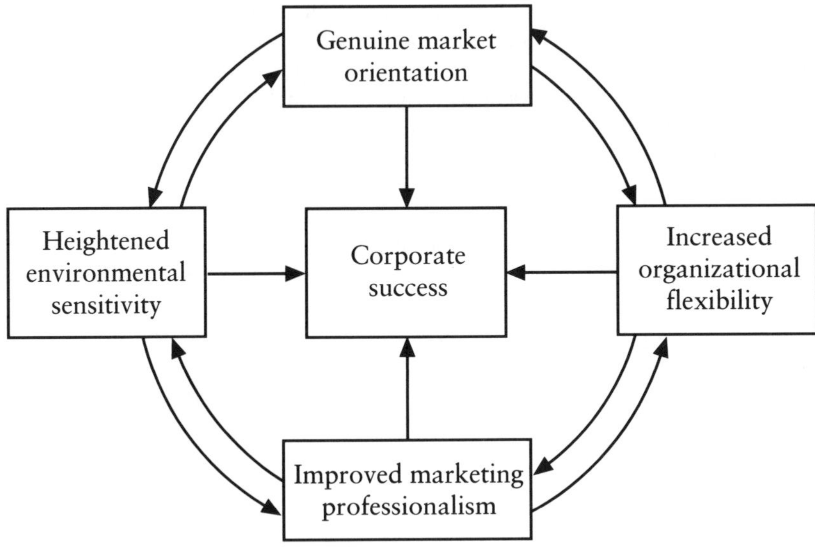

Figure 11.1 The virtuous circle of best marketing practice (Hooley *et al.*, 1984)

Hooley's 'virtuous circle of best marketing practice' (Figure 11.1) quoted in Baker and Hart (1989). Figure 11.1 captures all but one of the key features of corporate success. The omission of this key feature encapsulates the main failure of marketing in its progress to date–a failure highlighted in Malcolm McDonald's critique mentioned above–and offers the best future opportunity for marketing to fulfil its all-pervading role. The missing key feature is strategic direction, and when this becomes the force that drives the virtuous circle the strategic role of marketing will truly be fulfilled.

References

Baker, Michael and Hart, Susan, *Marketing and Competitive Success*, Philip Allan, Deddington, 1989.

Fifield, Paul, *Marketing Strategy*, Butterworth-Heinemann, Oxford, 1992.

Handy, Charles, *The Empty Raincoat*, Hutchinson, London, 1994.

Henry, L., 'Brand advertising targeting system', *Sunday Times*, 18 April 1991.

Hooley, G.J., West, D., and Lynch, J.E., *Marketing in the UK: a survey of current practice and performance*, Institute of Marketing, 1984.

Hughes, Arthur, *Strategic Database Marketing*, Probus, London, 1994.

Kotler, P., *Future Directions for Marketing*, Marketing Science Institute, 1979.

Lambin, J.-J., *Strategic Marketing*, McGraw-Hill, New York, 1994.

Levitt, T., *The Marketing Imagination*, Free Press, New York, 1986.
Lorenz, C., *The Design Dimension*, Blackwell, Oxford, 1986.
McDonald, Malcolm, 'Report on status of marketing', *Marketing Business*, 1994.
Naisbitt, J., *Global Paradox*, Nicholas Brearley, London, 1994.
Naisbitt, J. and Aburdene, P., *Megatrends 2000*, Futura, London, 1991.
Ohmae, Kenichi, *The Borderless World*, Fontana, London, 1991.
Reinertsen, D. and Smith, P., *Developing Products in Half the Time*, Chapman and Hall, London, 1991.
Sadler, Philip, *Managing Talent–Making the Best of the Best*, Pitman, London, 1993.
Waterman, Robert, *The Frontiers of Excellence*, Nicholas Brearley, London, 1994.

Mission statements

APPENDIX 1

Mission statements are difficult to write and often read like 'statements in support of motherhood'. They are subject to change in the light of reaction and experience (British Airways changed its 1986 Mission Statement in 1990) and fall into disrepute if not reflected in the daily actions of all employees. At their best, mission statements convey positive information about a company in much the same manner as strong brands; indeed failure to live up to the values projected in a company's mission statement effectively devalues the brands which it is marketing.

A good, crisp mission statement is that of British Airways written in 1990 and still valid today:

Mission and goals

Mission

To be the best and most successful company in the airline industry

Goals

- *Safe and secure* To be a safe and secure airline
- *Financially Strong* To deliver a strong and consistent financial performance
- *Global leader* To secure a leading share of air travel business worldwide with a significant presence in all major geographical markets
- *Service and Value* To provide overall superior service and good value for money in every market segment in which we compete
- *Customer driven* To excel in anticipating and quickly responding to customer needs and competitor activity
- *Good employer* To sustain a working environment that attracts retains and develops committed employees who share in the success of the company
- *Good neighbour* To be a good neighbour, concerned for the community and the environment

To achieve these goals, we must:

- Deliver friendly, professional service consistently through well-trained and motivated employees
- Search continuously for improvement through innovation and the use of technology
- Employ planning and decision-making processes that provide a clear direction and a sense of purpose
- Foster a leadership style throughout the organization which encourages respect for individuals, teamwork and close identification with customers
- Strive constantly to achieve agreed standards of quality at competitive cost levels.

Some businesses seek to give a harder edge to their mission statements both by calling them something different and by adopting a more 'business-like' tone. Williams Holdings, a financial conglomerate, offers the following:

Objectives and policies

Williams Holdings is an international manufacturing company. The principal business interests of the group are in fire protection, building products and security products. The group's objectives are:

- To achieve above-average underlying growth in earnings per share
- To maintain a progressive dividend policy
- To build businesses of lasting quality

The policies employed to achieve these objectives are:

- To own businesses which have significant shares in their relevant markets
- To avoid dependency on one specific market or geographic region
- To generate above-average margins and cash flow
- To market new products derived from a continuing commitment to research and development
- To invest capital to create the position of lowest-cost producer
- To decentralize management and to give high operational autonomy with short lines of communication

Williams Holdings is committed to the provision of high-quality and safe working conditions for the benefit of its employees and the adoption of sound environmental policies in the interests of the community. The management culture of the group is based on the principle of equal opportunity for all and rewards performance, stimulates initiative and encourages endeavour of the individual.

It is interesting that the word 'customer' does not appear anywhere in this statement. The financial strategy of the company is clear, the marketing strategy appears to be left to chance!

A third statement which is of interest is that of Tesco. Again the word 'mission' is avoided but the statement is wide-ranging and friendly:

Corporate objectives

Tesco is one of Britain's leading food retailers with 430 stores throughout England, Scotland and Wales and an additional 98 in France operated by Catteau. We are pleased to serve more than 8 million customers every week. Tesco is committed to:

- Offering customers the best value for money and the most competitive prices
- Meeting the needs of customers by constantly seeking and acting upon their opinions regarding product quality, choice, innovation, store facilities and service
- Providing shareholders with outstanding returns on their investment
- Improving profitability through investment in efficient stores and distribution depots, in productivity improvements and in new technology
- Developing the talents of its people through sound management and training practices, while rewarding them fairly with equal opportunities for all
- Working closely with suppliers to build long-term business relationships based on strict quality and price criteria
- Participating in the formulation of national food industry policies on key issues such as health, nutrition, hygiene, safety and animal welfare
- Supporting the well-being of the community and the protection of the environment

The real value of a mission statement lies in the process of involving employees (and, ideally, other stakeholders) in discussing and agreeing to its content. Often it is the mission statements which appear to be bland which have had a high degree of involvement by people other than management. They are a political document and show the marks of compromise and wide involvement. Few mission statements are able to define today's business without hindering a free and creative approach to shaping tomorrow's company. Tesco's focus on talents shows a recognition that companies are really a coalition of competences seeking markets in which to prosper, rather than prisoners of the markets in which they first achieved success. It is significant also that mission statements that have a sharp focus on shared values are usually more effective in use (see Chapter 8 for the values of Merrydown Wine–'quality, integrity and fun'). Those that are written by management to set a unilateral agenda are hollow and are as futile as the proud boast of the headless statue of Shelley's Ozymandias–"My name is Ozymandias, King of Kings: look on my works, ye Mighty, and despair!'.

APPENDIX 2

Strategic planning techniques and their practical application

(Reproduced from '*Strategic Leadership*' (Woodhead Faulkner, 1991) by kind permission of the publisher)

The value and pitfalls of techniques

This survey is intended to give marketers and non-planners a flavour of some of the techniques used by planners and to demystify them. Techniques are only as good as the quality of information which they manipulate and as the perceptiveness of those that use them.

Few subjects cause more dissention among planners than planning techniques. John Fawn sees them in a positive light: 'Planning techniques are potentially very attractive to senior executives at corporate headquarters for the following reasons:

(a) They give control back to top management. As companies grow larger and become more diverse, power probably shifted to divisional chief executives ... techniques ... bring it firmly back to corporate HQ.

(b) They enable rational decisions to be made. Top management can justify their decisions particularly to businesses which are to be run down/divested.

(c) Resource allocation (particularly capital) between totally diverse activities can be solved.

Top-down planning techniques cannot be used in isolation. Messages received from any particular technique are only indications. If the same message is received from several techniques that message starts to gain credibility' (Fawn and Cox, 1987). On the other hand, John Argenti (1989) says:

> 'I do not believe that directional policy matrices, computer models, assignment charts, or any of the dozens of other modern planning techniques, can inject the necessary level of belief and conviction into the

> average senior executive to be worth more than a passing mention in my book... What most [other authorities] have done, it seems to me, is to devise planning TECHNIQUES; they have not developed what I hope this book describes–an entire complete planning SYSTEM.'

John Chandler and Paul Cockle (1982) dismiss criticism of the use of models 'in the context of social sciences':

> 'We can ... assert that men think in terms of models [quoting K. W. Deutsch]. Only by mental manipulation of experience can rational decisions be made about future courses of action. Those who do not think in this way are called insane.

R.T. Lenz (1985) warns about excessive rationality:

> 'Although to some it may seem ironic, corporate planners are often victims of excessive rationality in planning. In their efforts to attain organizational respectability as vital contributors to strategic decision-making, the trappings of the 'science of planning' sometimes create a snare. The snare is slowly fashioned out of the increasingly intricate network of models, data, analytical techniques and formal procedures. If the process goes too far, these factors establish an intellectual cocoon of abstraction whose relationship to the administrative experiences of line managers is, at best, tenuous. Increasing sophistication can breed increasing irrelevance and the development of a ponderous planning apparatus.'

The value of techniques in the strategic planning process is as auxiliaries. Human beings think in terms of models and, as Ben Heirs (1989) demonstrates clearly, we use our experience, imagination and reason both to construct and interpret those models:

> 'The need to make sense of events and to construct a model of reality, which yields accurate and useful predictions about the future, is a fundamental human requirement. The obvious danger is that, faced with the monumental complexities of today's world, we may try to cope with them by devising models which are simplistic and artificially rigid, or by shutting our eyes to reality and constructing a model of the world which shows it as we would like it to be rather than as it actually is.'

Techniques can be helpful in assisting the process of thinking but they cannot be any substitute for that process.

As John Fawn points out, one value of techniques is to give credibility to a given model by multiple corroboration. One of the dangers in planning is to produce a model of one person's reality; techniques such as scenario planning help to remove idiosyncrasies and form wider-based judgements. The various matrix techniques and morphological analysis enable factors to be plotted spatially against different criteria. This can help to provide insights and establish meaningful patterns.

The building of scenarios is helpful in forcing managers to look outside their business and to identify the exogenous factors which may impact on it in a significant way. Building models helps to form working hypotheses of the inter-relationship between key factors within and outside the business. Both scenarios and models are likely to be considerably less than perfect but the challenge of building them helps to shape the internal model of the mind which in turn will refine the external models over time.

In all use of techniques it is important to be aware of Lenz's warnings. Planning is a process which seeks to identify and explore the issues facing a company. It is not a science and should not be prescriptive. Techniques should support the process but must not usurp it. In his article, John Robinson (1986) sets this memorably in context:

> We conclude that the job of the planner is not to state the objectives but to elicit them; is not to predict the future but to help understand it; is not to make the key decisions but to help managers do so; and is not to produce a plan so much as to conduct the planning process.

Scenarios

Traditional corporate planning systems have developed a single 'base case' and tested it for sensitivity to identify any weaknesses or factors imposing high risk on the outcome. The danger of the 'base case' is that it is consciously or unconsciously an extrapolation of past trends or is too much influenced by internal wishes. To think unconventionally is not always politically expedient in a business proud of its proven formulae for success and yet to 'think the unthinkable' is often crucial when a major discontinuity looms or a sudden change in predicted circumstances can wreck not just strategies but the companies which launched them.

In the late 1960s and early 1970s Pierre Wack of Shell developed a number of alternative scenarios for the future of the oil business. Scenarios were not new, Herman Kahn of the Rand Corporation had been writing scenarios in the 1950s, but Shell had taken scenarios to a higher level of sophistication. The insights obtained from Pierre Wack's work enabled Shell to foresee the likelihood of oil crises in 1973 and 1979 and, although these insights challenged received wisdom, they were accepted by the management.

As a result the technique of scenario planning has developed credibility and it provides a method of 'thinking the unthinkable' that is politically acceptable. Scenarios are basically qualitative in content, rather than complex numerical models, although variations of the technique generate and derive varying amounts of quantitative data.

While Herman Kahn was developing all-encompassing scenarios, his colleague Olaf Helmer developed the Delphi technique, which exploited a judgemental approach to forecasting. This technique itself is explained in a later section but has been developed into a scenario technique known as 'cross-impact analysis' which is explained below.

One key decision to be made in scenario planning is the number of scenarios to be developed. Theoretically the number is unlimited but the marginal value of extra scenarios declines rapidly. The minimum possible number is two and this has been championed by Peter Beck of Shell and has a strong following. Two scenarios imply that one is the 'base case' and the other the 'worst case'. The juxtaposition of these two scenarios provides, in practice, nearly all the insights that management really needs for the least expenditure of time, effort and money. Three scenarios were popular at one time but this forces attention on the middle position which can be chosen as the 'base case' almost by default. In an article in *Long Range Planning*, Stokke, Ralston, Boyce and Wilson (1990) describe the scenario planning used by Norwegian Oil and Gas ('Statoil') for R&D which develops four scenarios, reflecting four distinctive environments in which the company might have to operate in the long term. It would seem that four scenarios are near the practical limit for most purposes, although the CEGB developed five scenarios for the Sizewell enquiry (Figure A2.1) (Hankinson, 1986).

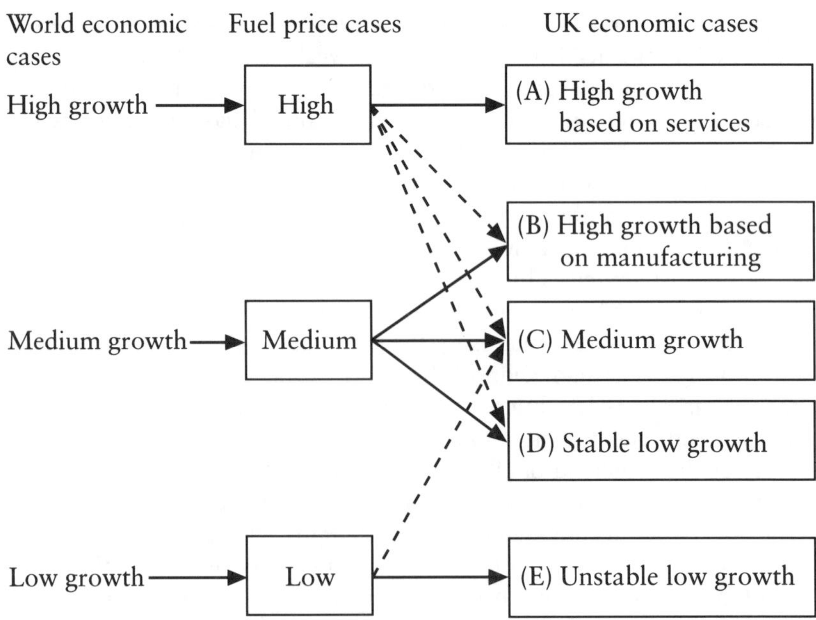

Figure A2.1 Scenario cases–world and United Kingdom (Hankinson, 1986)

It is interesting to note that scenario planning was developed primarily by companies with long planning horizons (oil companies, power utilities, etc.) since it is, in practice, virtually impossible to plan realistically for periods beyond five years without an imaginative and judgemental forecasting tool. The insights which protected Shell from the oil crises of the 1970s were obtained by scenario planning in the 1960s and given increasingly sharp focus as the critical moment approached. This does not invalidate short-term scenario planning, which is a highly effective form of sensitivity analysis at the least, but short-term plans tend to be rich in detail which may obscure deeper messages. Longer-term scenarios are not cluttered by familiar details and require considerable work to shape out of the unknown. This allows 'weak signals' to be picked up early and gives time for those signals to be monitored and validated as their meaning becomes more apparent.

Scenarios provide insights and assist the choice of strategies in the shorter term also. Dr Stephen Millett (1988) of Battelle identifies six such insights:

(a) Whether future demand for the company's existing products and services will expand, stay constant, or decline

(b) Whether market conditions are becoming more or less favourable to existing products and services

(c) Are there opportunities for new products and services which the company could provide?

(d) Whether there are changes in technologies affecting the mode of producing products and services

(e) Whether there are changes in competition, including the possibility of substitute products and services

(f) What is the degree of uncertainty facing the company and how much flexibility is needed in choosing strategies?

There are numerous variants of scenario planning. In an article entitled 'Scenario planning: what style should you use?' William Huss and Edward Houton (1987) identify three major categories:

(a) Intuitive logics as described by Pierre Wack in his articles in *Harvard Business Review* and as systematized and practised by SRI International and Royal Dutch/Shell *inter alia*

(b) Trend-impact analysis as practised by the Futures Group

(c) Cross-impact analysis as practised by the Center for Futures Research (INTERAX) and Battelle (BASICS), etc.

SRI International defines scenarios as 'devices for ordering one's perceptions about alternative environments in which one's decisions might be played out'. Its method has the following steps:

Step 1–Analysing the decisions facing the company with long-range implications and the company's strategic concerns.

Step 2–Identifying the key factors affecting those decisions

Step 3–Identifying the key environmental forces shaping the key decision factors

Step 4–Analysing those key environmental forces

Step 5–Defining scenario logics (themes, principles and assumptions which shape the scenario)

Step 6–Elaborating the scenarios (combining logics with the environmental analyses)

Step 7–Analysing the implications for the key factors affecting the company's decisions

Step 8–Analysing the implications for the company's decisions and strategies.

The SRI International approach relies strongly on intelligent and perceptive teamwork but can produce flexible and internally consistent scenarios over extended periods.

Trend-impact analysis relies on an independent forecast of the chosen key dependent variable which is adjusted under the impact of events. The Futures Group uses the following steps:

Step 1–Select topic and identify the key scenario drivers, e.g. GNP, regulatory environment

Step 2–Create a scenario space, picking the likeliest combinations of drivers (one of which might be median GNP/loose regulatory environment)

Step 3–Identify important trends and collect time series data

Step 4–Prepare a naive extrapolation (using standard time series)

Step 5–Establish a list of impacting events (by scenario planning, Delphi or by literature search)

Step 6–Establish probabilities of events occurring over time, including years to first impact, years to maximum impact, level of maximum impact, years to steady state impact and level of steady state impact

Step 7–Modify naive extrapolation to reflect impacts

Step 8–Write narratives.

The Futures Group approach is useful since it combines traditional forecasting techniques with qualitative factors. It forces the identification of specific impacting factors and an evaluation of their probability and importance. It does not, however, evaluate the impact of events on each other and is based on one key variable which is quantified based on historical data.

Cross-impact analysis was developed as a method of interrelating intuitive forecasts. From this concept two major scenario planning methodologies have been developed–INTERAX (Interactive Cross-Impact Simulation) and BASICS (Battelle Scenario Imputs to Corporate Strategies). (See Figure A2.2.) INTERAX's approach consists of the following steps:

Step 1–Define the issue and time period of analysis

Step 2–Identify the key indicators (the primary variables to be forecast)

Step 3–Project the key indicators (using econometric models, etc.)

Step 4–Identify impacting events (Delphi, interviews, etc.)

Step 5–Develop event probability distributions over time period

Step 6–Estimate impacts of events on trends

Step 7–Complete cross-impact analysis (events on events, trend impacts of events on trends)

Step 8–Run the model (using Monte Carlo random selection of events) to build a set of probable future paths.

INTERAX combines the strengths of trend-impact analysis with those of cross-impact analysis. It also allows a picture to develop over time and corrections to be made in the light of events. There is a weakness in the random selection of events in the model and little identification of which scenarios are more likely than others.

BASICS does not use Monte Carlo simulation and does not require the independent forecast of key indicators in Step 3 of INTERAX. BASICS has the following steps:

Step 1–Define and structure the topic including unit of measure, time frame and geographic scope

Step 2–Identify and structure the areas of influence

Step 3–Define descriptors (refined from areas of influence), write essays

Generic scenario generation steps	*SRI*	*The Futures Group*	*INTERAX*	*BASICS*
The topic	1 Analysing the decisions and strategic concerns	1 Identify key scenario areas 2 Create scenario space	1 Define the issue and time period of analysis	1 Define and structure the topic
Key decisions	2 Identifying the key decision factors		2 Identify the key indicators	
Trend extrapolation		3 Collect time series data 4 Prepare naive extrapolation	3 Project the key indicators	
Influencing factors	3 Identifying the key environmental factors	5 Establish list of impacting events	4 Identify the impacting event	2 Identify areas of influence
Analysis of factors	4 Analysing the environmental factors	6 Establish probabilities of events occurring over time	5 Develop event probability of distributions	3 Define descriptors write essays assign initial probabilities

Figure A.2.2 Comparison of the stages included in each scenario analysis technique (Battelle). *Source*: Millett, 1988

Cross impact			6 Estimate cross-impacts 7 Complete cross-impact analysis	4a Complete cross-impact matrix
Initial scenarios	5 Defining scenario logics	7 Modify extrapolation	8 Run the model	4b Run the program 5 Select scenarios for further study
Sensitivity analysis				6 Introduce uncertain events conduct sensitivity analysis
Detailed scenarios	6 Elaborating the scenarios	8 Write narratives		7a Prepare forecasts
Implications	7 Analysing implications for key decision factors 8 Analysing implications for decisions and strategies			7b Study implications

Figure A.2.2 (Cont'd)

for each and assign initial probabilities of occurrence to each descriptor outcome or state

Step 4—Complete the cross-impact matrix and run the model

Step 5—Select scenarios for further study including the writing of narratives

Step 6—Introduce low probability but high impact events and conduct other sensitivity analyses

Step 7—Make forecasts and study implications.

BASICS generates scenarios which are consistent and likely to occur. It is structured using influencing variables ('descriptor states') and uncertain events, giving a broader set of outcomes and giving extra flexibility. Its main weakness is that it generates 'state' scenarios, i.e. the scenario at the end of the time frame. This means that work is needed to interpret the paths to the 'state' through the time frame of the forecast. The different approaches may be compared more readily by reference to Figure A2.2.

Another interesting approach to scenario planning is that developed at Reed International by John Chandler and Paul Cockle. Their system is described in detail in their book *Techniques of Scenario Planning* (1982); but in outline, it takes the plan offered by the managers who contributed to building it as a 'base case'. This plan is then subjected to changes to see how they and their underlying strategies respond. The system is seen as a wheel with the centre representing the company and the rim the external environment (see Figure A2.3). The operation of the system depends on the interaction of changes in scenarios upon a number of structured models (macro-economic, market demand, market supply) and a series of financial models representing the company. This is a very flexible system whose strength depends on the quality of the models, the building of which is described in great detail in the book.

Scenario planning is a demanding exercise and difficult to justify for smaller companies. Its real benefits are derived over the longer term, providing insights which might be difficult to obtain without the discipline of the technique. Scenario planning also helps to set boundaries to uncertainty and risk and to help in the evaluation of strategic options. Most importantly it can be a powerful stimulus to strategic thinking particularly when it involves numerous people in that most demanding and yet rewarding of mental exercises and spreads ownership of the insights achieved.

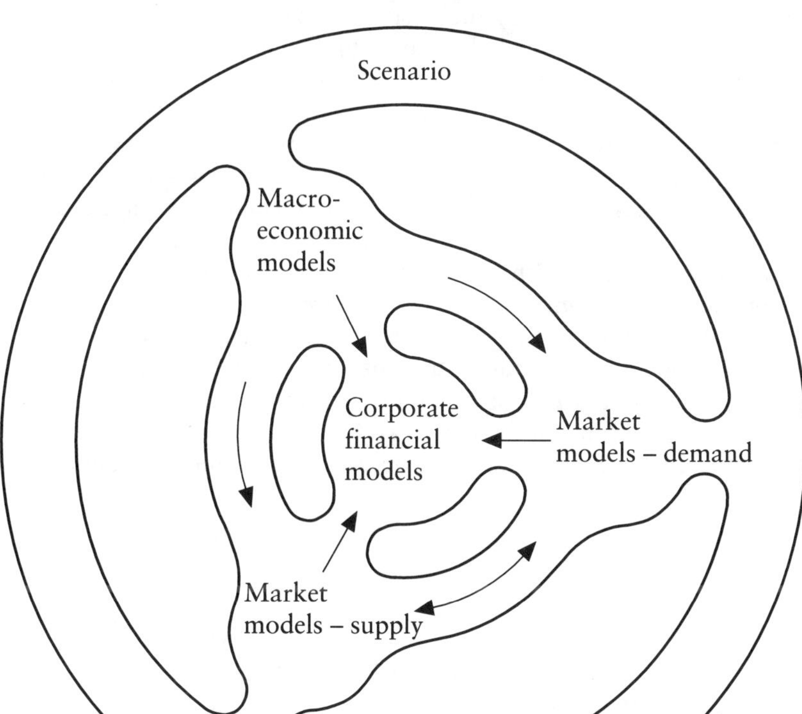

Figure A2.3 Transmission of influence through the planning system (Chandler and Cockle, 1982)

Analysis tools

Planners have long been interested in refining and using techniques to assist them in the development of strategies. A key stage in that process is the analysis of all available data in order to shape judgements. Tools to assist analysis include the following.

Experience curve

This tool was developed by the Boston Consulting Group and helps to quantify the well-established observation that as production increases, unit costs fall to a certain irreducible level. It is to be expected that when production doubles, unit costs will fall by a given percentage, characteristically 20 to 30 per cent. The working of the experience curve is recognized by Michael Porter, who emphasizes that it is valid for most business activities, not just production. John Argenti points out the danger of taking experience curve theory as a justification for maximizing market share by acquisition which has not always been successful in practice. In his article 'The uses and abuses of experience curves' Jean-Paul Sallenave (1985) demonstrates examples of experience curves derived from his computer model. He concludes that they can provide insights and early warnings but should not be taken too literally due to limitations in the quality of input data and the difficulty of making cross-comparisons with competitors whose technology and operating conditions may differ from yours.

Matrices

The classic tool of portfolio analysis (deciding in which businesses to invest) is Boston Consulting Group's 'Directional Policy Matrix (DPM)'. This is a two-dimensional matrix setting relative market share against business growth rate and is divided into four quadrants (see Figure A2.4) (Grieve-Smith, 1985):

- 'Stars' are businesses which are growing rapidly and whose cashflow is at least in balance.
- 'Cows' are well-established businesses which generate surplus cash.
- 'Dogs' are likely to have low profits and should be disposed of, especially if needing further investment.
- 'Question marks' may become 'Stars' if cash is invested to increase relative market share or may become 'Dogs' if growth should fall.

The individual businesses of a company can be located in the matrix and the shape of the portfolio estimated at some future time if certain strategies are followed. The DPM is a useful if simplistic tool for bringing out issues but its assumption that maximizing market share is always advantageous in terms of profitability is dangerous. The DPM has been developed further by BCG and others.

One development is the 'Directional Policy Matrix' of Robinson, Hichens and Wade (1978), which merges a number of key factors into two factors,

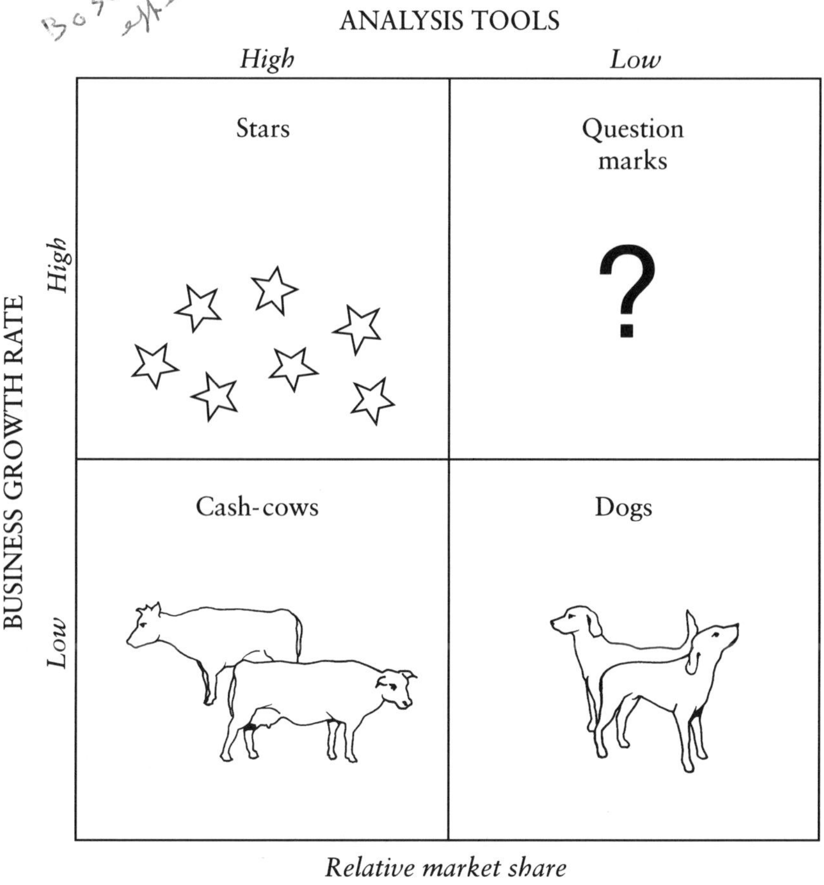

ANALYSIS TOOLS

High *Low*

Stars

Question marks

?

Cash-cows

Dogs

BUSINESS GROWTH RATE *High* *Low*

Relative market share

Figure A2.4 The BCG matrix (Grieve-Smith, 1985)

the business sector prospects and the business position of the company. The matrix is again two-dimensional but has nine boxes (see Figure A.5).

The principle is similar to the Boston DPM but the build-up of factors is more complex and the savings more nuanced. Given matrices for competitors the search for competitive advantage can be both structured and creative. It is also possible to project an ideal portfolio and determine how to move towards it.

A more comprehensive matrix is that of Hofer which plots competitive position against 'stage of product/market evolution'. A typical Hofer matrix is shown in Figure A.6 (Hofer and Schendel, 1978).

A more financially driven matrix is that of Patel and Younger. This plots the Return on Net Assets against Internal Deployment of Funds (i.e. the percentage of funds generated which are reinvested in the particular

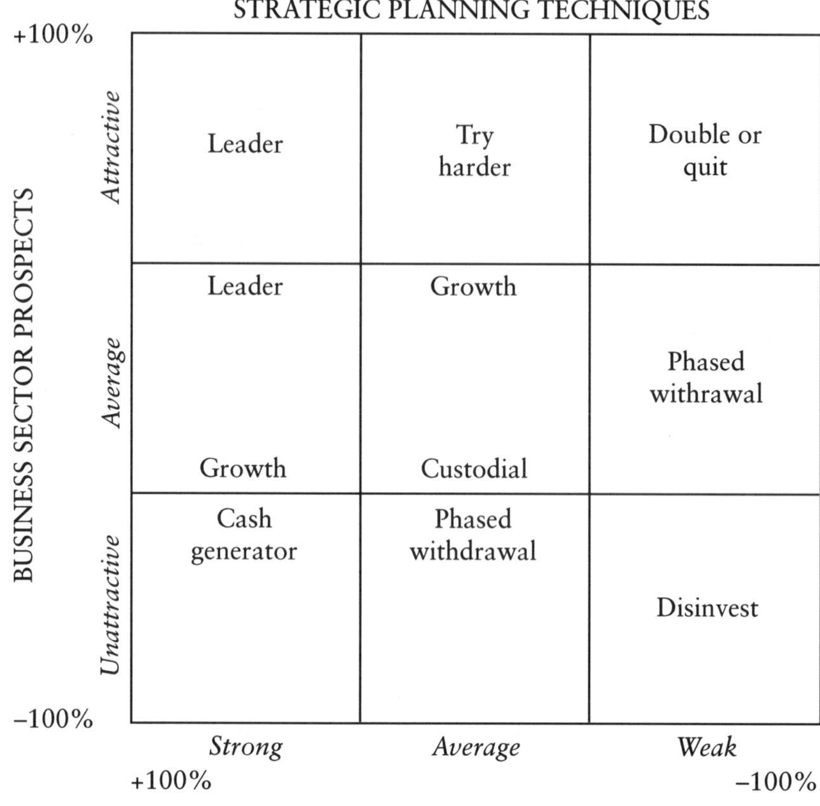

Figure A2.5 A company's competitive positions (Robinson *et al.*, 1978)

business). Businesses are categorized as 'embryonic', 'growing', 'mature' and 'ageing' and are plotted on the matrix as shown in Figures A2.7 and A2.8.

Matrices are a convenient way of displaying quantitative information spatially and of seeing situations in relative terms. They have an impact which raw figures lack and are as much a means of presentation as an aid to creative thought. (Examples in this section are taken from Patrick McNamee's article in *Long Range Planning* (1984)).

Profit Improvement of Market Strategy (PIMS)

The Strategic Planning Institute was set up in 1975 and has developed an increasingly sophisticated database of individual strategic business units covering a wide range of manufacturing, extractive and service businesses.

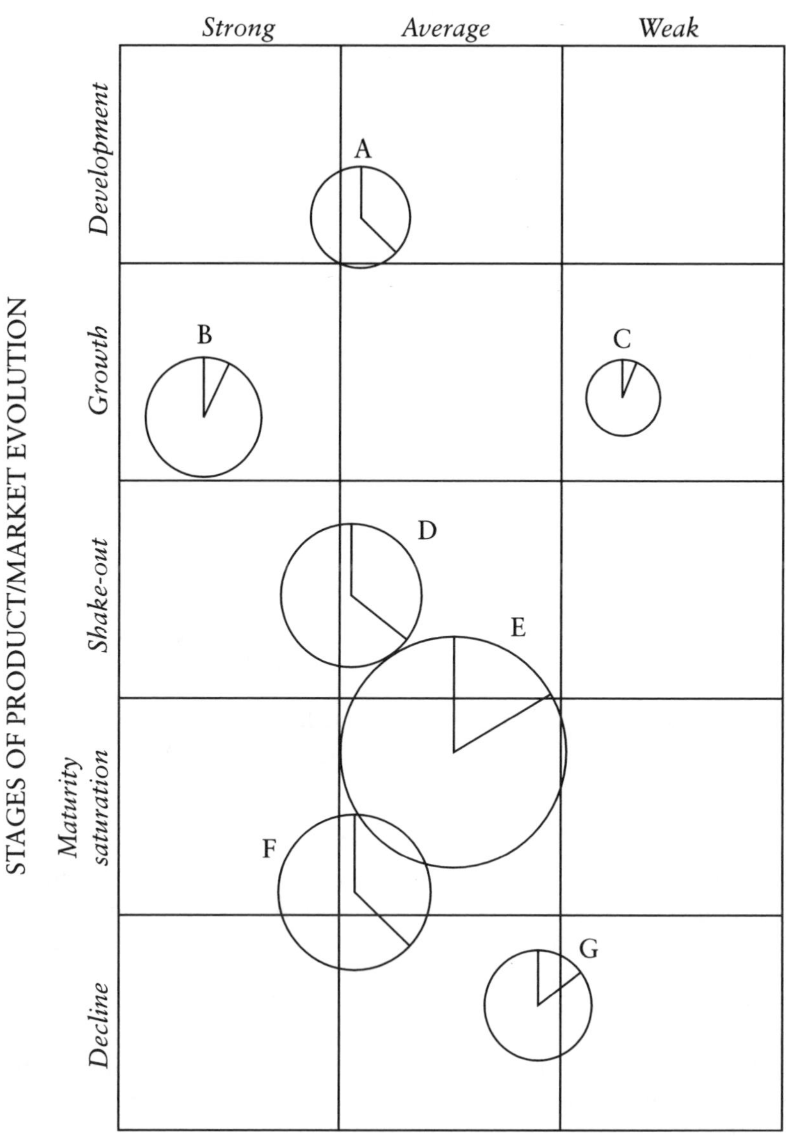

Figure A2.6 The Hofer matrix (Hofer and Schendel, 1978)

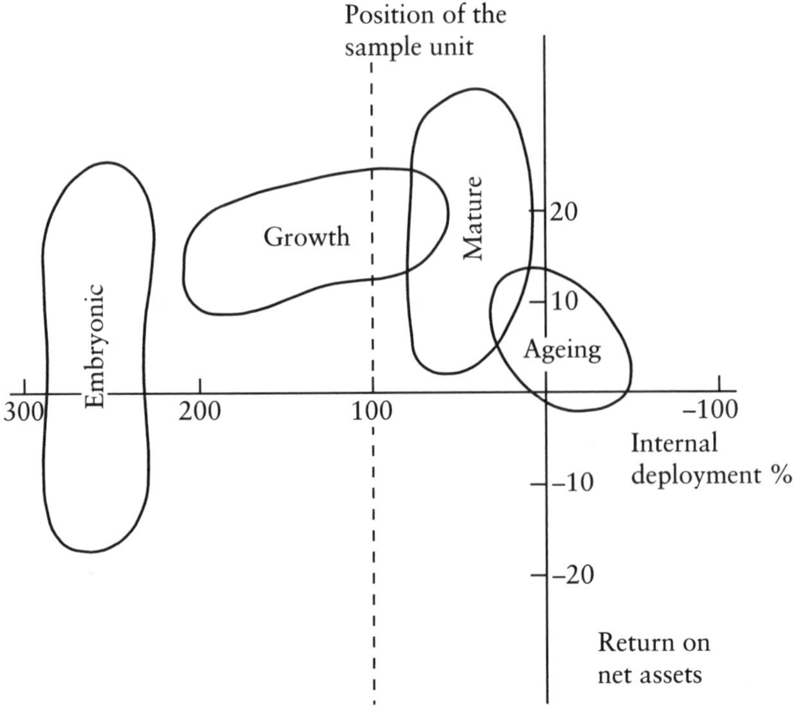

Figure A2.7 Patel and Younger's profitability and cash position matrix (McNamee, 1984)

The information recorded on each business includes its market environment, competitive position, state of competition and structure of its production process. The strategic moves made by the business over at least the last five years and its operating results are also logged. The database comprises more than 2500 distinct businesses in the USA and Europe and is used to generate global strategies by identifying the global potential of the industry in which a particular business operates, the extent of that business' and its competitors' globalization, the appropriate level and type of globalization for the business and its capacity for sustaining a global strategy. The steps involved are:

(a) Work with participants in the programme to identify the business and countries to be studied

(b) SPI staff spend time on site to help collect the data

(c) SPI staff help manage the data collection process to completion

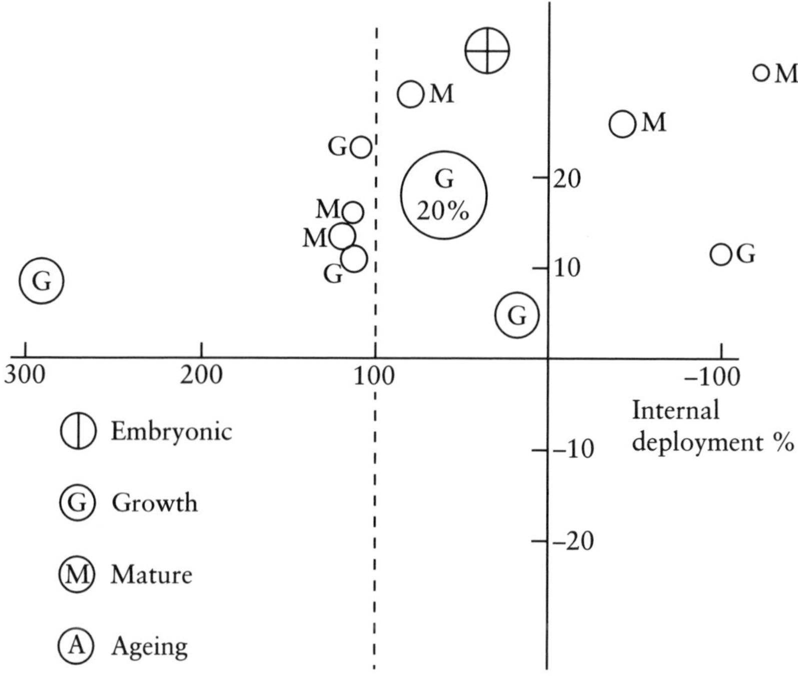

Figure A2.8 Patel and Younger's profitability and cash position matrix of a corporation by business unit (McNamee, 1984)

(d) Conduct a data review session

(e) Analyse the global data against the PIMS global strategy framework

(f) Analyse the core data against the PIMS database of over 2500 business units

(g) Develop and present strategy recommendations.

In an article entitled 'PIMS: a tool for developing competitive strategy' (1984), R. G. Wakerly of PIMS Associates claims that PIMS research has identified some 30 major universal factors which, taken together, explain some 70 per cent of the profitability variations between businesses on the database. These factors relate to the 'shape' of businesses and not to their products. In particular they relate to the structural characteristics of an industry (e.g. growth rate), the competitive position of the specific business (e.g. market share and quality rating), and capital and labour productivity (e.g. capital intensity).

Wakerly quotes Bismarck: 'Fool you are to say you learn from your own experience. I prefer to profit by others' mistakes and avoid the price of my own.' The PIMS database constitutes a unique record of business experience on a wide scale. It has been found to give useful pointers to many companies and has no doubt saved many of them from expensive mistakes. Whether PIMS is a substitute for the learning curve of experience is more debatable.

Value chain

The value chain is a concept which has been popularized by Michael Porter though it has been used in various guises by consulting firms for some years. The value chain represents the selling price of a given product broken down into its various elements (cost of components, assembly costs, overheads and profit). This enables tactical make-or-buy decisions to be made, and provides a basis for evaluating vertical integration and acquisitions. The manufacturer of a final product might examine carefully the value chain of a supplier and conclude that he could run that business more profitably. He might equally look at the economics of distributing his product and find synergy in that direction. Value chain analysis can also be a timely warning of danger. Christopher Clarke (1989) quotes an example of a manufacturer of power semiconductors who was interested in forward integration by acquiring a leading manufacturer of variable speed drives. Value chain analysis showed that the power semiconductor was only 4 per cent of the value chain of the variable speed drive manufacturer. This meant that the benefit to the value chain of that manufacturer of even a 50 per cent fall in the cost of power semi-conductors would not be significant.

Force field analysis

Force field analysis is a technique for evaluating forces affecting change which was developed by social scientist Kurt Lewin in the early 1950s. It involves a careful analysis of internal and external forces supporting and resisting a specific change targeted by an organization. These are mapped against the present equilibrium point and the desired equilibrium point after the targeted change has been achieved. Examples of the types of forces involved are shown in Figures A2.9 (Ajimal, 1985) and A2.10 (Thomas, 1985); (the lengths of the arrows indicates the relative impact of each force).

An interesting case study in the use of force field analysis is written up by Dr Joe Thomas in *Long Range Planning* (see above). It is admitted that the use of the technique for strategic planning has been limited so far but force field analysis can provide useful insights. It is a technique which is

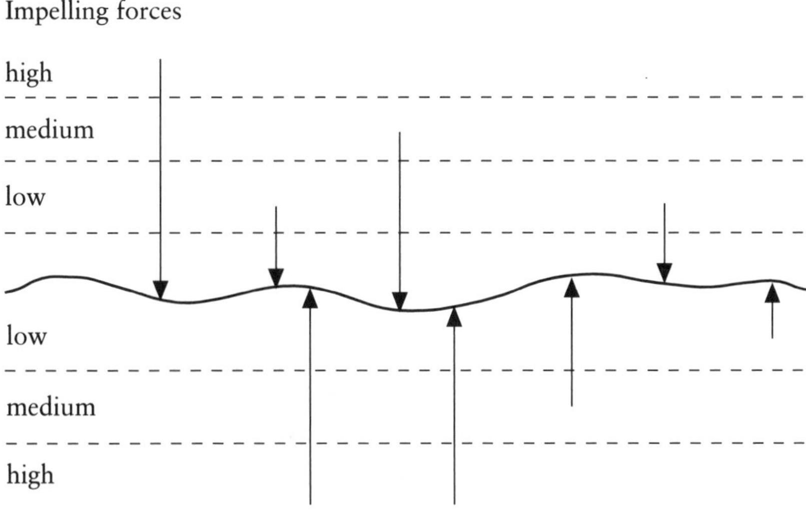

Figure A2.9 Force fields (Ajimal, 1985)

best practised by a group both to remove individual bias and to widen ownership of the possible solution.

Delphi

Delphi is a method of forecasting based on structured interaction between chosen experts. It avoids direct confrontation between the experts which is a recognized weakness of panel discussions and is based on a series of face-to-face interviews or anonymous questionnaires. These seek reactions to hypothetical future events in a structured form which allows a statistical pattern of probability to be derived. The process is renewed, showing the range of answers and inviting respondents to revise their estimates. Interaction continues until a meaningful consensus develops.

The Delphi technique is valuable as an intuitive approach to forecasting and complements more mechanistic techniques, such as extrapolating past trends, using heuristic models based on a causal mechanism or morphological analysis (see below). Although the technique uses statistical methods to drive for a consensus, it does allow for comments which challenge and may change the basis of that consensus. Its main

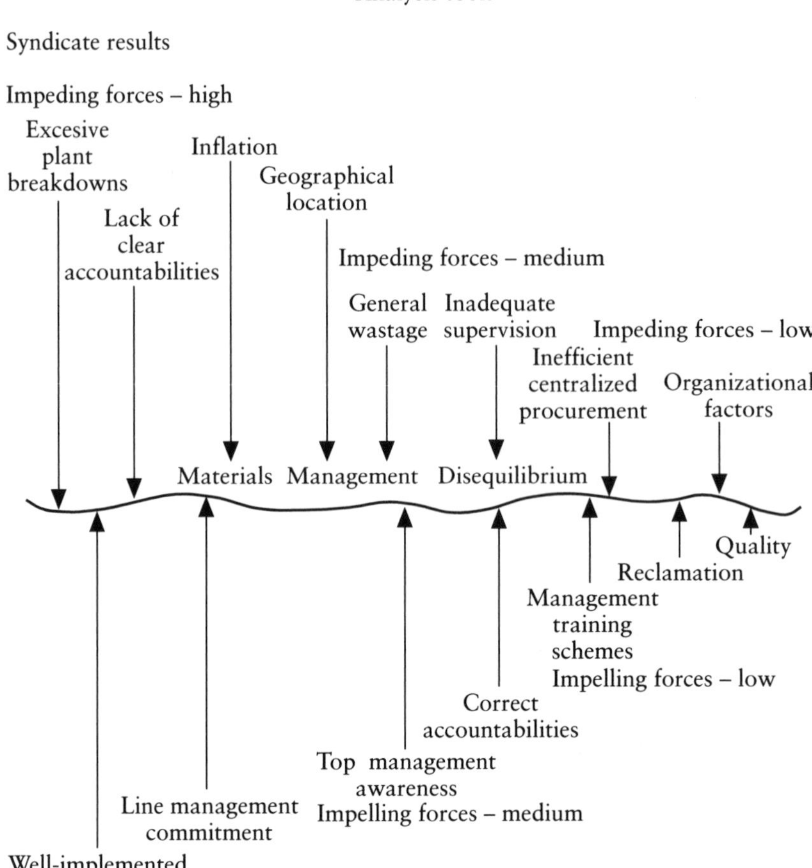

Figure A2.10 A force field analysis of a materials management problem (Thomas, 1985)

potential weakness is the ability of experts to foresee discontinuities in their area of expertise which are driven by factors outside the scope of their specialisation. Much of the skill lies in the formulation of the questions put to the experts and these should allow for such outside eventualities wherever possible.

Morphology

Russ Shurig (1984) characterizes morphology as 'a technique for lateral thinking, for interdisciplinary problem solving, prophecy or forecasting, fundamental research and creative speculation'! The *Concise Oxford English Dictionary* defines morphology as 'the study of the form of words' (and, in biology, of plants and animals). Morphology is essentially a method of classification, e.g. the periodic table of chemical elements, which is very comprehensive and painstaking. The technique is often used for innovation since it is wide-sweeping and well-structured and is non-numeric in concept, even though numeric values may be attached to its results.

A simple example of morphological analysis is provided by Shurig in respect of information media, analysed against each other in their order of historical evolution, and analysed against the needs of the modern office (Figures A2.11 and A2.12). An analysis of this type assists the differentiation of information and knowledge. Knowledge is meaningful information and is derived by the use of human reason. To equate information with knowledge is to equate machines with people. Knowledge is a specifically human faculty and only human beings can turn information into knowledge. 'Computers, telecommunications and databases are information tools whereas human brains, languages and morphology are knowledge tools' in the words of Russ Shurig.

Wargames

Like the concept of strategy, wargames are another contribution from the military to business practice. Wargames have been developed by most major powers as an aid to strategic and tactical decision making and as a valuable training tool for staff colleges. The analogy between the operational circumstances and objectives of military and business is strikingly similar in Figure A2.13, taken from Ginter and Rucks (1984).

Wargames are models based on military, political and scientific principles. Some factors in the model can be quantified accurately, e.g. artillery rates of fire, other factors are more variable or indeterminate. Like scenarios and models used for corporate planning, wargames need to have a framework of assumptions and judgement can be tested by varying these.

In practice most of the business models are built on a smaller scale and have less exogenous factors than military wargames. This is partly a function of cost but also due to difficulties in making such models 'user friendly' to decision makers. Staff officers see wargames as central to their practical needs; decision makers in business see them all too often as a theoretical self-indulgence of planners and a head-office overhead.

Strategic planning techniques

Information media preferences

	Voice (24,000 BC)	Image (12,000 BC)	Text (6,000 BC)	Data (3,000 BC)
Voice	(Voice is a medium for personal contact)	People prefer the use of speech rather than text, image or data when message is urgent, informal or personal		
Image	Message cannot easily be verbalized but can be displayed pictorially	(Image is a medium for visual display)	Message is complex, precise, external in origin or signed	Message is intricate or overview is needed or impact is important
Text	Message is complex or hard copy record is needed	Message is brief and/or verbal in nature	(Text is a medium for the preservation of thought)	Message is qualitative and/or non-numeric
Data	The use of data is preferable to the use of voice, image or text when the message is quantitative or precise			(Data is a medium for the preservation of measurement)

Figure A2.11 Comparison of information media with each other (Shurig, 1984)

	Information technologies			
	Voice	Image	Text	Data
Voice	Telephone Audio conferencing Audio processing Voice messaging	Audio graphics Video conferencing Picture phone	Dictation Voice annotation Display phone Text-to-speech	Voice recognition Voice ordering Voice I/O
Image		Micrographics Image processing Facsimile Photocopy Video	Fiche base Videotex Electronic blackboard Telecommuting Photocomposition	Graphics Computer aided drafting Aperture card base Optical character recognition
Text			Word processing Teletext Text messaging TWX/telex Electronic mail Text processing	Text base Computer conferencing Word processing and data processing
Data				Database Computation Data processing Electronic banking

Figure A2.12 User needs and application areas or technology information media combinations (Shurig, 1984)

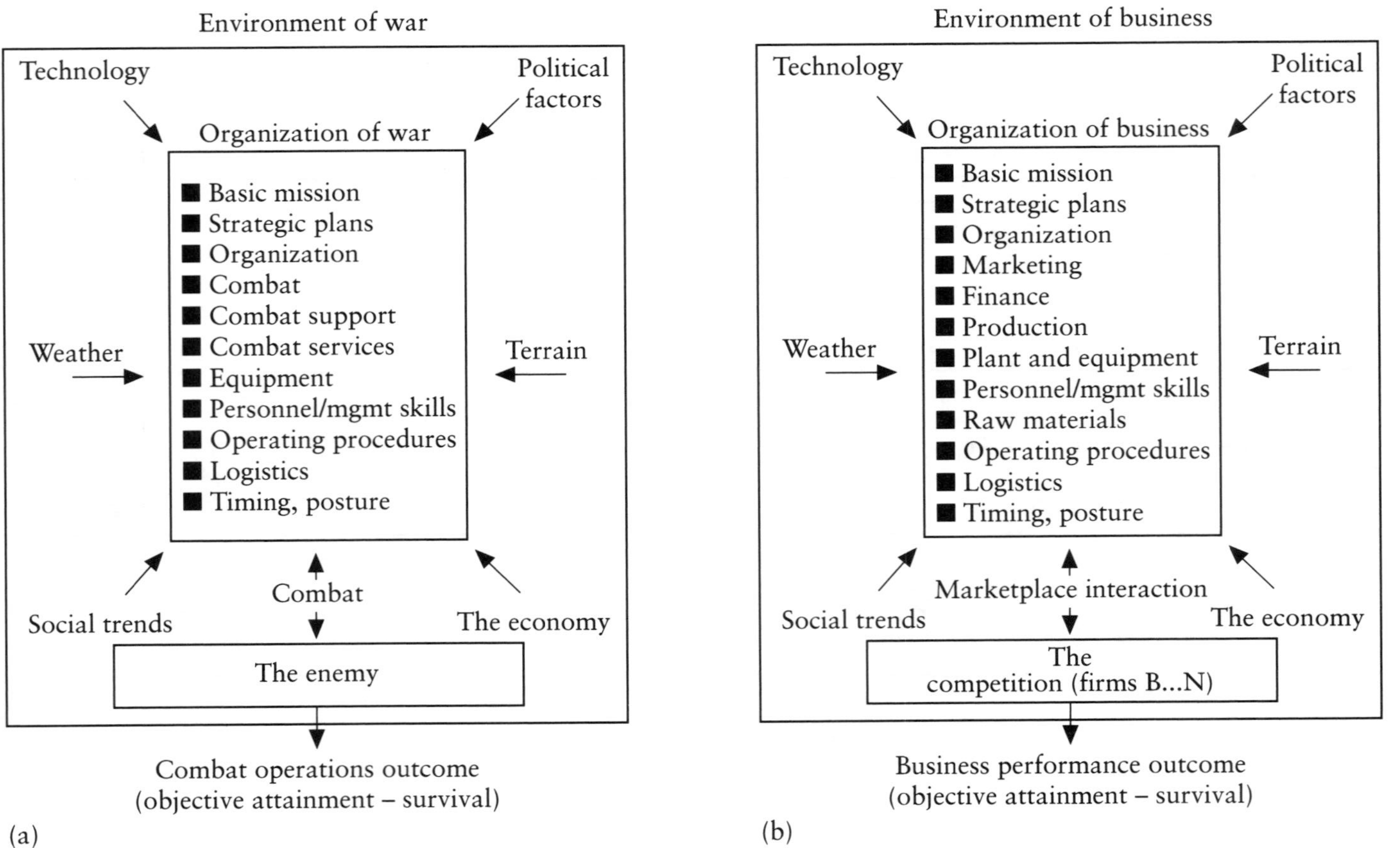

Figure A2.13 The military-business analogy (Ginter and Rucks, 1984)

Modelling

Earlier in this section we have referred to models which are attempts to formulate the relationship between different factors in order to predict a probable outcome. Models may be no more than equations which have been developed, tested and found to be useful. In these days of considerable computer power, models are more often developed to run on computers and may be of considerable complexity.

Models have often been developed initially to reflect the conventional accounting framework within which most businesses are managed. Such models enable the dynamics of the company's management and financial accounts to be captured and are mainly monetary in nature. Many companies use such models for budget building and budgetary control and the relationship between the different parameters in the model is usually established by convention or experience.

When models are developed for use in strategic planning it becomes necessary to distinguish between factors which the company can control and those outside its control. For the former norms have to be established and built into the model; for the latter assumptions have to be made and quantified for use in the model. In each case the relationship between parameters needs to be defined and expressed as a set of linear and non-linear differential equations.

In an article entitled 'Using computer models in corporate planning' (1989) Dr Kumar and Professor Vrat identify the following models classified by modelling strategy:

(a) Optimization models (to identify the optimum among alternatives)

(b) Econometric models (to forecast performance in the light of exogenous variables)

(c) System dynamics models (which bring feedback into consideration)

(d) Simulation models (used to imitate the realities of the system)

Models are also classified by Kumar and Vrat according to their characteristics:

(a) Deterministic models (with fixed values and no randomness)

(b) Probabilistic models (with multiple estimates with at least one operating characteristic given by a probability density function)

(c) Static models (which do not explicitly take the time variable into account)

(d) Dynamic models (which include time varying interactions)

Classifications by methods of consolidation and the existence of recursive models, simultaneous models and logical models are also recognized.

The main areas of application for models include forecasting and scenario generation, evaluation of alternatives ('what ifs'), budgeting, cash planning, investment and financial planning.

Kumar and Vrat suggest that system dynamics modelling offers considerable potential advantage for corporate planning, providing a 'flexible framework within which to view the interdependent operations of a system in a coherent and orderly manner'. Building such a model is an iterative process with seven identifiable steps:

(a) Problem identification and definition

(b) System conceptualization

(c) Model formulation

(d) Analysis of model behaviour

(e) Model evaluation

(f) Policy analysis

(g) Model use and policy implementation

Schematic diagrams of systems dynamics modelling are shown in Figures A2.14 and A2.15.

The advantage of such a model for corporate planning lies in its 'causal view of reality' enabling it to break away from past patterns of behaviour by searching out meaningful patterns of interaction between individual components of the system which are often highly non-linear.

Models are also used for other planning applications, including manpower planning. Users are mainly large employers with well-defined hierarchies, long service patterns and ongoing training needs. Such models are usually constructed to show manpower patterns at yearly intervals, based on past experience and projected ahead on structured assumptions. Manipulating such models can give a better insight into the dynamics of the manpower system and the results of possible policy changes. Models usually work on aggregate members rather than on identified individuals. The latter approach is difficult to work effectively and may be subject to the Data Protection Act 1984. Data in the model can only be really useful, however, if it is based on computerised personal records and kept up to date.

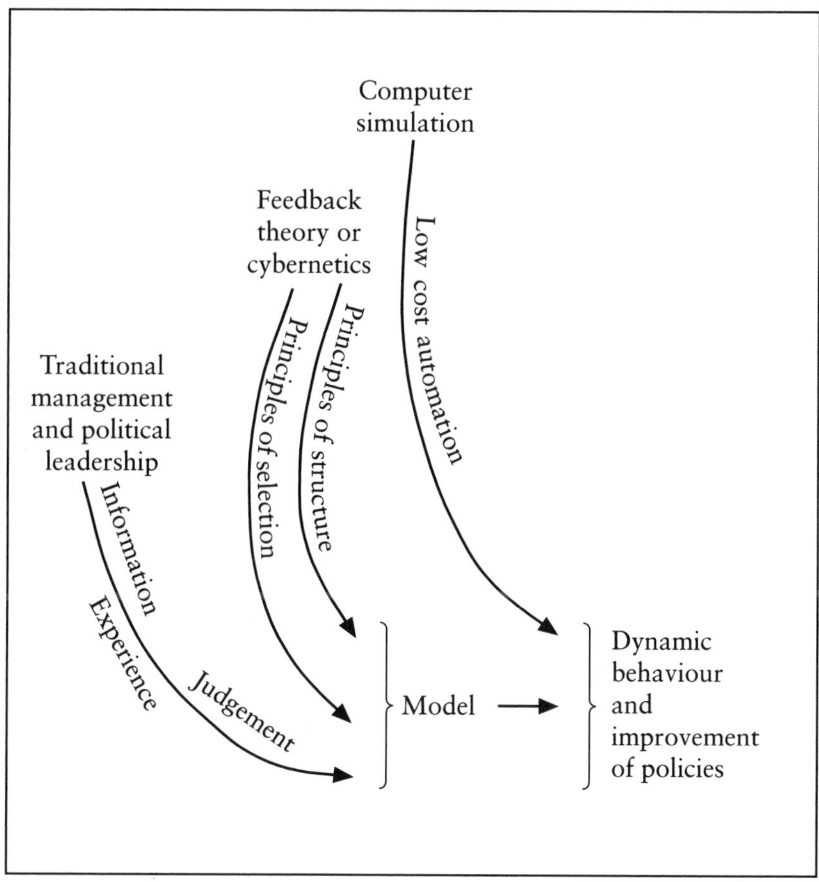

Figure A2.14 Background of the systems dynamics method (Kumar and Vrat, 1987)

Portfolio analysis

Earlier we examined the application of matrices, based on the BCG Growth Rate Market Share matrix. Such matrices are used for gap analysis and, by mapping competitor data, for competitive analysis. They are also a key tool in portfolio analysis.

The theory behind portfolio analysis is that the company is an investor in a number of businesses and attempts to optimize its return over the long run by a skilful choice of businesses which are diversified to spread risk and meet seasonality, and are at different stages of development to ensure

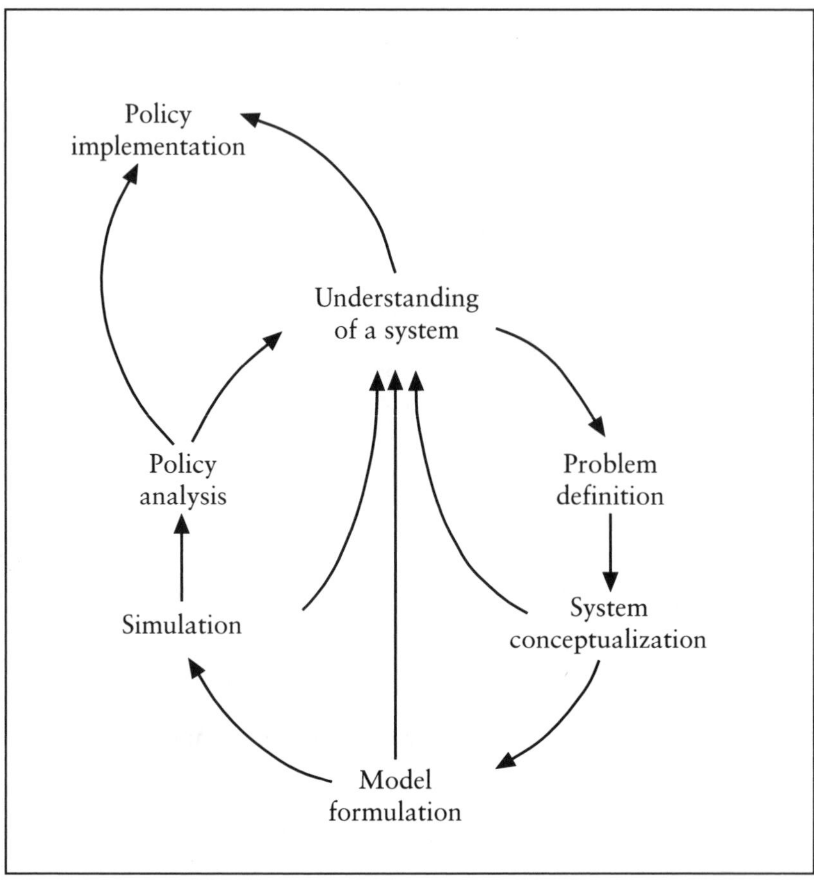

Figure A2.15 Overview of the systems dynamics modelling approach (Kumar and Vrat, 1987)

continuity. This theory was manifested in the earlier conglomerates, most of which have now disappeared or have been restructured. New conglomerates such as Hanson, concentrate on mature businesses and avoid commitment to cash-hungry 'start-ups' or high-technology businesses requiring heavy research and development expenditure. The earlier concept has now evolved into 'portfolio management' which requires involvement in running the businesses rather than mere investment. To adapt portfolio analysis to make it contribute to a practical operation planning system requires, in the view of Robert Walker, the resolution of the following problems:

(a) The business units have to be defined fully

(b) The validity of available data is at best variable

(c) The growth rate market share (GRMS) matrix does not show in itself how the company intends to respond to the environment in terms of sales

(d) The response in terms of returns and profits is similarly not portrayed

(e) Only one competitor is considered for each business in the GRMS matrix

(f) A full profile of competitors is not provided

(g) The varied characteristics of fragmented as opposed to concentrated markets are not differentiated

(h) Differing market and competitive situations in the multinational environments are not considered.

This approach interlinks portfolio analysis with competitive analysis and adds an extra degree of realism. As John Grieve-Smith (1985) says:

> 'The limitation of portfolio analysis is that it is primarily concerned with which individual businesses should comprise the corporation, rather than how they are run, or even their individual long-term strategies (save in the very restricted sense as to whether they are to expand, be run down or even liquidated).'

Other limitations of portfolio analysis have been pointed out by Derkinderen and Crum (1984). Because the technique is largely focused on cashflows, there is no easy way to reflect the effect of non-financial factors such as skill shortages, knowhow, management capability, and 'resilience'. The latter comprises the risk and endurance profile of the company and is crucial to the choice of sustainable and robust strategies. Portfolio analysis is therefore only one of a series of tools needed to analyse the strategy challenges of diversified companies, and is normally used to give pointers to areas where intensive work is likely to be fruitful. Linking portfolio analysis with competitive analysis to achieve a more involved 'portfolio management' approach is likely to provide better insights but is no substitute for full analysis of key businesses, markets, competitors and products.

References

Ajmal, K.S., 'Force field analysis: a framework for strategic thinking', *Long Range Planning*, October 1985.

Argenti, J., *Practical Corporate Planning*, Unwin Hyman, London, 1989.

Carson, R., *Silent Spring*, Penguin, Harmondsworth, 1982.

Chandler, J. and Cockle, P., *Techniques for Scenario Planning*, McGraw-Hill, New York, 1982.

Clarke, C., 'Acquisitions: techniques for measuring strategic fit', *Long Range Planning*, June 1989.

Derkinderen, F. and Crum, R., 'Pitfalls of using portfolio techniques, assessing risk and potential', *Long Range Planning*, April 1984.

Fawn, J. and Cox, B., *Corporate Planning in Practice*, Kogan Page, London, 1987.

Ginter, P. and Rucks, A., 'Can business learn from wargames?' *Long Range Planning*, June 1984.

Grieve-Smith, J., *Business Strategy: An introduction*, Blackwell, Oxford, 1985.

Hankinson, G.A., 'Energy scenarios: the Sizewell experience', *Long Range Planning*, October 1986.

Heirs, B., *The Professional Decision Thinker*, Grafton, London, 1989.

Hofer, C. and Schendel, D., *Strategy Formulation: Analytical concepts*, West Publishing, St Paul, MN, 1978.

Huss, W. and Houton, E., 'Scenario planning: what style should you use?' *Long Range Planning*, August 1987.

Kumar, R. and Vrat, P., 'Using computer models in corporate planning', *Long Range Planning*, April 1989.

Lenz, R. T., 'Paralysis by analysis', *Long Range Planning*, August 1985.

McNamee, P., 'Competitive analysis using matrix displays', *Long Range Planning*, June 1984.

Millett, S., 'How scenarios trigger strategic thinking', *Long Range Planning*, October 1988.

Robinson, S.J.Q., 'Paradoxes in planning', *Long Range Planning*, December 1986.

Robinson, S.J.Q., Hitchens, R.E., and Wade, D.P., 'The directional policy matrix: tool for strategic planning', *Long Range Planning*, June 1978.

Sallenave, J.-P., 'The uses and abuses of experience curves', *Long Range Planning*, February 1985.

Shurig, R., 'Morphology: a tool for exploring new technology', *Long Range Planning*, June 1984.

Stokke, P.R., Ralston, W.K., Boyce, T.A., and Wilson, D.P., 'Scenario planning for Norwegian oil and gas', *Long Range Planning*, April 1990.

Thomas, J., 'Force field analysis: a new way to evaluate your strategy', *Long Range Planning*, December 1985.

Wakerly, R. G., 'PIMS: a tool for developing competitive strategy', *Long Range Planning*, June 1984.

Glossary

Some of the terms used in strategic management may not be familiar to all readers and many have been corrupted by lax usage. The following is an attempt to find working definitions, using authorities such as the Strategic Planning Society where possible, and offered on my own responsibility where necessary. In some instances other definitions are given in the text (e.g. mission).

Strategic planning

The following definitions have been prepared by Basil Denning and approved by the Strategic Planning Society.

Corporate Purpose: The social and economic justification of an organization In a free society the variety of organizational purposes is legion, (e.g. a bank, an airline, a university, a club, a professional society, a charity). Virtually all organizations have one dominant purpose which is common, namely, autonomous survival. One condition of autonomous survival in all organizations is some threshold level of performance which attracts sufficient resources (financial and others) for survival. Once that threshold is achieved, a wide variety of value-orientated purposes may be generated (e.g. becoming a technical leader, maximizing profits, achieving pre-eminence in a field of learning, meeting family needs). These value-generated purposes will be a reflection of the values of the directing group.

Strategic Vision A short succinct statement of what the organization intends to be at some point in the future. This should embrace key areas of activity, geographical scope, size and shape, and distinctive competences. Vision acts as a filter for corporate options.

Mission The core tasks which an organization intends to carry out to achieve the corporate purpose within the constraints of the corporate vision. It is often accompanied by a statement expressing a corporate philosophy to its employees and other stakeholders. In large or complex organizations missions are particularly valuable when applied to discrete units of the organization. This is sometimes achieved through the concept of a 'charter' for the XYZ division.

Corporate objectives A coherent set of desired achievements over an extended period which, if achieved, will make the organization what it wants to be, i.e. realizing its vision and thus fulfilling its purpose.

Strategy A coherent set of policies, programmes and projects which defines the path to be pursued. Strategy provides a framework for plans, should identify the competitive stance, and should reconcile trade-offs between conflicting objectives (e.g. growth and short-term profits). In a large complex organisation one will expect to find:

Corporate strategy – for the whole organization
Business strategy – for units of the organization
Functional strategy – for functions within the business units.

Policy A standing decision rule which gives guidance to those with executive responsibility on acceptable and unacceptable types of action.

Goal A specific desired achievement at a particular point of time. It will usually have a shorter time dimension than an objective and will often be a milestone on the road to an objective.

Programme A coherent, coordinated set of actions embracing a variety of tasks designed to achieve a goal (e.g. a productivity-improvement programme will embrace actions on machinery layout, training, work flow, and information technology).

Project An identifiable, specific increment to the existing pattern of operations capable of separate analysis, planning and control (e.g. a factory extension, an acquisition, a new product).

Target Short-term (frequently one year) specific desired achievements.

Financial projection The best guess at possible financial results (usually over a 3-5-year span).

Budget The short-term financial plan (usually one year).

Corporate planning The organizational process within which strategic planning, major project planning and the forward planning of ongoing operations are integrated.

Strategic planning The organizational work and process through which purpose, vision, missions, objectives, strategy, major policies and key goals are developed in a systematic way. Strategic planning in large complex organizations is required to develop:

Corporate strategy
Business strategy
Functional strategy

Strategic planning should provide an integrative framework for other forms of planning and is a necessary preliminary to financial projection, project planning, operational planning and budgeting in any strategically managed organization.

Strategic control The organizational process which assesses or measures progress along strategic paths. It will rely heavily on monitoring milestones and achievement of key goals and tasks.

Budgeting The organizational process through which the first year of any plan period is quantified financially.

Capital budgeting The organizational process through which capital projects are evaluated, approved and the relevant sums are earmarked for disbursement at the appropriate time.

Financial control The monitoring of financial results against budget, both capital and operating.

Performance assessment The monitoring of performance, usually in the short term against targets and budgets.

Strategic management Finally, the expression 'Strategic management' has been coined over the last few years. What does it mean? The essentials of strategic management centre on the creation of a clear concept of purpose, vision and objectives at corporate level, the dissemination of these in a meaningful way, the development of relevant strategies, goals, policies, etc. right through the organization so that resultant action builds towards achievement of purpose, vision and objectives. Strategic management in large organizations is most likely to be expressed in effective and relevant processes of planning and control and in appropriate organizational structure and culture where strategic criteria are continuously and evidently applied. Strategic management also requires leadership–but that is another subject which requires another book with definitions. The random buzz-word generator is particularly active in that field at the moment!

Other terms used by strategic planners include:

Assumptions the expected status of key factors affecting the plan (e.g. interest rates).

Bottom-up plans plans prepared by operational/functional staff within a framework set for the business as a whole.

Chaos theory non-linear dynamics and how to cope with them.

Contingency plans action programmes to meet foreseeable events which may significantly affect the business.

Emergent strategy a strategy derived from an unforeseen opportunity or threat as opposed to a deliberate strategy.

Gap analysis the process of matching bottom-up and top-down plans.

Key action programme see **Programme**.

Risk analysis identifying potential risks and their possible effect on the business.

Sensitivity analysis testing the effect on plans of changing key assumptions.

Strategic benchmarking use of external best practice to set strategic goals.

Strategic direction the process of setting and pursuing a clear mission and objectives.

Strategic intent the single most compelling strategic objective of a business.

Strategic management accounting the techniques of accounting used to support strategic management.

Strategic objectives the limited number of very long-term objectives needed to accomplish the mission of the business.

Strategic process establishing mission, objectives and the strategies to achieve them and ensuring that these are effectively implemented.

Top-down plans plans prepared by the directors/managers of a business to reflect the objectives needed to be met and when to meet them.

Strategic marketing

Account management the process of building systematic and multilevel contacts with a customer.

Aspirational marketing the techniques of appealing to a customer's need to achieve self-improvement.

Direct marketing the process of engaging customers directly rather than through intermediaries or the use of media advertising.

Global marketing marketing addressed at global rather than just individual markets.

Internal marketing the process of creating client/supplier relationships within a business (total quality systems are based on internal marketing).

Marketing audit the review of marketing processes and effectiveness using independent external persons.

Marketing concept the philosophical basis of marketing, i.e. the search for a customer.

Offensive marketing the techniques for making the marketing process proactive.

Relationship marketing the techniques for maximizing ongoing customer relationships and repeat business.

Societal marketing an approach which focuses on the long-term well-being of the customer and of society rather than just the satisfaction of immediate needs.

Strategic marketing marketing directed to achieving sustainable competitive advantage.

SWOT analysis a process of evaluating the strengths and weaknesses of a business relative to the opportunities and threats that it faces in order to identify potential strategies.

Technical market research a technique which allows customers to evaluate potential products in the supplier's laboratory.

Time-based marketing an approach which focuses on the value of time (and timing) to the customer.

Word-of-mouth marketing the process of personal recommendation which is at the heart of marketing professional services and also powerful in other sectors.

Index

AA Autoquote, 111, 112
Aburdene, Patricia, 9
Account management, 196
Adaptation of plans, 60
Akers, John, 134
Alcon, 19
Aldi, 91, 123
Allan, John, 118
Alliance & Leicester Building Society, 110
Alliances, 91, 123
Aluminium manufacturers, 40
American Express (Amex), 28, 134
Amersham International, 28
Analysis tools, 173
Ansoff, Igor, 13
Argenti, John, 163, 174
Arndt, Johan, 81, 133, 134
Aspirational marketing, 150, 196
Assumptions, 46, 92, 98, 195
Audit committee (of the board), 139

Baker, Michael, 5, 9, 10, 94, 157
Baker Perkins (APV), 19
Ballantyne, David, 96
Banesto, 145
Bank of America, 17
BBA, 64
BCCI, 60
Beck, Peter, 166
Beckman, Bob, 69
Belbin, Meredith, 81
Benton, Peter, 69
Benchmarking, 29
Benetton, 153
Berlik, Leonard, 132
BET, 78, 107, 117
Bhide, Amar, 105
Biffa (Severn Trent), 117
Binney, George, 14
Black Death, 1
BMW, 44
Board approval of plans, 52
*Body Shop, The, 13, 14, 64
Boeing, 26
Bonoma, Thomas, 106
Booms and Bitner '7P' model, 96
Boots plc, 59, 121
Bordon, Neil, 94
Boston Consulting Group, The, 174
Bottom-up plans, 49, 56, 195
BP, 52, 97
Brands, 37, 85, 119, 121
British Aerospace, 72
British Airways, 14, 60, 143, 159
British and Commonwealth, 57, 139
British Antarctic Survey, 28
British Standards (BS 5750), 63
Britoil, 52
Brittan, Samuel, 3
Brookes, Richard, 106
BSA, 145
BTR, 17, 52, 117
Budgets, 53, 55
Bulmers Cider, 115
Buonaparte, Napoleon, 105, 125
Burmah Castrol, 26
Business Process re-engineering, 156

Campbell, Andrew, 14, 64
Canon, 29
Cap Gemini Sogetti, 144
Capital expenditure, 54
Cardin, Pierre, 68
Carson, Rachel, 61
Caterpillar, 28

CEGB (Sizewell enquiry), 166
Chandler, John, 164, 170
Changing the rules, 107
Chaos theory, 43, 196
Chevron Oil, 17
Choice, 11
Christopher, Martin, 96
Churchill Insurance Services, 111
Churchill, Winston, 146
Clarke, Christopher, 180
Clowes, Peter, 60
Coca Cola, 28, 129, 154
Cockle, Paul, 164, 170
Comet, 123
Competitive advantage, 21
Concorde, 65
Concurrent engineering, 137
Conglomerates, 17
Consumer panels, 10
Consumer rights, 61
Consumers, 6, 10
Consumerism, 61, 62
Consumers Association, The, 62, 150
Continental system, 3
Contingency plans, 47, 196
Cook, Thomas, 8
Cooperative Retail Services, 122
Coopers and Lybrand, 73
Corbishley, Douglas, 132
Corporate planners, 43, 44
Corporate purpose, 193
Corporate state, 3
Cost drivers, 25
Costco, 124
Courtaulds, 17
Critical Success Factors (CSFs), 40
Crocker Bank, 17
Cross-impact analysis, 167
Crum, R., 191

Daimler Benz, 144
Dark Ages, 2
Data sources, 36
Database marketing, 148
Davidson, Hugh, 71, 85, 155
Davies, Adrian, 33, 139, 142
Decomposing the centre, 131
Defence companies, 87
Delphi technique, 77, 166, 181
Denning, Basil, 193
Derkinderen, F., 191
Design, 83
Design Council, The, 84
Deutsche Aerospace, 144
Differentiation, 20, 24, 26, 117
Digital Equipment Company, 17, 79, 133
Dior, 83
Direct Line, 111, 112
Direct marketing, 196
Directional Policy Matrix ('DPM'), 174
Discount retailers, 123
Doyle, Peter, 4
Drivers in society, The, 65
Drucker, Peter, 4, 18
Dun and Bradstreet, 36
Dupont, 144

Economist Intelligence Unit, 36
EDS, 143
Electronic data interchange (EDI), 112, 152
Elida Gibbs, 72
Empowerment, 60
English Electric, 59
Entrepreneurial planning, 105
'Environmental wheel', 33, 34
Essex University database, 75
Euromonitor, 123
European Community, 3
Exel Logistics, 107, 125
'Existential organization', 14
Experience curve, 174
External environment, 35
Exxon, 53

Fawn, John, 163
Fifield, Paul, 140, 148, 155
Financial planning, 48, 77
Firstdirect, 28, 107
Flores, Fernando, 80
Force field analysis, 180
Ford, Henry, 163
Ford Motor, 124, 134, 154

Free trade, 3
Functional expertise, 72
Functional plans, 56, 57
Futures Group, 167, 168

Gap analysis, 51, 56, 99, 196
Gardner, Howard, 151
GATT, 3, 7, 63,
Gaymer Cider, 115
GEC, 17
General Electric (GE), 30
General Motors, 62, 133, 143
Gerstner, Lou, 134
Gillett, John, 134
Girobank, 107, 110
Global marketing, 130, 154, 196
Goals, 16
Goodwill, 37
Goodyear, 75
Goold, Michael, 16
Grieve-Smith, John, 191
Gulf Oil, 17
Guinness, 10, 62, 155

Haggerty, Patrick, 142
Hamel, Gary, 29, 141
Handy, Charles, 14, 127, 146, 150
Hanson, 17, 37, 51, 59, 117, 190
Harris, Lou, 14, 44, 64, 131
Harrison, Frank, 17
Hard Rock Cafe, 129, 154
Hart, Susan, 9, 10, 94, 157
Heineken, Freddie, 147
Heinz, H.J., 73, 78
Heirs, Ben, 164
Heller, Robert, 4
Henley Centre for Forecasting, 60
Hewlett Packard, 30, 144, 156
Hierarchy of plans, 56
Hill, Rowland, 19
Hitler, Adolf, 105
Hofer matrix, 175
Honda, 14, 127, 146, 150
Hotpoint, 59
Howie, Ian, 114
Hughes, Arthur, 148
Humble, John, 79

Iaccoca, Lee, 107
IBM, 71, 77, 84, 107, 133, 144
ICI, 17
ICL, 71
Implementation, 16, 53, 107
Information systems (IS), 77
Initial Towel Services, 118
Innovation, 55, 68
'Internal Communication Focus', 78
Internal marketing, 196
International Network Services, 127
Internet, 36, 148

Jaguar cars, 68, 84
Johnson, Samuel, 151
Jones, David, 72

Kaas, Philippe, 123
Kahn, Herman, 165
Kay, John, 107
Kennedy, John F., 55, 61
Key action programmes, 47, 100, 196
Key issues, 45
Kinsey, Joanna, 98
Komatsu, 13
Kotler, Philip, 152
Kumar, R., 187
Kwik Save, 123

Laing, Henry, model of segmentation, 125, 148
Laissez-faire, 3
Lambin, Jean-Jacques, 74, 102, 152
Law, relating to marketing, 62
Learning, 80, 150
Lennon, John, 101
Lenz, R.T., 164
Lever Brothers, 72
Leveraging alliances, 133
Leveraging control, 125
Leveraging differentiation, 117
Leveraging information, 121
Leveraging reach, 129
Leveraging value, 113
Levi's, 154
Levitt, Edward, 5, 11, 154
Lewin, Kurt, 180

Lewis, John (Partnership), 60, 122
Lifestyle segmentation, 125
Lindblom, L.E., 107
Lingrain, 155
Lipton Tea, 122
Listening, 80
Lloyds Bank, 28, 60
Lloyds of London, 28
Loblaw, 124
London International Group, 139
Logistics, 125
'Long Range Planning', 14
Lorenz, Christopher, 84, 154

Malthus, Thomas, 7
Manpower Inc., 136
Market research, 75
Marketing audit, 86, 139, 140, 197
Marketing, Chartered Institute of, 5, 63, 113, 156
Marketing concept, 59, 197
Marketing, definition of, 4, 5, 59
Marketing ethics, 63
'Marketing in developing countries', 98
Marketing mix, The, 76, 83
Marketing objectives, 93
Marketing, origin of, 4, 5
Marketing planning, 57, 89
Marketing quality, 139
Marketing research, 75
Marketing review, 90
Marketing strategies, 94, 97
Marks and Spencer plc, 26, 74, 122
Marlboro, 73, 122, 124
Marshall, Sir Colin, 143
Masefield, John, 2
Maslow, A., 14, 69, 150
Matrices, 174
Matrix organization, 84
Matsushita Corporation, 131
Matsushita, Konosuke, 48
McCarthy, E.J., 94
McCormick, Cyrus, 19
McDonald, Malcolm, 11, 89, 100, 102, 139, 156
McDonalds, 154
McGregor, Douglas, 60
McKinsey ('7S' Model), 65
McLuhan, Marshall, 129
Measurement, 101
'Megatrends', 8
Megatrends 2000, 9, 10
Mercantilism, 3
Merck, 144
Merrydown Wine, 107, 113
Merrill Lynch, 109
Microsoft, 84, 133
Michelin guide, 19
Midland Bank, 86, 108, 140
Migros, 122
Millett, Stephen, 167
Mills, David, 108
Minnesota Mining and Manufacture ('3M'), 11, 144
Mintzberg, Henry, 20, 43
Mission, 14
Mission statements, 159
Mitsui Corporation, 146
Modelling, 187
Mondial Assistance, 112
Monte Carlo simulation, 169
Monte dei Paschi, 145
Morgan Cars, 26
Morgan Crucible, 144
Morita, Akio, 84, 133
Morphology, 183
Motorola, 72, 79
Multilevel marketing, 118, 130

Nabisco, R.J.R., 134
Nader, Ralph, 6, 9, 62
Naisbitt, John, 8, 9, 69, 147, 155
National Heritage Fund, 151
National Lottery, 151
National Starch and Chemical, 107, 129, 155
Natwest, 17
Nestlé, 81, 85
Network marketing, 5, 155
New marketing, The, 106
Newman, Kevin, 109
NFC, 60
Nielsen, 121
Nissan, 131

Non-executive directors, 141
Novon, 123, 124

Objectives, 15, 45, 90
Ocean Group, 118
Offensive marketing, 71, 85, 197
Office of Fair Trading, 63
Ohmae, Kenichi, 13, 105, 131, 154
Olivetti, 83
Omron, 131
OPEC, 35
Options, 99
Ordnance Survey, 28
Ouchi, William, 64
Ownership, 100
Own-label products, 122, 123

Packard, Vance, 6, 61
Pascale, Richard, 64
Patel and Younger matrix, 178
Payne, Adrian, 96
Pepsi Cola, 154
Persil, 122, 124
Peters, Tom, 10, 11
Philips, 154
Planning cycle, 48
Planning framework, 49
Planning process, 49
Plans (drive business), 55
PLJ (ex-Beecham), 115
Porter, Michael, 18, 21, 26, 28, 117, 125
Portfolio analysis, 189
Post Office Counters, 28, 110
Pralahad, C.K., 29, 141
Process teams, 72
Proctor and Gamble, 85, 129, 155
Product managers, 84
Product, price, place, promotion
    ('Four Ps'), 94
Profit Impact of Marketing Strategy
    (PIMS), 77, 176
Programmes, 100, 194
Projects, 46
Purchasing and Supply, Chartered
    Institute of, 136
Purdey, Richard, 113
Purpose of business, 13

Quality, 63, 139

Reckitt and Colman, 37, 85, 129
Regional pivot, 130, 131
Relationship marketing, 5, 62, 77, 96,
    130, 134, 152, 197
Report on the Year 2000, 7
Resale Price Maintenance Act, 33
Resources, 46, 56
Resources analysis, 37
Resources evaluation, 38
Retailing, 122
Review of plans, 54, 101
Risk analysis, 46, 196
Robinson, S.J.Q., 165
Robustness, testing for, 52
Rolls-Royce Cars, 28
Rome, Club of, 7
Rover Cars, 44, 73
Royal Society of Arts, 143, 153

Sadler, Philip, 156
Safeguard Insurance, 111
Sainsbury plc, 91, 122, 123
Sale of Goods Act, 63
Salomon Brothers, 37
Samuelson, Paul, 1
Savundra, Dr., 60, 111
Scenario planning, 34, 52, 77, 165
Schumpeter, Joseph, 145
Self-development, 7
Self-employment, 151
Self-fulfilment, 7
Self-renewal, 118, 139
Sensitivity analysis, 46, 196
Service businesses, 117
Seven intelligences of the individual,
    151
Severn Trent, 79
Shareholder value, 59
Shell, 17, 34, 52, 165
Shloer (ex-Beecham), 115
Shorrock, 118
Shurig, Ross, 184
Siemens, 136
Simmonds of Kensington, 28
Slave trade, 2

Smith, Adam, 3
Societal marketing, 152, 197
Socioeconomic classifications, 10
Sony, 84, 131
Sorrell, L.C., 18
SRI International, 168
Stacey, Ralph, 20
Stakeholders, 13, 59
Statism, 3
Statoil, 166
Stevenson, Robert Louis, 4
Stora, 145
Strategic analysis, 33, 36
Strategic benchmarking, 29, 30, 196
Strategic control, 16, 17
Strategic database marketing, 148
Strategic direction, 86, 196
Strategic intent, 29, 196
Strategic management, 195
Strategic management accounting, 48, 196
Strategic marketing, 5, 73, 74, 147, 197
Strategic marketing planning, 102
Strategic objectives, 15, 196
'Strategic Planning Society', 14, 193
Strategic planning techniques, 163
Strategic process, 196
Strategic procurement, 134
Strategic relationships, 134
Strategic vision, 14
Strategies, 18, 19, 46
  emergent 18, 20, 33, 55, 196
  tailored 18, 55
  generic 18
Strategy, 13, 18
Strategy and policy, 13
Supply chain (value chain), 21, 125
Supporting plans, 47
Swinton Insurance, 111
SWOT analysis, 90, 197
Systems integration, 134

Target, 194
Taunton Cider, 115
Teambuilding, 81, 136
Technical Market Research (TMR), 75, 197
Techniques, planning, 163
Technological leadership, 29
Telesure, 107, 111, 112, 113
Tesco plc, 122, 123, 128, 155, 161
Tetra Pak, 11
Texas Instruments, 142
Time-based marketing, 153, 197
Timex Products, 26
Timotei, 122
Toohey, 116
Top-down plans, 195
Toshiba, 136
Total quality management (TQM), 56, 73, 78
Townsend Thorensen, 53
Trend impact analysis, 167
Trends analysis, 77
Triumph Motorcycles, 60
TSB, 37
Turner, Jim, 9

Unilever, 72, 73, 86
Union Carbide, 53
Unipart, 72, 73, 86
Uruguay Round, 3, 7, 9, 10, 63, 69, 124

Value-based marketing, 113
Value chain, 21, 26, 28, 180
Values, 14, 16, 53, 64, 80, 117
Vickers, 145
Virgin Airways, 60
Virtuous circle of best marketing practice, 157
Vision, 14
Volkswagen, 83
Volvo, 11
Vrat, P., 187

Wack, Pierre, 165
Walmart, 124
Ward, Keith, 48
Wargames, 183
Waterman, Robert, 10, 11, 155
Watson, Gregory, 29
Wellington, Duke of, 20
Wells Fargo Bank, 17
Whyte, William Hyde, 10

Williams Holdings, 160
Wilson, Aubrey, 59, 66
Wilson, Harold, 65
Wilson, R.M.S., 4
Womach, James, 72
Word of mouth marketing, 197

Yamaha, 14, 131

Xerox Corporation, 19, 29, 144